WHAT HAPPENED IN LONDON

A DI ADAMS PREQUEL

KIM M. WATT

Buy the book. Gift the book. Read the book. Borrow the book. Talk about the book. Share the book. Just don't steal the book.

Book thieves will be fed to the bridge monsters. *Snap-snap-snap.*

But keep some chocolate handy.

For further information contact www.kmwatt.com

Cover design: Monika McFarland, www.ampersandbookcovers.com

Editor: Lynda Dietz, www.easyreaderediting.com

ISBN this edition: 978-0-473-66812-9

ISBN Ingrams paperback: 978-0-473-66810-5

ISBN ebook: 978-0-473-66811-2

First Edition January 2023

10 9 8 7 6 5 4 3 2 1

CONTENTS

To Terry,
for so many reasons.
Thank you.

BEFORE WE BEGIN

Lovely people, thank you for joining me. If you've come here from the Beaufort books, welcome! And be warned that the tea and cake levels are shockingly low in this book. *Shockingly.*

If you're new around here, welcome! Sit down, make yourself comfy, and please ensure you have plenty of snacks. Also, trust no one. Especially not the cats.

Now, as to that before we begin thing: apologies to all Londoners and everyone who loves London for my cavalier attitude toward the geography of your city. It's bad enough that I'm accusing your rivers and bridges of being up to mischief, but I'm not even being specific about which ones I mean.

I love London. I can (and have) walked for hours around it. But I've only lived there for about six months many, many years ago, and despite quite a few 'research' trips (anything can be research to a writer), my knowledge is far from complete. So I will apologise here for my geography being wonky, my knowledge of the Met police and their districts being iffy, and the feckless additions of Christmas markets, alleys, and strange creatures.

And let's not mention the aspersions cast on your bridges and toasties …

Happy reading, lovely people.

And keep your ducks close.

Kim x

1

NO ONE PREDICTED THE BIN

THE BIN WAS LOOKING AT HER. WITH INTENT. THE BIN WAS looking at her *with intent,* and she had no idea how she knew that, or how it was even possible (obviously it *wasn't*), but that was the current situation.

Detective Sergeant Adams of the London Metropolitan Police had no time for problematic (and impossible) bins. She glared back at it, daring it to … she didn't know. Bins were not something she'd considered a hazard before, other than in the olfactory sense, or as hiding places, but this one was different. Everything about it was just a little *off.* It was marginally too big, or too small. The colour was fractionally too intense, the familiar red on white of the logo too sharp, or the logo itself too big, or too small, or too *something.* And she could smell curry spices for some reason.

"No," she muttered, and the world around her lurched, the yellow light stuttering. "No, what's wrong with me? It's just a *bin.*"

She looked away, peering deeper into the maze of slope-walled alleys, looking for her quarry. They had to be in here somewhere. She'd been right on their heels as they'd plunged off the street and into the dim-lit, secret ways that ran like veins just beyond the skin of London. They couldn't have got far. She should've been able to see them, unless they'd hidden, but there were no turnings, no doorways, just—

"You," she said, and turned her gaze back to the bin. It seemed closer. "But I'd have heard the lid go," she added, frowning, and was sure – *sure* – that said lid creaked just slightly upward in response. It almost looked smug.

"It's just a bin," she muttered, and shifted her grip on her telescopic baton. "You're just a *bin.*"

Now she was *sure* it looked smug, but she stepped forward anyway.

She wasn't going to be beaten by a bin.

THE EVENING HADN'T STARTED with ominous bins. It had started at the Christmas market by the river, where warm yellow strings of lights sliced the riverside market into smooth wedges of rich colour and deep shadow. The scents of mulled wine spices and fatty sausage and frying onions fought against a persistent, fishy musk that the concrete-and-exhaust scent of the city couldn't quite defeat, and the air rang with chintzy Christmas music, the grumble of cars, and the shrieks of excited children, as well as the shouts of adults who'd had a little more Christmas cheer than was probably necessary. A Christmas tree of inadvisable height, cinched into place by hefty cables, towered over the wooden stalls and glittered with baubles and ribbons and bells and even more lights, which somehow still did nothing to illuminate the mass of people swelling around it. Hats were pulled low over cold-pinched ears, scarves rolled high to shut out the ever-present wind from the Thames, and the swirl and hulk of winter coats robbed the crowd of definition, turning them into blurred swatches of colour.

Deep russet scarf/black coat/black hat. Navy scarf/maroon coat/cream hat. Brown/grey/grey. Stripes (colour unidentifiable in the yellow light)/black/blue. White on white on white, standing out a little against the rest, then lost again in the sea of revellers. People washed and surged around the market cabins like the tide, clutching mugs of hot chocolate and mulled wine, gnawing potato spirals on sticks or popping mini doughnuts into mouths sticky with spilled sugar, shrieking with delight at glittering glass ornaments and dancing metal candle toppers. The rich, low light rendered the stalls oddly intimate despite the crowds, an oasis against the city looming on its shoreside edges and the river curling past on the other, dark and muscular and indifferent.

DS Adams tucked her hands deeper into her pockets and stared at the crowd, watching a small girl in a bright orange puffer jacket wrestle an equally small boy for ownership of an enormous lollipop. Either they'd been let loose with their own pocket money or someone hadn't realised the potential of large lollipops to start international-level incidents. The boy was clinging to the sweet grimly, pressing it into the chest of his jacket, and the girl had lost her hat, her hair wrapped around the stick somehow. They were both screaming, and the gloves were literally off on both sides. A woman with a takeaway coffee mug had picked the loose clothing up and was watching the struggle with such awed fascination that Adams decided she was an aunt or cousin – someone who wasn't going to have to get the lollipop out of everyone's clothes, anyway. The woman looked up, as if aware of Adams' scrutiny, and gave an embarrassed little wave with the handful of gloves.

"I think they're a bit overexcited," she said.

"I think you need another lollipop," Adams said.

"Ellie dropped hers."

"Ah. Well, then."

They both watched the kids for a moment longer, then the woman sighed, finished her drink, and went to pull them apart.

Adams shifted her gaze back to the crowd, wanting to say to the woman, *Never mind the lollipops. Just keep them close.* She spotted Zahid beneath the Christmas tree, heavy arms folded across his chest, beard half-swallowed by a wide red scarf, and caught the alarmed yellow flash of high-vis jackets drifting through the mass of people. *Maintain a presence.* That was where they were at. Never mind trying to catch whoever the hell was behind it all, just try to stop it happening again, because right now they had nothing. *Nothing.*

She took a handheld radio from her coat pocket and keyed it. "DS Adams, north quarter. Nothing seen. I'm taking a walk."

"Adams, Mirza. Copy." Zahid's answer was short. It was quite possible their quarry had access to police radios – anything was possible, really, and anyone covering their tracks so bloody effectively had to know *something.* Adams supposed they could have kept to their mobiles, but there didn't seem much point in it with all the uniformed officers squeezing through the crowds, less in the hope of spotting someone than in the cause of being seen to be Doing Something.

Adams nodded to a uniformed constable standing on the edge of the pavement, where a road came down in a loop toward the river. An ice cream van was parked at the kerb, doing unfeasibly brisk trade for the fact that it was cold enough to make her nose sting, and beyond it there was a posh lavender tea stall housed in a wood-panelled trailer decorated with dreamcatchers and twinkling lights. The last space was taken up by a battered Land Rover attached to a trailer that was old less in a vintage manner and more in a one-careless-owner-for-thirty-years one. The shutters were lifted, and there was a queue three deep outside it. Adams caught a whiff of melting cheese, and her stomach reminded her that coffee was not a food group, no matter how much of it she drank.

She hesitated, then decided that a quick tour of the market's edges should earn her a toasted sandwich on her way back. It wasn't like she didn't have time. No one was going home any time soon.

THE SCREAM WAS LONG, and drawn out, and it seemed that the music simply fell away beneath it, crumbling to nothing. Adams broke into a run before the cry had even ended, shoving unceremoniously through the crowd and cursing the after-work happy hour partiers who were still swilling drinks and insulting each other good-naturedly. Her radio spat names, calling urgently for check-ins, and she almost tripped over a small girl in a dinosaur suit and a Christmas hat as she plunged toward the river. The crowd felt determined to hold her back, swelling in the same direction, drawn by the promise of drama, and for one moment she was half suffocated by the thick, mingled scents of burnt sugar and hot alcohol and old oranges. There was another scream, and someone shouted, and then she was elbowing a tall man in a fluffy hat aside and bursting through the crowded marketplace onto the quieter riverside walk. The cold air coming straight off the Thames snatched at her breath, and for a moment her nostrils were filled with salt and rusting metal.

She spotted a detective constable staring blankly up at the

nearest bridge, its span dark and heavy across the water. "Harry!" she shouted. "You see anything?"

He looked around at her, then shook his head. No, of course he hadn't. He'd have to have been actually paying attention for that, and she was willing to bet the thermos mug he was clutching held more than just coffee. She jogged toward the river, her breath harsh in the back of her throat, scanning the faces of the crowd as she went.

More police were emerging from the direction of the market, in uniforms and not, all of them checking the jostling mass of revellers and searching for the screamer. No one came running out of the night looking for help, and no one cried out again. Even the crowd that she thought had been pulled toward the shout had either lost interest or had never really been interested in the first place. There was barely anyone walking the cold banks of the river in the dark, just one teenaged couple swaddled in puffer jackets, scurrying back toward the market with their heads down. She angled toward them.

"Excuse me," she said, then, when they didn't look around, *"excuse me."*

The young woman gave her a startled, alarmed look, but there was a smile playing around the corners of her mouth, and her companion gave a snort that threatened to tip into all-out laughter. They didn't slow, and Adams was about to intercept them when Zahid loomed into their path, chest out and legs planted wide.

"DI Zahid Mirza," he said, and the woman's smile vanished. "Can I have a word?"

Adams left Zahid to deal with them, the adrenaline already fading. The scream hadn't meant anything. Just some kids messing around at the edge of the river, tasting the shock of delighted fright that came from almost falling, and gave a better taste to the night.

She balled a fist and struck her thigh with it lightly, tasting frustration like old wine at the back of her throat. Not that she *wanted* anyone else to get taken, not with four kids already gone, vanished from the market and the riverside, but she'd like to have caught someone at it. *Arrested* someone.

Harry was still loitering at the edge of the crowd with his hat pulled down over his ears, his thermos swapped for a brown paper bag, and now he trotted over to her.

"Just those kids, huh?" he said, nodding at Zahid.

"Looks like," Adams agreed, peering down the riverside walk. "You didn't see anything?"

"Nah, nothing." He glanced over his shoulder at the bridge, a quick, twitchy movement, then looked back at Adams. "They probably won't come when it's so busy."

Adams gave him an unimpressed look. "The last kid was taken at seven on a Wednesday night. It wouldn't have been any quieter." Just taken. Whipped away into the dark, the parents turning away from the hot chocolate stand with cups in hand to find their daughter just *not there.* And no one had seen anything. No one had heard anything. One small girl just gone, like a stone swallowed by the river.

"We weren't all here last time, though," Harry pointed out. "That's different."

Adams nodded, squeezing the bridge of her nose with one hand and closing her eyes for a second. They felt scratchy. No one had been getting much sleep. The first kid had been one thing – one terrible, terrible thing – but the second had made them all sit up, both of them going missing from the Christmas market within a week of each other. The third had been five days later, and the fourth four days after that. All the stories were horribly identical in all the ways that mattered, and no one could doubt that this was a pattern. Someone was hunting the market, using it as their own personal honeypot. And they weren't leaving a single sign behind.

She opened her eyes, looking to the sky as she did so, searching for a moment's relief from the stark shadows and heavy lights down here. The bridge loomed at the corner of her vision, all tight lengths of cable and steel on top, hard grim brick and girders below. It dragged at her attention, and something *moved.* Her head snapped toward it, her body tensing with expectation. A jumper? The bridge was low, like so many along the Thames, but the water was hungry and treacherous, and teemed with hazards. Currents, shoals and drop-offs, the jagged skeletons of old structures hidden in the murky waters, fun things like Thames tummy and Weil's disease. And that water was *cold.*

There was no one that she could see. No one perched on the high metal sides, nothing crashing to the water from the hulking metal struts. But she kept staring anyway, the sounds of the city weirdly remote, as if her ears had suddenly filled with water. Harry was saying something, but she couldn't hear him, and the unceasing rumble of traffic was a murmur on the edge of her consciousness. The night was all sharp edges and strange colours, and there was movement on the bridge. No, not on it, under it. *In* it. Nothing she could be sure of, just a whisper of something almost out of sight, too big to be a pigeon, moving with too much intent to be a drifting piece of rubbish on the wind. Something twisted in her chest, a hungry, primal fright, because the movement didn't make sense, it was—

The whiff of hot cheese dragged across her senses like a slap of cold water, and she blinked at Harry. He was holding half a sandwich out to her.

"Toastie?"

Adams wrinkled her nose. "No." She looked back at the river, but Harry waved the sandwich at her again.

"I took the ham off this half."

"You know it doesn't work like that, right?" She couldn't see anything on the bridge now. It was just stark angles and hard shadows, and nothing could really be under there. Although she supposed there must be workers' access and stuff.

"Why not? It's just cheese now. And they're really good toasties." He took a bite of the other half and nodded at her encouragingly as he chewed.

"It's still got meat gunk on it," she said. "You can't just take it off and say, oh, now it's veggie."

"I don't see why not," Harry muttered, but he turned his attention back to eating.

Adams ignored him and walked down to the river with her hands in her pockets and her gaze fixed on the bridge. That strange moment of dislocation had gone, the traffic back to its normal assertive snarl, the constant hum of people and buildings and trucks and cars and *everything* re-establishing itself. She glanced warily up and down the path, but Zahid was looking the other way, into the crowd – where her attention should be too, she knew – and the riverside walkway was all but empty. It looked as if it should be fiercely lit by the stalking limbs of the streetlights that lined it, sown at regular intervals along the bank. Between them, and the ever-present glow of the city, and the heavy yellow wash of the lights on the bridge, it didn't seem as if there would be much room for darkness at all. Even the Thames reflected the light back off its surface, catching it here and there on the crests of wind-driven waves, and glowing in the foam that followed them. But in practise, there was more dark here than Adams was entirely comfortable with. The bridge loomed large and shadowed, none of the illumination reaching its squatting girders, and the lights seemed to accentuate the dark rather than push it back.

She paced down the path, her stride measured and wary, still looking for that strange movement. It had to have been some scaffolding, perhaps, left behind by workers and shaken loose by the wind. Or it could be rubbish caught among the uprights, but it had seemed to own too many straight lines for that. Maybe some loose canvas, part of a protest sign or a tarp used for covering up repairs, still daubed with logos or slogans. Or … or it could be *something.* A handy way to hoist kids out of sight once they'd been grabbed. It was possible.

She quickened her pace, rubbing a hand across her eyes. Spots of weariness stayed behind when she opened them again, leaving swimming motes that threatened to spread, and a dull throb started up in her forehead. Great. Was this a migraine? She'd never had one, but it was that sort of thing, right? One of her friends at school used to get them, and she'd had to go to the nurse and lie in a darkened room with a facecloth on her forehead, like some Victorian heroine, and— Adams shook the thought loose. Why the hell was she thinking about migraines? Bridges. Bridges and kids.

She stopped under the loom of its arches and stared up at it, all vast grey girders stalking out across the Thames, indifferent to the sharp edges of the wind and the scrape of the waters at its supports. It should have been clear-cut, the night winter-close and heavy but still full of ever-present city light. The bridge should have been nothing but firm angles and straight lines, and as she followed its stretch across the river it *was,* but here, above her … she pinched the bridge of her nose again and blinked hard. The bridge was just a bridge. Not even one of the attractive ones the tourists all loved. It was brutal and utilitarian, and there was nothing interesting about it at all.

She was tired. She might even need to get her eyes

checked. Or she really could be starting with migraines. That'd be brilliant. Just what she needed.

A duck quacked from the edge of the river, and she frowned at it. It waggled its back end and stomped up to her, examining her from one eye then the other.

"Seen anything unusual?" she asked it, then looked around a little guiltily. That was all she needed, being seen talking to a duck. Hardly add any credibility to the Met Police, would it?

She looked up at the bridge one last time, unsure of what she was looking for, but it gave back nothing.

"You're no help," she said to the duck, which looked put out. She started to turn back to the market, and as she did so her radio blared into sudden life, startling an answering quack out of the duck.

"All stations, all stations. MISPER reported, repeat, MISPER reported *now.*" There was an edge of both panic and triumph in the officer's voice, and Adams' heart slammed into high gear. MISPER. Missing Person.

"IC3, male, six years old," the officer continued, and Adams turned on the spot, moving fast but taking time to really *look*, scanning the river and the path and the low banks of scrubby vegetation that had been poorly planted on the embankment further along. IC3. That meant he was Black, and in her head he was suddenly her little brother as he'd been years ago, shrieking next to her as they ran down the river path with their arms out and the winter wind carving past them, wild with the excitement of Christmas.

"Blue hat, red jacket, ski trousers. Name Alfie Penn."

The path toward the market was empty, the underside of the bridge cold and hostile. There was no one near the water she could see, no one clinging to the waist-high river wall. Other side of the bridge, and there was the embankment with a patchy covering of low bushes— She stopped, straining to see in the dim light. There was someone there, standing frozen amid the undergrowth, hands clamped to their head. She took a step toward them, the hair on the back of her neck rising, and felt their attention shift to her.

"DS Adams, Met Police," she shouted. "Stay where you are."

Predictably, they didn't.

Also predictably, she gave chase, leaving the startled duck behind.

It wasn't until she reached the bin that things got unpredictable.

2

DON'T FALL FOR THE DOUGHNUTS

ON THE FAR SIDE OF THE BRIDGE THERE WAS A SENSE OF having stepped into a different postcode. The path continued, well-kept and with lights leaning protectively over it at regular intervals, but rather than the crowded joviality of the Christmas market and the gloss of bars and restaurants beyond, an embankment swelled up to divide the path from the road. Bushes pocked it, straggling into untended shrubs, and it looked as if it had been planned as some sort of park. Nicely spaced benches faced across the Thames, but the wind channelled along here with too much purpose for DS Adams to imagine anyone wanting to sit on them, even on a good day. Right now she may as well have been sprinting into a wind tunnel.

Her quarry raced through the bushes with his hands held high, as if he were trying to prove his innocence – or at least his weaponless status – while also trying to put as much distance between him and DS Adams as he could. The nearest light was broken, rendering the passage through the bushes treacherous and tangled, but Adams charged straight through them anyway, trying not to think about what she was stepping in.

"*Stop!*" she shouted, as they neared the road. "Met Police!"

The person ahead didn't stop. They bolted straight across the bike lane, making a woman in skinny jeans and a dramatically flowing scarf yelp as she swerved, and the fleeing figure shot through a gap in the traffic with their skinny ankles and bare feet flashing under the cuffs of a lime green one-piece ski suit.

For one moment Adams considered just letting them go, because they certainly weren't dragging any kids with them, but there was still a chance they'd seen something. You didn't run from the police for no reason. And right now she was willing to try anything, because that made five kids. Alfie made *five.*

She went across the road as fast as she dared, dodging cars that swerved and braked in alarm. It wasn't busy, at least, and as she hit the pavement on the other side she saw her quarry plunging into a narrow alley between the worn-down buildings. Even right on the Thames, you didn't have to go far to find the pockets that hadn't quite made it onto the developers' drawing boards yet, or been populated by those determined to reenergise places that had never had much energy in the first place. The stained brick buildings looked across the road at the river with blank faces, their doors scarred, some of the windows lit and others boarded. She hesitated at the corner of the alley, checking for ambush, but it was empty, just graffiti blooming across the brick. It was rough, shouting stuff, less art than screams of fury and dislocation, rendered in dripping paint on the old walls.

The alley carried the usual reek of rotting food and human waste, damp and hurt and weariness. Adams wrinkled her nose, breathing shallowly, and padded in cautiously, checking for doorways and hiding places. The alley ended at a T-junction, a slightly brighter and wider passage running across it at right angles. It seemed empty, the walls smooth and devoid of places to lurk, but the skin on the back of Adams' neck was tight and prickling, and the light seemed somehow wrong, a low yellow sogginess that cast the shadows in sagging, unfamiliar angles.

To her right, the alley ran on behind the buildings, but she couldn't see any skinny green form racing down it. To her left the stretch of old, potholed tarmac finished in a dead end only ten metres or so away, and that was where the bin sat. Just a big commercial bin, grey and featureless. She couldn't see any shops it might belong to, or even the back doors to any buildings. It just crouched there, its lid firmly shut, and it was just a *bin,* for God's sake.

Except that she couldn't shake the feeling it was watching her. She scowled at it, then looked the other way down the alley.

"DS Adams, Met Police," she tried again. "No one's in trouble here. I just want to talk to you."

No one replied. There was only a heavy, expectant silence that made her swallow hard, her throat clicking. She keyed her radio. "DI Mirza, DS Adams," she tried.

There was no answer, not even the spit of static, and she clicked the mic a couple of times, but there was nothing. Maybe the battery had died, although it had been fully charged when she left the car. She fished in her pockets instead, coming out with her telescopic baton in one hand and her phone in the other, and put her back to a wall as she snapped open the baton. The noise rang dully against the brick and stone.

And then she looked back at the bin.

There was definitely something off about the bin.

It was closer, for a start.

THERE WAS A MOMENT, leaning there against the wall and scowling at the large, grey bin with its four wheels and slightly crooked lid (because they were *always* crooked, and she half-thought they came out of the factory like that), where she wondered if she really did need to stop drinking so much coffee. Or get more sleep. Or … she didn't know. Meditate, or something. Because she was seriously considering the possibility that the bin was not only creeping closer, but possibly had nefarious designs on her.

She pointed a finger at it, barely stopping herself from saying, "*Stay,*" as if the thing were a badly trained terrier, then unlocked her phone and hit Zahid's number. The phone bleeped in her ear sadly, and she took it away to give it a disbelieving look. *No service.*

"You're kidding me," she muttered, then shivered at the way the words fell dead around her. For the first time she was aware of how *quiet* it was in here. Not the usual city quiet, underscored by the rustle and hum of countless lives being lived just beyond the walls, the constant background of traffic and footfalls and sirens and planes hurtling past far overhead. No, this was an entirely different sort of quiet. It was the quiet of something waiting to happen, and she examined the bin again.

Was it closer still? It had been right up against the dead end just before, and then it had been a few metres from the wall, and now it seemed to be halfway down the alley toward her. But that wasn't possible. Bins didn't move. Unless there was someone behind it, pushing it? She took a wary look behind her, back the way she'd come, then down the T-junction in the opposite direction to the bin. A small, niggling voice at the back of her mind assured her she should have been able to see out to a street or *something* that way, but instead the cobbles (and why was it cobbled? That was a bit flashy for this part of town, wasn't it? To still have *cobbles?* They'd usually been tarmacked over, or at least gunged up with dirt, but no, here were *cobbles)* seemed to just stretch on into darkness.

"Bollocks to this," she told the quiet night, then wished she hadn't. That was too close to talking to herself. She dropped to her knees and peered up the alley to the dead end, toward the bin, expecting to see bare feet behind it.

There was nothing, and as she stood up again, brushing her knees off, the bin *creaked.* She stopped, hands still hovering over her trousers. The bin creaked again, and now she was sure it was closer. It couldn't be, though. Could it?

"No," she muttered, the word falling flat. "No, what's wrong with me? It's just a *bin.*" It couldn't move. Not unless ... there was a slope. There *had* to be a slope, even if it was a very slight one, so slight she couldn't see it. Or— she almost hit her forehead with the palm of her hand, but that was too theatrical for even an empty alley. *Of course.* She really did need more sleep, not to have seen this straight-away. Ski Suit had run in here and jumped in the bin, and their momentum was what was moving it. If there was a tiny slope, it'd keep moving, too. All she had to do was open the top.

"You," she said to the bin, putting her full authority into the word, then hesitated. "But I'd have heard the lid go."

There was no response to that. Not that she expected one, of course. Although the damn thing still seemed to be looking at her.

"It's just a bin. You're just a *bin.*" She took a deep breath, and addressed the missing Ski Suit, because obviously she wasn't talking *to an actual bin*. "DS Adams, Met Police. Come out now."

There was no response, just the bin staring back at her

blandly, and she caught a whiff of curry from somewhere that made her belly rumble.

"Come on. I know you're in there. You're not in any trouble, I just want a word."

The bin creaked slightly, and she didn't exactly see it move, but it had inched forward a couple of cobblestones. She was taking note now.

"Last chance. Don't make me drag you out of there."

There was still no response, and she shifted her grip on the baton, keeping it close to her leg but ready to swing up and around. Her mouth was abruptly dry, and she licked her lips, daring another quick glance back to the street and down into the depths of the alley. No one.

She squared her shoulders and stepped forward, and someone grabbed her.

DS Adams wasn't the sort of person who did much screaming, but she definitely bit down on *something* as she spun to face her assailant, twisting her arm out of their grip and taking two fast steps back, the baton coming up over her shoulder instinctively.

Ski Suit cringed in front of her, almost dropping to a crouch as he raised his hands to protect his head. "Don't!" he yelped. "Please don't!"

"Where the hell did you come from?" Adams demanded, then twisted around, suddenly aware of the bin at her back. It stared at her blandly, and she tried to tell herself she was just worried about an as-yet-unseen Ski Suit 2 popping out of it.

"I was hiding. I was running, and hiding, and I wasn't going to come back, but then I thought, you don't know."

"Know what?" she asked, turning her attention back to

him now that it looked like the bin wasn't going to pounce on her.

He pointed, and she managed not to look behind her. That was the sort of thing decent detective sergeants didn't fall for.

"So there is someone in there?" She took a step backward, toward the bin, still not looking at it. The skin on the back of her neck was crawling, and Ski Suit squawked again.

"Don't! Don't go near it!"

"Why not? Who's in there?" She stopped, trying to look at both the bin and him at once. Not that he looked like much of a threat. He was tall, but even in the suit everything about him was bony and angular. His wrists were knobbly where they hung out of the grimy green cuffs, and he had a scraggly ginger beard under a woolly orange hat. His accent was hard to place, one of those almost-posh voices that has been carefully scoured of its regionality.

"No one's in there. But it's a trap," he whispered.

"It's a *bin,*" she said, annoyed to find herself whispering as well.

"Have you seen a bin like that before?"

She glanced at it, opening her mouth to say *of course* she had, they were in every alley all over the city, probably all over the *country,* bulging with rubbish and scraps, with the inevitable broken lamps and lopsided chests of drawers abandoned next to them. But the words died before she could speak. The damn thing still seemed to be watching her, as ridiculous as that was. She scowled at Ski Suit and said, "Well, how's it a trap, then?"

"I don't know. I just know it's dangerous."

"Dangerous how?"

He reached out as if to grab her arm again, but her frown deepened and he let his hand drop. He started to back away toward the street instead, beckoning her. She didn't follow, and after a few steps he stopped, scratching anxiously at his chest. "It just is. I don't think it's really a trap for us, but if you're alone, or unwary ..." He spread his fingers. "It takes its chances, you know? Like a crocodile."

"I'm police," Adams said, not sure if she was protesting the accusation of unwariness or the idea of a crocodile bin.

Ski Suit shrugged. "It doesn't care. And you *see,* so it means it can see you, too."

Adams looked at the bin, then back at him, sorted through the many possible things she could say, then said, "Sorry, what?"

He thought about it, then said, "People walk past this alley all the time, and they never even see it. People who fit into the world don't. But then I look down here and I swear there's boxes of doughnuts left out. Just boxes and boxes and *boxes* of them, all warm and fresh and they smell *so* good." He sighed. "I like doughnuts."

"And?"

"And sometimes people who don't fit into the world go missing. And maybe they liked doughnuts, too, or maybe it showed them something else. My friend Edith always saw scones with clotted cream and raspberry jam, all set out on a little table with a checked cloth, and daffodils in a jug on the table." He looked at the bin thoughtfully. "She's gone now."

"You think the bin ate Edith." She wanted to laugh – or at least to *want* to laugh – but somehow she didn't.

Ski Suit shook his head firmly. "No. She knew not to go too close. It can only catch you if you're not careful. The others, though ... they *hunt.*"

Adams shivered despite herself. "The others?"

"By the bridge." Ski Suit's voice was a whisper, and in the strange light his eyes were washed of colour, left flat and grey and lifeless. "The new monsters. The ones who steal you. *Snap-snap-snap.*"

Adams flinched at the *snap,* the man's voice suddenly hard and high, then she said, "You saw something? You saw someone at the bridge?"

Ski Suit gave her a wary look. "I tried to tell the police, but they said I was lying. They can't *see.* They can't even listen."

"Talking about crocodile bins might not have been the best way to start."

He pointed at her. "*You* see."

"Well, I've got eyes. What's your name?" He was off his head, obviously, but he *had* been at the bridge, and if he'd seen something it meant he was the best lead they had. The *only* lead they had.

He looked past her at the bin. "I can't tell you. Not here. Names matter."

"Would the station suit you better?" Adams asked, then immediately held both hands up as Ski Suit skittered away from her. He stared at the baton with wide eyes, pressing himself into the wall, looking more frightened than he had of the crocodile bin. She collapsed the baton hurriedly and shoved it into her coat pocket. "Sorry, sorry. I'm not arresting you."

"I didn't do anything," he said. "I'm just looking for my friends, but the police all say, no, Jack, go away, go away and tell stories somewhere else or we'll lock you up, lock you up in the walls and away from the sky." His fingers were digging into the brickwork, and she could see the knuckles whitening with pressure.

"I'll listen," Adams promised him. "And is that your name? Jack?"

"It's *a* name."

"Alright, Jack, I'm DS Adams—"

"That's not a real name."

"It is."

He frowned at her. "You should have a real name."

"Like Jack?" She raised her eyebrows at him.

"Jack could be a real name. DS isn't a real name at all. And *Adams* is a last name, which means it isn't even yours. It's your family's."

Adams rubbed a hand across her face and looked up at the invisible sky. Twenty minutes ago she'd been patrolling a crowd in a perfectly normal manner. Now she was considering crocodile bins and arguing about the relative real-ness of her name. "D'you want me to help find your friend or not?"

"Friend*s*," he said. "Plural. Edith and Lilith and Tommy and Weird Al and Bertie."

She stared at him. "Five people?"

He nodded. "But not people anyone cares about. No one cares when we go missing, because we're missing from the world already."

"Well, I'll help if I can." She couldn't apologise for no one listening before, because that wasn't how things were done. Or she could, but it wouldn't mean anything. And it wouldn't change anything, because he was right. Not everyone was listened to in the same way, and they should be. Not just because it was human to need to be heard, although that was reason enough, but because it might be the one lead that unravelled everything – this case, or a different one.

He examined her. "You will, won't you? And you can see, so maybe you really can."

She tried for a reassuring smile. "Yes. But you've got to tell me everything. You've got to tell me anything you know about people vanishing around here. Kids are going missing too, you know."

Jack smiled at that, an oddly charming grin that revealed neat white teeth. "And everyone cares about the kiddies. At least the ones with the money and the cute smiles."

She didn't argue it, just shrugged. "Can we help each other?"

"Maybe. But you really have to *see.* See properly, you know. Because they're everywhere. And we feel them at some level. Most of us, anyway. If we're smart, we pay attention. If we're not … well, doughnuts." He sneaked a sideways look at the bin. "*We* know. We know we have to be careful."

"We?" Adams asked.

"We." Jack pointed at his own chest. He smiled, revealing those neat white teeth again. "You lot don't see us, but we see *everything.*"

"And who are *they?* The ones who are everywhere?"

Jack nodded past her, and she followed his gaze. The bin creaked, and Adams caught a whiff of curry that made her stomach growl. She wondered if she should march up to it and fling the lid open, confront whatever – *whoever* – was in there, but she couldn't seem to make herself do it. The headache from the bridge was starting to spread across her forehead.

"See?" Jack whispered. "It's still trying. Bet it'd love to catch a human. Must be nice after all those rats and pigeons and stuff. And there's much more than bins out here."

"This is ridiculous," Adams said, without much conviction. She stared at the bin. It seemed to have edged even closer while they were talking.

"You said you'd help," Jack reminded her.

"You need to give me details. Proper ones, not fairy tales and … and urban myths." Although she'd never heard myths about carnivorous bins before.

"I'm trying. It's not … it's no one *human*. We know what's out here. We do. And so we can usually stay safe, usually avoid them, but there's something new. Something we don't know. And it's catching up to us. So we need help. You *have* to help. And if you're going to help, you have to see."

DS Adams took a careful breath. The air in the alley felt too close, too tight. "You can't really mean that. It's ... what? You think aliens took your friends? *Monsters?*" She tried to laugh, but it fell flat and breathless.

Jack gave her a strange look, some mix of despair and pity. "*No.* Not aliens. And monsters – well, not like a river monster or something. But they're *not human*. You have to *see.*" He pointed down the alley. "You *have* to!"

She followed his pointing hand, feeling as much as seeing shadows flocking at the corners of her vision, more nasty little migraine-motes. The strange yellow light of the alley was murky and diffuse, with no real source, as if it were coming from the walls or the thick, claggy air itself. She hadn't seen any streetlights since she'd left the main road, and there were no windows in the buildings around them. Just old brick forced into awkward, pointless patterns, like a child's first attempt at LEGO. The walls were dark and damp, and the dead end behind the bin seemed undefined, as if the alley both went on forever beyond it, and at the same time was no more than a painted backdrop hiding some horrifying backstage that she had no desire to see.

And the bin ... the bin was closer. There was no doubting it now. It crouched on the slick stone, vibrating with expectation, and she was aware again that it was all but silent in here. The sounds of the city were lost, as indistinct as lights seen through a fog bank, and she glanced back toward the street. Dimly, she could see the road beyond, a mirage of the world she knew, but even as she watched, someone – some*thing* – passed the end. It was all slouching, multi-angled limbs, disproportionately tall and thin and bending in all the wrong angles and places. She tried to swallow against a tightening in her throat, but her mouth was too dry, and she looked at Jack with her face as hot as a fever. He stared back at her, reflecting her panic, and the bin creaked closer, the air pressing even tighter as it did so.

"Not that much!" Jack's voice was a hoarse yelp. "You can't see that much! Then they *know* you see!"

But Adams didn't know how she was meant to stop. The world had cracked open, and she was falling.

3

ALFIE MAKES FIVE

The blare of her mobile cut across the alley with a brutal digital clarity that hurt her ears. And it hurt something else as well. Adams felt a hiss at the edge of her hearing, and the walls of the alley snapped back into grimy focus, the thick yellow light splitting and scattering. The heavy, inviting reek of spices evaporated, leaving behind the sharp and strangely welcome stink of urine and stale beer. The bin was right where it should be, back against the wall of the alley, its colours familiar and unremarkable, and the figure passing on the street was just a tall man in a trilby hat.

DS Adams fumbled the phone out of her pocket with fingers that didn't want to bend properly, stabbed the answer button, and managed a dry-mouthed, "Yeah?"

"Adams, where the hell are you?" Zahid shouted in her ear. "It's a complete sodding circus down here!"

"Um, I saw someone." She couldn't seem to get her voice above a whisper.

"Adams?" Zahid's irritation gave way to sharp, urgent edges. "You alright?"

"Yes. Yes, I'm fine." She cleared her throat, looking around for Jack. The alley was empty in all directions, and she tapped one fist off the brick lightly, grimacing. "All good. False lead. I'm on my way back. Meet you there."

"Move yourself, then."

Adams hung up, and leaned back against the wall for a moment, staring at the entirely ordinary bin, and the damp brick walls of the entirely ordinary alley. She made some small, not quite articulate noise of disgust and turned on her heel, marching back the way she'd come. She didn't look back at the alley as she left, just strode out into the streetlights and across the road, her shoulders aching with tension, and turned along the pavement in the direction of the Christmas market. She avoided the scraggly descent through the bushes to the riverside path, with its roots and rubbish and human leavings, and avoided passing under the bridge.

The ever-present river wind rushed to greet her with bony, chilled kisses, and the lights of the city shattered on the surface of the water as it came into view. For one moment all was silent, and her chest tightened as she was gripped by the conviction that she'd somehow slipped out of the world, that she was walking alongside it, not quite touching it, in a plane where she could see but not hear, another invisible person fallen through the cracks that others couldn't – or wouldn't – even see.

Then a motorbike blatted past, and a siren screamed further down the bank, and the lights of a riverboat dislodged themselves from the clutter of the shore, accompanied by the sharp blast of a horn. She took a deep, shaky breath, and looked along the river at the bridge. The shadows under it were dark with promise, and for one moment she felt the world *shift* around her. She closed her eyes, letting it steady, then headed back toward the market. There was nothing to see there, or anywhere else. Bins don't eat people, and nothing lives in the arches of bridges. The world doesn't work like that.

It can't.

THE CHRISTMAS MARKET was a chaos of complaining shoppers and stallholders, all of them demanding to know why the police were shutting them down early, and, more importantly, why they were being channelled through one narrow gap in some rapidly erected cordons to leave. The official line was security threat, which was enough to get most people hurrying along. Families and couples flowed past the watching officers, heading for cars and homes and hot dinners, and only the most stubborn – or most inebriated – took it as an invitation to get in some officer's face and shout about their rights. Most of them just wanted to get home and warm, although Adams passed a couple of young men being rather enthusiastically helped into the back of a police van by a displeased looking uniformed sergeant who had lost her hat, and a skinny constable who was going red in the face with the effort.

"Alright, Liz?" Adams asked the sergeant as she went past.

"Oh, aye. There's always someone thinks it's all about them, isn't there?"

"Every time," Adams agreed, and kept going. The toastie van was still doing a brisk trade, and as she drew level with it a young man leaned out and called to her.

"Something to keep you warm, detective?"

She turned to scowl at him, but he was just holding out a brown paper bag. "No thanks."

"No charge for police." He waved the bag, then examined her and frowned. He put it back behind the counter and said, "Brownie, perhaps?"

A woman grabbed his arm and pulled him back into the van, and DS Adams kept going.

Zahid was standing by the back of an ambulance that had pulled around to the far side of the market stalls, his arms crossed over his chest. He scowled at Adams as she hurried to meet him.

"Where the hell have you been?"

"I saw someone legging it when the call about the kid went out, so I followed him."

"On your own? Without telling anyone?"

"It was all a bit rushed. This the father?" She peered past him at a man sitting in the back of the ambulance, a blanket around his shoulders and a paper cup in one hand. He was holding his phone in the other, staring at it blankly.

"Grandfather. Brought the kid down for a bit of a treat, and swears he barely took his eyes off him. They went down to the river to look at the ferries, and the next thing he knew the kid was gone."

"By the bridge?" Adams asked, wondering if the words sounded as stiff as they felt.

"Yeah. Don't know how they're bloody doing it." Zahid shook his head. "Nightmare, this. The same thing all over again – no one saw anything, heard anything, just bloody nothing. What was with the person you saw?"

"It wasn't anything." *Just a hungry bin.* She rubbed the back of her neck and looked at the man in the ambulance again. "He alright?"

"Oh, great. He's just called his daughter to tell her he lost her kid."

"I mean …" Adams waved vaguely, then gave up. She'd meant was he injured, but it hardly seemed relevant. Physically the man didn't even look old enough to be a granddad, his close-cropped hair still more black than grey, but the way his shoulders slumped as he curled forward over his cup told a different story. Adams wondered what good the traditional hot, sweet tea was doing. Not enough, she thought.

Zahid inclined his head and walked a few paces away, and she followed him.

"Think he's got anything to do with it?" she asked, once they were out of earshot.

"Not really. Not unless he's behind the others as well." Zahid took a couple of protein bars from his coat pocket and offered her one. Adams shook her head, and examined the dwindling crowd.

"Really, no one saw anything at all? *Again?*"

"We can't exactly interview the lot of them," Zahid said. "If we even told them a kid had just vanished it'd be mad panic. Best we can do is interview the stallholders, and for the rest just make sure no one looks like they're leaving with a kid that isn't theirs."

"Cameras?"

"In the van. It'll catch everyone leaving."

It was something. So far the CCTV on the market had revealed nothing, not even an idea of who might've been here on each of the nights where a kid had vanished. Between all the big scarves, brimmed hats, umbrellas, and the dim lighting, it was all but impossible to tell people apart.

"And our lot?" Adams asked. "They come up empty too? It wasn't far short of a copper convention down here."

Zahid sighed, and took his hat off to scrub a hand through his thick hair. "Absolutely sod all." He tugged the hat back down over his ears and looked at her. "You sure you didn't pick up anything?"

"Yeah. It was a mistake." She hesitated, thinking of the bridge, and the alley, and Jack hissing, *You have to **see**.*

"Sure? It must've been quite a mistake for you to be heading away from the action."

"Yeah. No. I'm sure." She caught the whiff of browned

onions and melted cheese, and turned to see a slight woman in baggy trousers and a striped apron over her T-shirt heading toward them. She had a pile of grease-stained brown paper bags in her hands, and she handed a couple to the ambulance crew, one to Alfie's granddad, who opened it with the same mechanical motion he'd been using to drink his tea, then approached Adams and Zahid.

"Toastie?" the woman said. "Goat's cheese, rocket, and red onion."

"Carbs *and* dairy?" Zahid said, and patted the flat of his belly. "No chance. You go on, Adams."

"I'm not hungry. Thanks."

"Sure?" The woman wafted the bag in front of her, grinning, and just for a moment her eyes were flat pools reflecting the light like a cat's, and her teeth were crowded and sharp. Adams drew back half a step, and the woman gave her a puzzled look. "You alright? Look like you've seen a ghost."

"Fine," Adams said, and shoved her hands deeper in her pockets. The woman was just a woman, a little older than Adams herself, her hair pulled back in a heavy plait of rich, chestnut brown. Adams needed sleep, or, failing that, more caffeine.

"Suit yourself." The woman wandered off, and Adams watched her go.

"That was weird," she said.

"What, offering up toasties? Probably had extras left after we shut things down," Zahid said. He was scrolling through his phone. "Bollocks. I missed saying goodnight to the girls."

Adams looked at him, at the tight lines of his shoulders, hunched over the phone. Maya and Aisha were six and eight. Right in the age range. She rocked on her heels and puffed air, watching it curl away in a soft white plume into the night. "They alright? And Amira?"

He pocketed the phone with a sigh. "First time I've seen Ami really worried. Won't let them come anywhere near the river. Not even the pond by us, to feed the ducks."

Adams nodded. "Can't blame her."

"No." He looked back at the river. "The scene of crime bods are on the way, and so's the DCI. We best find something, or someone's getting it in the neck."

"That would be you," she said. "Senior officer on the scene and all."

"And if you think I won't pass it down the line— *Harry!* What the hell, mate?"

Harry had emerged from behind one of the stalls with a large paper mug clutched in one hand and a half-eaten doughnut in the other. The mug was topped with a tower of whipped cream, chocolate sauce oozing down it, and he looked at them guilty. "Just fuelling up, boss."

"Jesus Christ. Herself is going to be here in five, and you're …" Zahid gestured futilely, then looked at Adams. "Come on. Let's walk."

He headed for the river, and she fell into step with him. She'd found the DI's affection for silent walks in the areas of crime scenes irritating when she'd first transferred and started working with him. It seemed like an affectation, and it filled her with a bubbling impatience that verged on anger. Why weren't they *doing* anything? What was the point of *walking?*

Until a few months into the transfer when, as she strolled next to him, barely able to stop herself voicing the relentless monologue running in her head, she'd glared at a box of recycling sitting innocuously at the kerb. It was collection day, and she noticed that someone had put the bottles in with the cans. Her circling, irritated mind had seized on this outrage, worrying at it, and a block after that, as they still walked on, Zahid with his long, stalking stride that somehow made his barrel chest barely noticeable, rendering him slight and unrecognisable, DS Adams had remembered it had been bin day at her flat yesterday and she'd missed it again, and somehow …

Somehow she'd known, the pieces sliding into place with a delightful frisson that she'd come to anticipate and savour even more than arresting people, that it had been bin day – garden waste to be precise – when the robberies had taken place in a leafy street in Kensington, and so there never needed to be a getaway vehicle. There just needed to be a rubbish truck that looked legit but came through an hour before the real one did, and a bin put out with the goods hidden neatly under a few leafy branches of rhododendron. Easy.

She could never say just how she'd made the connections, but that was how walking worked, Zahid said. The brain did its thing as long as you simply *looked,* and tried not to think too much. So she walked, her hands tucked deep into her pockets and her chin into her scarf, trying not to think about carnivorous bins. She let her eyes drift across the path and onto the river and back again, flicking away from the buildings across the road, the ones that held the alley. None of that could have happened. Or not the way she seemed to remember it. She touched her head, working her fingers into the tight bonds around her bun, looking for bumps or blood, and slowed as they approached the bridge, stealing glances up at its underside. From here it looked just as it had every other time she'd been down here. Stolid, boring, a triumph of practicality over beauty.

"Adams! Are we sightseeing or something?" She'd fallen behind while Zahid continued up the path, and now he turned back to her, the bridge vast and hungry overhead. "You need a selfie?"

"Me? I'm not the hashtag gym-bro hashtag little shorts or

whatever you are." She forced herself to catch up, the skin on the back of her neck crawling. She was being ridiculous.

"Those are workout shorts. Don't try and clothes-shame me." He looked up at the bridge, and for a moment Adams wanted to say, *Do you see it? Do you **feel** it?* But she didn't. It'd be like asking a Labrador if they'd ever heard of portion control. Half-seen things didn't exist in Zahid's world. Or hers. "What're you thinking?" he asked her.

About carnivorous bins and hidden places. She took a breath and said, "All the kids were taken along the river path."

"A statement of the astoundingly obvious," Zahid said, with no heat.

"We've pulled every scrap of CCTV we can find," Adams continued. "Pulled boats, vans, cars, bloody rickshaws."

"We have." Zahid's voice was grave, and she shivered, glancing up at the bridge again. It was raw-edged and disinterested, and the wind funnelling around it seemed to accelerate over them, forcing harsh fingers down the back of Adams' collar, evading her scarf. Something scratched at the nape of her neck, a piece of debris swirled in or a rough tag on her shirt, and she slapped at it irritably.

"What if they didn't leave?" she asked.

Zahid looked at the surging mass of the Thames, the surface opaque and choppy with the conflicting currents of tide and flow and turbulence. "You mean …" He mimed grabbing someone and pitching them in.

"Maybe," she said, although she hadn't exactly been thinking that. All she could seem to think of was the damn bridge. "But what if they were whipped into a nearby building? Some maintenance entrance to an office block, a parking garage, something?"

"There's been half a dozen door-to-doors. It'd be seriously high-risk, keeping them in the area."

DS Adams finally dared a proper look up. The bridge

looked just as a bridge should. Solid. Bridge-y. She nodded at its fat brick supports where they met the bank, and the ladder climbing up into the girders beyond. It was locked with a spike-topped barrier and gate, but there was no saying who had access. "What about up there, then?"

Zahid frowned at the bridge, then craned his neck as he followed the ladder up into the tangle of girders and arches. "It's not exactly high, is it? Anyone could see. And hear."

"Not so easy to see at night. And who looks up, anyway? No one *ever* looks up. The parents take off running up and down the path in a panic, or rush to check the river. If the kids are incapacitated, someone could easy climb with them."

"Then what? They come back down later? It's not like they could just walk out past the searchers. We're packed out right now." He waved along the path, where high-vis jackets were splashed in pairs at regular intervals.

DS Adams shrugged. "You can probably get right across the river on those walkways."

Zahid regarded the bridge for a little longer, then looked back at her. "Interesting theory. Worth looking into."

"But you don't think so."

"Five kids now. All snatched from parents who were *right there,* either in the Christmas market or just outside it, all at busy times." He pointed back the way they'd come, at the huddle of wooden huts and the huge tree sprouting from the centre of them. The lights should have made it look cheerful, but Adams could see the ambulance from here, and the press of people still straggling out into the city. The stalls were already closing up, and a sick taste of fright hung about the place. "A couple were in the market itself, and others by the river. They'd have had to get the kids from there to here. Someone would have seen something. It's an interesting thought, and we'll take a look at it, because we really do have nothing, but I don't see it. Not unless our abductor was also a ring bearer."

DS Adams nodded and puffed air over her bottom lip. "I just have a feeling they're closer than we realise."

"A *feeling?* Don't let the DCI hear you talking about those. She's allergic." But he didn't move on straight away, still scanning the riverside and the bridge with his big shoulders straining at the seams of his coat. "It's a weird one, though. Bloody high-risk tactic for trafficking, and they've been taken so close together that it seems unlikely to be your average nutter. There's been no escalation. From nothing, to *this.*" He shook his head, then turned and started walking again. "I hate the weird ones."

DS Adams didn't answer, just fell into step with him, smelling salt and car exhausts and rusting metal in the sharp teeth of the wind.

THEY KEPT on despite the chill wind, not talking, just watching, until they were in sight of the next bridge along. The bank had hulked up into red brick walls, holding back the city behind them, and Zahid finally stopped, squinting against the spitting rain that had started.

"Anything?" he asked.

"No. Not really. Just ... I don't know."

"That's how it goes." He pointed at his head. "Stick your bridge idea in the mind muck and let it swill around for a bit."

"Poetic. Didn't Sherlock have a mind *palace?*"

"Yeah, but he was a posh git," Zahid said comfortably, and took another protein bar out. "Sure you don't want one?"

"No. They taste like cardboard."

"Better for you than all that bloody coffee you drink."

"Sure it is."

"You don't know what you're missing." He turned and started to head back, checking his phone as he went. "Nothing from Herself yet."

"What're you going to say?"

"I'm going to give her your bridge idea. If she hates it, I'll blame you. If she likes it, I'm taking all the credit."

"Naturally." Adams took a breath, then said, "I did see someone before. Not a suspect, but maybe a witness of sorts."

Zahid stopped short and glared at her. "*What?*"

Adams raised one hand and kept walking. "He wasn't very lucid, and he seemed to think some of his friends had been eaten by a carnivorous bin, but he was by the bridge. He could've seen something."

"Oh, right." Zahid caught up with her. "So some junkie, then? That sounds helpful."

"Like you said, we've got nothing. Isn't it worth a try?"

Zahid sighed heavily as a stocky figure in a long coat appeared on the riverside walk ahead of them. "Yep," he said, and raised one hand to the DCI. "Anything's worth a try right now."

4

A LITTLE TOO X-FILES

DS Adams, whom even her brothers didn't call Jeanette (especially since she'd pointed out that having a sister in the police could be a nice thing, or it could be a real pain, depending on said sister's current disposition), did not sleep well in general. She wasn't sure police work – or police work in any major city, at least – left one inclined to peaceful nights.

That night she didn't sleep at all.

The morning had edged into the wee small hours by the time she got in, having walked the river path more times than she cared to think; fended off more toasties from Harry, who seemed to have set himself up as some sort of sandwich reseller; and been forced to tell her highly edited story of spotting Jack by the bridge to the DCI, who had declared he was worth talking to further. The DCI had seemed less impressed by the idea of the bridge as an escape method, but she'd still dispatched a couple of uniformed officers to find some keys and get them access to the walkways.

By the time it had become clear that there was no one remotely fitting Jack's description in the vicinity, and that no one was getting into the bridge superstructure without protective gear, banks of lighting, harnesses, and an hour-long safety briefing from a city official no one could seem to name, let alone locate, the DCI had dismissed half the team. Most of them were lurking around slurping coffee and pretending to be busy anyway. Not long after that she dismissed everyone but a handful of officers she tasked with watching both ends of the bridge.

"We won't get in there till morning," she told Adams and Zahid. "Marine police are watching for any water escapes, and we've got shoreside covered, so no one's going anywhere. Get some sleep and come back fresh."

Adams wondered when the DCI slept, but she didn't argue, any more than she did when Zahid declared that he was starving and needed chips. He found a greasy caff that was still open and ordered a large serving slathered with curry sauce, which he balanced on his knees and ate as he drove them back to the station, explaining that anything eaten between the hours of one and four a.m. didn't actually count as part of your daily calorie allowance. Adams tried to enter into the spirit of things, but her own chips tasted too greasy, even when drenched in vinegar, so she'd binned them before she got in her own car. At home, she'd eaten a slice of toast standing over the sink instead, the Marmite pinching at her nose, and stared at her coffeemaker for a while before deciding she should at least try to sleep.

By the time she'd showered and pulled some pyjamas on she already knew it was going to be a pointless exercise, but she practised lying down for a bit anyway, staring at the floral '70s curtains her mum had given her (she kept meaning to change them, but somehow it was one of those things that wasn't even at the bottom of the to-do list for the simple reason that it had never made it onto the list in the first place). Her head was full of crouching bins and lurking bridges and deep, hungry shadows, and eventually she got up and went to the window, ducking under the curtains and leaning her head against the cool glass.

She wasn't sure what she expected to see. The wheelie bins rolling in grimly regimented ceremonial circles as they plotted their attack on the city, maybe? She'd looked out of this window plenty of times. Her flat was quarter of the second floor of a three-storey Victorian terrace, one of countless little boxes cramming a bedroom, a bathroom, and a combined kitchen and living area into the same space that the original inhabitants had probably designated as barely sufficient for a dressing room. But she liked it. She liked not sharing, and she liked that whoever had designed the place had decided that her flat should be long and thin, running right across the width of the house, so that she had one window in her bedroom that looked out the back, and another over her kitchen sink that faced the street. They were overly tall things that flooded the tiny flat with light, and while her bedroom was barely wide enough for her small double bed, it did have a little built-in seat below the window where she could sit and look out over the gardens at the back. Not that she had much chance to do so, or that there was much to see – the gardens were skinny strips of grass and desultory flowers, for the most part, coveted by the ground floor inhabitants but overlooked by everyone else.

But now, in the orange of the streetlights bleeding through from the road at the front, everything was sepia-toned and unfamiliar. Playhouses were shrunken, haunted edifices, and garden sheds hulked ominously, seeming disproportionately large in comparison. The winter grass was curtly short and frozen, and the paved yards glittered with damp, like dark and treacherous ice. There was no sign of life, no other lights visible from this angle, no glowing eye of a cigarette as some other insomniac leaned in a doorway and drank up the night with weary eyes. She was looking at a wasteland.

Movement below her, and she caught a yelp at the back of her throat as something dark and shaggy leaped lightly to the top of the wooden fence at the back of the garden. The low light gave it weird dimensions, rendering it oddly indistinct, as if it were somehow not quite in focus, and Adams leaned closer to the window. It had to be a dog of some sort, a scruffy-looking, terrier-sized stray with long matted hair and a sweeping tail, although she hadn't thought dogs were usually that good at climbing fences. It looked up at her, and she could feel its regard even though its eyes were hidden behind a mass of hair. They stared at each other for a long, fragile moment, then the dog-thing lifted its chin just slightly. Adams found herself nodding in reply, and the dog jumped off the wall, landing on the top of a playhouse in the next garden, then vanished out of sight. Off to investigate the bins, probably, and Adams was seized by the sudden conviction that she needed to go and warn the creature, to tell it not to venture too near them, that some bins were *dangerous* …

She pressed her cheek to the window. Her face was too hot, and the back of her neck itched with it. She closed her eyes, thinking about hidden paths and hidden lives. All the things that lie unseen, just out of reach. Out of *notice,* until one falls into them and out of the world. What was that thing about never being more than a metre from a rat in most cities? She wondered what else might pass so close, yet never seen.

She opened her eyes again, suddenly feeling less like she was looking out at an unseen world, and more like one was looking in on her. She pushed back from the window, letting the curtains fall back into place, and pulled a hoody on over her pyjamas. What had her old DCI said? "Sleep is nice, but coffee fills the void," she muttered to herself as she padded into the living room.

Anything sounded like wisdom if you said it with enough conviction.

ADAMS LIKED PRINTOUTS. She liked notebooks. She liked lists, and sketches, and anything she could scribble on the margins of, and cross things off of, and draw arrows and question marks on, and, on particularly irritating days, underline so hard that the pen snagged the paper. She thought better that way. Connections that eluded her on computer screens were suddenly evident when she spread papers out across a desk – or some chairs, or the floor, or whatever other space she could find. It was just how her brain worked – how it had always worked – and neither Zahid asking her if she'd ever heard of this snazzy new thing called a personal computer, nor DC Harry McMartin rushing past her desk in his permanent, aimless haste and sweeping half a dozen sheets of paper to the ground in his wake, gave her any cause to rethink it. Which was what he did now, and she made an exasperated noise. Coffee might fill the void, but it wasn't doing as much for her mood as a few hours' sleep might have.

"Sorry!" Harry yelped. He'd had a haircut this morning, by the look of things. It had been cropped brutally short, and did nothing to hide the grey coming in at the sides. It did help make the slowly expanding bare patch at the top of his head a little less obvious, though. He stooped and snatched up the papers. "Um …"

"It's fine. Give them here." DS Adams waved at him, and he thrust the notes at her, blinking a little too fast.

"Any luck?" he asked.

"Not really." She looked down at the desk, the woefully

thin files on each of the missing children. There were plenty of interviews, of course, but nothing of worth in any of them. They'd gone to different schools, played for different sports teams, swum at different pools. Their parents frequented different pubs, shopped at different supermarkets, had subscriptions to different food delivery apps. They were almost as separated as it was possible to be for five families from central London. The only thing that tied them together was the Christmas market, and the river, and the fact that each of their children had simply disappeared. One moment there, one moment gone.

The first to vanish had been seven-year-old Toby Green, skipping school with his older cousin. It had taken them a while to connect his disappearance with the others to start with, since the cousin initially swore Toby just hadn't turned up to walk home after school as he usually did. School CCTV cameras had told a different story, of them sneaking out over the roof of the maintenance shed, and once the cousin was presented with that, he'd broken.

"It was a Christmas present, right? He was having a rough time, and I said I'd buy him a hot chocolate and maybe a toy or something, and it was like this adventure, right?"

Until it wasn't, and Toby was gone.

Noah Doyle had been feeding the remains of his toasted sandwich to the ducks, flinging scraps of bread over the railing into the Thames. His dad had been telling him it was bad for the birds, and had turned to see if anyone was selling duck food. "It's important," he'd said to DS Adams in the interview, wiping his eyes with the sodden sleeve of his jumper. His nose dripped onto the table, but he didn't notice it. "It's important to care about these things. Noah knew that, but he said the birds were hungry, and …" He stopped, staring at the table without seeing it, and he didn't speak again until Zahid gently asked him if he wanted a tissue. It was as if he'd simply run down, a clockwork doll out of spring. Noah had been gone when he turned around. Simply gone.

Dotty Lambert – Dotty seemed such a strange and old-fashioned name for a seven-year-old, but her skinny, flowing mother had whispered that old names were back in fashion, it was honouring the past, these things mattered – Dotty had gone to buy a Christmas ornament shaped like an octopus, because she liked octopuses, and her mother had stood back to allow her to spend her own pocket money, and because she knew it was likely a present for her. "I don't really like octopuses," she confided, her fingers picking and plucking at a scarf. "But Dotty does, so I get a lot of octopuses." The scarf had octopuses on it, Adams noticed. Dotty's mum had looked away while her daughter was buying her ornament, just long enough to look for her own mother, who was buying hot chocolates, and then Dotty was gone.

Alfie Penn had wanted to go home, his granddad said. "But I told him no. I told him no, because all he does is get on his damn computer games, you know? And it was Christmas, and I wanted him to be *here,* be *present,* with the family. With me." He pressed both hands to his face, pulling them down so that his whole face followed, a man young to be the grandfather of a six-year-old, but right now looking older than Adams' own grandfather. "We got chestnuts, because he hadn't had them before, and he didn't like them much, so he ran ahead to the river to see if there were any ferries. He likes ferries. And then he just wasn't there. *He just wasn't there.*" He pulled at his face again, and DS Adams had the feeling he'd have pulled it straight off if he could have. If in doing so he could change things.

And Safa Hasan, the first they really noticed. Out with her little brothers and their parents, and their grandparents, and half a dozen cousins and some aunts and uncles besides.

All of them descending on the Christmas market to celebrate the end of school and to beat back the winter chill with hot chocolate and sugary pastries and the simple heat of the kids' excitement and the thrill of being out late on the banks of the wilding Thames. It was the sort of raucous, rushing group where anyone outside wonders how they keep track of each other at all, let alone of one small eight-year-old who never went anywhere without a book in her bag. The DCI had even suggested just that, but Zahid and Adams had looked at each other, then at her, and Adams had said, "Some big families are just the opposite. We sort of know where everyone is, even more than if it were smaller."

"Group responsibility," Zahid agreed. "Everyone's looking out for everyone else."

DCI Halloran looked from one of them to the other, then nodded. "Sure. But she's still gone."

She was. They all were.

Now DS Adams took a mouthful from her to-go mug and regarded Harry again. "Have you heard about any missing homeless people?"

He shook his head. "Don't think so. Why?"

"Someone told me there's been a number gone missing recently. All around the bridge area."

"Huh." He rubbed a hand over his head cautiously, as if hoping to discover some of his hair had come back. "That wouldn't come here, though. It'd be reported down at a local station. Battersea, maybe?"

"Well, obviously. But they don't have any reports."

He blinked at her. "Then maybe it didn't happen."

"That's it? That's the two choices – there's a report on it, or it didn't happen?"

"Well … yeah."

"You haven't heard of rumours, or conjecture, then? Lost reports? Misfiled ones? *Unofficial* statements?"

"Um …"

"Adams, leave Harry alone," Zahid said from his own desk. He was scrolling through something, and didn't look up. "It's not his fault that your mystery junkie put the wind up you."

"He didn't *put the wind up me.* And whether he's an addict or not is irrelevant. He seemed perfectly lucid when he was telling me about people going missing." *Perfectly* was probably stretching things, but still.

"But he still gave you nothing." He looked up at her finally. "Focus, Adams. We've got five missing kids and no leads. Don't start making up extra cases to confuse things."

"I'm not—"

"Did he actually say he saw anything?"

She rubbed a hand over her face, eyes stinging with weariness, seeing the dog staring back at her in the night, the bin lurking at the back of the depthless alley, the desperate *wrongness* of the figure passing. "He claims people are going missing. It's the same area. He also says that he's tried to report it, but no one takes him seriously. What if this is some sort of escalation?"

"Starting with adults and moving on to kids?" Zahid frowned at her, but he was leaning back from the computer at least, giving her his attention.

"Maybe."

"I've never heard of that," Harry said. "And you're just going by what some junkie says?" His nose was wrinkled. "There'll be a reason no one's taking him seriously."

"Sure," Adams said. "But is it a good reason?"

"What?"

Zahid looked at them both, then said, "Adams, follow it up. Get hold of the station. See if your mate really has tried to make some complaints."

"I already tried," she said. "All I get is, 'nothing on the system'."

"Computer says no," Harry said, grinning, and Zahid gave him an unimpressed look, then turned back to Adams.

"You're not going to let this go, are you?"

"I don't see any reason to. It's *something,* isn't it?"

He nodded. "Fair. Head down there and remind them about interdepartmental cooperation. Try to be nice about it."

"On it. Thanks, boss."

Zahid pressed a hand to his heart. "*Boss.* I should let you do what you want more often."

"You should," Adams agreed, gathering the scattered papers.

"What should I do?" Harry asked.

"Go with Adams," Zahid said. "Try and dissuade her from vanishing down dark alleys with dubious men."

"Joy," Adams muttered, and Harry looked equally enthused.

LONDON TRAFFIC WAS LONDON TRAFFIC, but half an hour later DS Adams pulled into the parking garage attached to the local station. There was no one on the barrier, just an automated arm, and her pass from her own station didn't let her in. She pushed the intercom button, waited, then pushed it again, holding it down longer this time.

"What?" someone finally asked, irritation plain even over the static of a dodgy speaker.

"DS Adams and DC McMartin. Can you buzz us in?"

There was a deep and breathy sigh, then the woman said, "Hold your ID up to the camera."

Adams obliged, and a moment later the arm swung up. It

seemed as reluctant as the woman had sounded, and she half expected it to slap down on them before they got through, just because it could.

The parking garage was poorly lit and smelled of damp, and the narrow halls that led them to the front desk weren't much better. A door with a push-bar release, like an emergency exit, let them into a small reception area. Three walls were lined with fixed grey plastic seating, leaving just enough room for the exterior door and the one they came in, and the fourth wall was taken up with a third door leading deeper into the building and a glass-enclosed reception desk.

Adams waited until the desk sergeant – a small woman with a thick crown of tightly curled blonde hair and a name tag identifying her as Sergeant Murphy – had finished dealing with a stolen bag reported by a tall man with thick dark hair and a heavy accent. He seemed very distressed, his forehead almost touching the glass as he mumbled to the sergeant inside, but finally he turned and headed for the door, his face pinched with worry, and Adams ambled up to the desk, ID in hand.

"Busy day?" she asked, trying for an understanding smile.

Murphy snorted. "Abdul there was making such a fuss I'm starting to think we should be more worried about what's in the bag than who grabbed it."

"Oh?" Adams said, holding onto the smile.

"Sounds about right," Harry said, grinning at the sergeant. "Probably got a goat in it, or something."

"Or an extra wife," Murphy said, and they both laughed.

Adams gave up on the smile, and just waited for them to finish. She needed the woman to actually help her, but she couldn't help saying, "Really?"

The sergeant examined her. "It was a joke."

"Hilarious."

"You lot are always so sensitive."

"Us lot?"

"Oops. You stepped in it there," Harry said, and laughed again.

Murphy flapped a hand at them both. "I meant detectives."

It was almost certainly not what she had meant, and Adams was getting a good idea why Jack hadn't got far with trying to report missing friends. But she just said, "Too much sensitivity training, I suppose." She was rewarded with a laugh from Harry and a grudging sort of snort from the desk sergeant, and added, "I just wanted to ask about someone making nuisance reports."

"Get plenty of that here," Murphy said.

"Do you?" Adams wondered how many really were nuisance reports, and how many were just too much hassle to do the paperwork.

"We do." Murphy crossed her arms and leaned back in her chair. "Place is crawling with junkies and all that sort. They're always coming in complaining about something. I just get them out the door quick as I can. Gets in the way of proper police work."

Adams looked at the hard chairs and the handful of posters above them, all screaming punishment instead of assistance. There was no comfort to be found in this place, no sense of safety. It even made *her* feel uncomfortable. She rubbed the nape of her neck, blinking away the weariness in her eyes, and said, "Any reports of missing persons over the last month? Specifically in the homeless population, and maybe with some strange circumstances indicated?"

"Oh, *him,*" Murphy said, and grinned. "You pull old Junkie Jack in for something?"

"I've been questioning him," Adams said, which was marginally true.

"About time. He needs moving on right quick. He was in

all the bloody time over the past couple of months. Claims his mates are being stolen by monsters no one can see." She snorted. "I started writing it all down just to send it round the station. Bloody hilarious, it is."

"Sure. Can I get a copy of those?"

The sergeant frowned at her. "Really? You're not taking it seriously, are you?"

"She's our own Dana Scully," Harry said, and would have elbowed Adams but she gave him such a look he subsided.

She turned back to Murphy. "Not the monsters, obviously. But I'm looking into patterns of missing persons, and it might be helpful."

The desk sergeant shrugged. "You're all a bit young and keen still, aren't you? There's always missing persons, love. And we did look into Jack's reports the first couple of times, but we couldn't even determine if he was talking about real people. He was the only person claiming they existed, let alone were missing. Fairy tales. Can't be wasting our time on that sort of thing."

"They didn't even exist?"

"Not that we could find. We threatened to do him for filing false reports, and he knocked it off a few weeks back. He's pretty entertaining, though. Monsters in the mist and trolls under bridges, all that sort of thing."

Trolls under bridges. Adams swallowed a shiver and managed a laugh. "Sounds it. I'd still like a look at those notes, if I could. Just out of interest."

"Sure. Bit of light reading for you. What's your email?"

Adams told her, and the sergeant busied herself on the computer, finishing with a theatrical tap of the enter button.

"There you go," she said, and looked past Adams as the exterior door opened. "Heads up. More missing bags, by the looks. Have people never heard of left luggage?" She waved a confused-looking couple forward, and DS Adams nodded her thanks, heading for the door back to the parking garage.

Harry trailed behind her. "Fox Mulder," he said. "He was the one that believed in monsters. Does that make me Scully, then?"

Adams looked back at him. He seemed quite taken with the idea.

5

DON'T THINK OF A BRIDGE

The afternoon was long and unpleasant. Zahid pointed at Adams as soon as she and Harry walked back into the room.

"Anything?" he asked.

"I've got an email to go through—"

"She's Mulder, and I'm Scully," Harry said. "Investigating monsters under bridges!"

"Trolls under bridges," Adams muttered, trying not to shiver.

"Come again?" Zahid demanded.

"I don't think there's anything," she said, before Harry could launch into a blow-by-blow account of the entire pilot episode of *The X-Files*. She'd already been subject to it in the car. "The desk sergeant didn't bother filing reports because they couldn't find anyone actually missing. Jack – the complainant, the guy from the bridge - didn't have any last names, and he seemed to be the only person who knew them."

"Missing imaginary friends?"

She grimaced. "Seems like it."

Zahid nodded brusquely. "Fine. We've checked it. All good. Now get your bums in some seats. I want to pull every bloody file we've got on *anyone* in the city who could conceivably fancy themselves some kiddies. Doesn't matter how tenuous. Herself has just had a visit from the big boss, and we're all going to be wearing the fallout if we've got nothing to give her."

"What about local ghosts?" Harry said, grinning. "Should we look into them?"

"Not unless you want to join them," Zahid said. "Get yourself on a desk, you divot."

"Yes, boss." He padded off, all scrawny angles, and Zahid turned his attention to Adams.

"How about the bridge?" she asked, before he could say anything. "Have SOCO been up there?" If anyone could find something, the scene of crime officers would.

Zahid shook his head. "Nothing. Nowhere they could be stashed, and no sign anyone had been cutting locks or anything else."

Adams swung into her chair with a sigh. "Sorry. All a bit of a waste of time."

"At least you're bloody thinking," he said, going back to his screen. "The rest of them are all hanging about scratching their collective rear ends."

Which was a better response than she'd imagined.

ADAMS LEANED back in her chair, pushing the heels of her hands into her eyes. Her tongue felt heavy and dry with too much coffee and not enough water, and her stomach was suggesting that food would be a good idea. She couldn't face it, though. Not after hours of trawling through a swamp of the sort of case files that were bad enough handled individually, never mind in bulk. She stole a glance at Zahid, hunched over his computer with his shoulders looming larger and larger around his ears. He was glaring at the screen like he was barely restraining himself from punching right through it, and the entire room had slowly descended into a simmering, uneasy silence, absent the usual off-colour banter and half-joking shouts.

She tapped her pen against her notebook. She'd flagged the files that had even the remotest possibility of potential, but she'd written the names down too, as if to give herself a handle on them. She considered another cup of coffee, but her stomach gave a roll of protest and she got up, stretching.

"I'm getting a Coke," she said to Zahid. "You want anything?"

He glanced at her, his face bare and haunted for a moment, then shook his head. "Rot your stomach, that stuff."

"I refuse to believe your sports drinks are any better."

"Scientifically formulated, Adams. *Scientifically formulated.*"

"Scientifically formulated bollocks," she said, and headed for the hall and the vending machine.

There were a couple of the same plastic, bolted-down chairs as at the other station by the vending machine, and above them a window looked out onto the afternoon, already heading rapidly into darkness. Adams could see her reflection in the glass, shadowy and insubstantial, as she leaned against the wall and opened her drink. She unfolded the papers she'd picked up from the printer on the way out, skimming them. They'd been in the attachment on the email the desk sergeant had sent her, all neatly typed up in Word, presumably in between engaging in a mix of light racism and borderline hostility toward tourists. Jack – named in the document only as That Nutter – had obviously tried to make serious reports, but he could never supply last names, and his descriptions were all along the lines of *He looks like a robin at the end of winter,* or *Her hair's the same colour as really good fish 'n' chips.* To give the desk sergeant credit, she'd taken everything down word for word, including her own questions.

– Back again, Jack?

– Yes, ma'am.

– Who've you lost this time?

– Edith.

– Edith who?

– She likes apples when they're just a little soft, because her teeth aren't good, and she smells like apples except when she has bad days.

– And what does she smell like then?

– Despair.

DS Adams shivered. For some reason she could imagine the scent, a steely, empty sort of damp, like the bottom of a dried-out well.

– And where did you see her last?

– At the river. She went to see if the toastie place was throwing anything out. The woman who runs it gives us stuff at the end of the night, you know.

– How nice.

– It **is** *nice. But she didn't get there. Edith, I mean.*

– How do you know?

– I asked. The woman – her name's Mirabelle, like sunlight in winter, Mirabelle – she said she hadn't seen Edith.

– Maybe Edith went somewhere else.

– She doesn't have anywhere else. She's gone.

– Well, we need a name. Or at least a description.

– Edith. She—

– Smells like apples?

– Yes. Will you look for her?

– Where? With some river monster, is she?

– I don't think it was the river monster.

– No?

– No. They only eat people who go in willingly, and it's not the bodies they eat. It's something else.

– Another monster, then? Or aliens this time? Ghosts?

– Ghosts aren't real.

– Well, that's a relief.

– You're not taking this seriously. Something ***took*** *her!*

– The big bad wolf?

– They're going to come for all of us. ***All*** *of us, and you don't even care, because we're already vanished to you.*

– You should write this down, you know. Bet you could sell it to Netflix or something. "The Monsters of London".

Movement in the window caught Adams' eye, and she jumped enough to spill Coke over her hand. She peered into the dim world beyond, overlaid by her own image, but there was nothing out there. "Pigeon," she muttered, and folded the papers in half. There was nothing there. Nothing but some poor lad, not quite connected to the world, telling tales of missing friends who'd never existed in the first place. There were enough monsters in the city without Jack's invented ones. Hadn't she just spent all afternoon looking at them?

Even so, she hesitated as she walked back into the cluttered sprawl of the office, her eyes drawn to the windows lining two walls and the reflections leering back in at them. There could be anything beyond that. Anything at all.

Adams had a steady headache throbbing behind one eye, a combination of exhaustion and hunger and too much caffeine, when Zahid pushed back from his desk and stretched. She heard his back crack from where she sat, and winced.

"What've you got?" he asked her.

"Not a lot," she said, her voice rough. She'd worked her way through her list of possibles, thin as they were, and it looked even thinner now that she'd made some phone calls. One was dead, two incarcerated, and five had solid alibis for the entire time. "I've got four who have alibis for more than one of the disappearances."

"Could still be working with someone else."

"Sure. They're on the more than unlikely list, as opposed to the just unlikely list."

"Do we not have a likely list?"

"Afraid not," she said, sighing. "Maybe someone else will."

"Yeah, well." Zahid scrubbed his hands through his beard. "I don't have one either. Give me the unlikely list, then."

"A porn type who still swears he had no idea the images were underage – he's only got a very shaky alibi for one disappearance, nothing for the others. Someone done for indecent conduct in Hyde Park with no alibis, but says he never goes out at night and reckons he can prove it. A sexual assault suspect also with no alibis, but a broken leg and a neck splint, and finally we have an eighty-three-year-old flasher who only accidentally targeted a kiddie who was with her gran. He didn't know the kid was there – thought the gran was his girlfriend and was just being a bit cheeky."

"Eighty-three. No one needs to see that."

"When it's uninvited no one needs to see it whatever its age," Adams pointed out.

"True." Zahid checked the time on his phone. "I've got even less than you. But we can follow them all up tomorrow. There's no point tonight."

"What about the trafficking angle?"

"Rafiq and Denison are covering it," he said, jerking his head at a small, intense-looking man who was hunched over his phone, and a bigger man with thick round glasses, who had his nose about an inch from his monitor. "They're liaising with NCA. Much as they can, anyway, unhelpful weasels that they are."

Adams nodded. Neither man looked as if they were having a much better day than her. "What now?"

"Now you get some dinner and go home."

"Not hungry. Not after that."

"No," he agreed, and got up, taking his coat from the back of the chair. "I'm going to the gym to punch things for a bit. But you, Adams, are going home whether you eat or not. You look like an extra from a cut-rate zombie movie."

"Thanks," she said, but without any heat. She *felt* like a cut-rate zombie, never mind someone playing one.

"Not saying it's much different to your usual look, mind, but it's unnerving. Can't have suspects thinking you're going to bite them."

"Might be useful," she said. "Threat of zombification."

He nodded. "Yeah, you're definitely tired. Get out of here, Adams. Before Herself catches you and gets you overtiming."

"Good point."

By the time she'd shut the computer down and tidied her desk, Zahid had vanished, and everyone else was sneaking glances at her. As soon as she went, they'd be gone too. But it wasn't like they were getting anywhere. Not unless an eighty-three-year-old-flasher was progress. She got up, grabbed her coat, and nodded to Denison, who gave her a bleary look through his heavy glasses. He nodded back, then returned to his slow scrolling, and she hurried through the door and headed for the parking garage. She was going home, and she was going to sleep, and she wasn't going to think about bridges.

She had been very clear on that, which made her wonder why she was currently standing in the middle of the Christmas village, her breath pluming in the cold air, scowling at the bridge straddling the river with possessive limbs. The market had been reopened that afternoon, once the SOCOs had decided there was nothing there to be found, and the stallholders had barely had time to set up before the crowds came back. Everyone knew *something* had happened, but the something always happened to someone else. Until it didn't.

The big tree loomed behind her, festooned with oversized gold baubles and red ribbons and lights, and the crowds surging through the little wooden huts of the stalls, trailing scarves and laughter, seemed almost as thick as last night. Not as many families, though. So maybe people weren't as entirely silly as she sometimes feared. She tucked her scarf a little more carefully around her neck and wondered what she was doing here. She'd fully intended to take the long way home, avoiding even a glimpse of this particular bridge (it wasn't like she could avoid *all* of them, when she worked north of the river and lived south of it), and yet here she was, staring at it. It was darker and heavier against the sky than it had any right to be, the lights that clung to its top side somehow serving to highlight its shadows rather than banish them.

But it was just a bridge. Her eyes watered as she watched it, the wind cold and hostile, and still she didn't look away. She didn't know what she was waiting for. For it to *move,* maybe? For a monster to jump out? For the bin to come lurching out of the shadows of the huts? There were plenty of shadows here, despite the festive lights. Or because of them, she wasn't sure. Just like the ones on the bridge, they seemed to serve to create shadows, not burn them away, and she wondered if they were the wrong voltage, if someone had swapped them out for some eco bulbs whose wattage didn't measure up to what they should. She blinked the tears from her eyes, and muttered, "Goddammit. What the hell am I even *doing* here?"

A woman passing close enough to hear grabbed her son and pulled him away, shooting DS Adams a suspicious look, but she didn't see it. Because as the water cleared from her eyes the world *shifted.*

The river that had a moment before been one-dimensional and opaque, featureless in the night, was riven with strange currents and luminescent bodies, the turbulence of their passage creating patterns full of meaning she couldn't discern. The sky swirled, the wind drawing fingers through clouds that suddenly had substance and motion, and someone shouted from the bank in a voice that wasn't human. Adams lifted her gaze to the bridge, her heart painful in her chest, and for one moment she glimpsed movement, deliberate and sharp-edged and spun silk, then it was gone. The world reasserted itself, draining of colour and meaning, and when the shout went up from the riverside again it was just someone a little too full of the spirit of the season. A little raspy, maybe, but human. How could it have been anything else?

She pressed the heels of her palms to her eyes, a teetering snake of nausea crawling through her belly, then dropped them away again. Spots swam in her vision, but the bridge stayed where it was, and the river remained empty.

"I need sleep," she muttered, just as someone loomed up in front of her.

"Ma'am?" they said, and she blinked at a uniformed officer in a heavy high-vis jacket, her dark hair gathered as severely back as DS Adams' own usually was. She had a feeling it was looking rather less well-groomed now, though. "Are you alright there?"

"Yes. Fine." She looked past the officer and saw the woman she'd startled before.

"I think you should move along," the officer said, her voice making it clear that there was no *think* about it. "You're creating a disturbance."

"DS Adams," Adams said. "Do you want ID?"

"Yes," the officer said flatly, and watched her warily as she fished her card from her pocket. The PC examined it, then nodded and handed it back, her stance barely relaxing. "I think you should go home, Detective Sergeant."

"I think I should too," Adams said, and managed a smile. "Sorry. Carry on." She turned and walked away, glancing back once to see the officer still watching her with a frown. Fair enough. She really did need some sleep.

She walked the length of the market on the way back to the car, and she almost missed the toastie van. It had lost its prime position at the end of the market to a coffee truck, and was instead tucked behind a stall selling personalised wooden nameplates and another dedicated to Christmas-themed pet clothing. There were a handful of people queued outside it, and the young man who'd spoken to her the night before was taking their money while the woman pressed bread onto a hotplate in the steaming heat of the interior. Fat, bare, multicoloured bulbs were strung along the outside, and a blackboard advertised *Best Toasties in Town,* and *Try our mulled wine!*

Adams frowned at it. They'd been here last night, she was sure, and then … which one was it? Noah, that was it. Noah Doyle, feeding the ducks with the crusts from his toasted sandwich. Of course, there might be another toasted sandwich van, but she was willing to bet this one had been here that night too. And yet she was near enough certain that she hadn't seen them on the lists of stallholders from the scene, and she was *completely* certain she hadn't seen any interviews with them. Which probably just meant they'd packed up and left before anyone could talk to them, or else Harry had been meant to do it and had been distracted by melted cheese. Probably.

DS Adams hesitated, looking toward the street and her car, parked in a loading bay with her permit in the windscreen, tantalisingly close. Then she turned toward the trailer and joined the queue.

The young man was cheerful but efficient, and a moment later he grinned at Adams and said, "Knew you'd cave eventually. Paneer and spinach toastie on a wholemeal paratha? We've got some tamarind chutney if you fancy it. Bloody nice it is, too. And different hotplate to the meat."

She frowned at him, and he grinned.

"I know a veggie when I see one."

"Do you?" She was suddenly almost overwhelmed by a wave of hunger, but there was something else, too. "You called me detective last night."

"Well, you are one, aren't you?"

"Yes. But how did you know?"

He shrugged. "You were walking into the market when everyone else was being shooed out. And no uniform. Now – toastie?"

Adams rubbed a hand over the back of her neck. She was jumping at shadows. "Right. Of course. I'll take one, then."

"Course you will." He held his hand out to take her money, and the woman at the hotplate turned to look at DS Adams, her eyes glittering in the multicoloured light. Adams had another sickening wave of that strange sense of dislocation, and, just like the night before, it seemed that the woman's teeth really were a little too sharp and a little too crowded. And now she was thinking about it, wasn't there something off about the young man, too? The way he stood, or the angles of his back?

Then it was gone again, and the woman said, "No charge for coppers."

DS Adams shook her head. "I'll pay."

"No one else does," the woman said, and winked. "Theo, love, run the line a second."

"Sure."

They swapped places, squeezing past each other in the tight confines of the trailer, and the woman leaned on the counter to peer down at Adams, her gaze curiously evaluating. "Can I help you? Other than the toastie, obviously."

"Maybe," Adams said. "Do you give food away to some of the homeless population at the end of the night?"

"If there's any left. No cause for it to go to waste when people are hungry."

"Have you noticed anyone missing recently?"

The woman lifted her chin slightly, and this time Adams was ready for the *swoop,* the twist of the world like turbulence on a flight. But the woman didn't change, even if, when she smiled, it seemed that she really did have an awful lot of teeth. "People come and go. But yes. Maybe more are going. It's winter, though. Dark, deep nights. If there's warm places to be had, they're better there."

"Someone called Edith? Do you remember her?"

The woman nodded, her mouth twisting slightly. "Not seen her for a bit. But things happen. The city's a hungry place."

"And last night – did you see anything? Anyone new? Anyone acting strangely?"

The woman laughed at that. "Humans are all bloody strange. We all are, I suppose." She turned and took a paper bag from the young man, offering it to DS Adams. "Enjoy your toastie."

"Is that a no?" Adams asked, taking the bag.

"Pretty much," the woman said. "People are impermanent.

They're fickle and strange, and never last. Only the city remains."

"What's that supposed to mean?"

"That things have patterns, and that I can't help you," the woman said, and turned away to swap places with the young man again. He gave Adams a wary glance, then looked past her.

"Burger, love?" he asked a woman in a pink feather boa. "All the trimmings?"

She gave him a thumbs up, and DS Adams stared at the bag in her hands, then at the slim back of the woman working the sizzling hotplate. She was craving the faintly resistant bite of cheese and the tangy slick of chutney, and her mouth was watering.

But she still had questions. Not even the best toastie could change that.

6

A CONFLICT OF TOASTIES

DS ADAMS FOUND A COFFEE STALL BY SCENT ALONE, AND GOT her mug refilled with what the painfully posh barista assured her was "Like, just the best coffee in London, yah?" while flicking a couple of blonde, gap-year dreadlocks over one shoulder. Adams supposed that meant she shouldn't be enjoying it in the same mouthful as London's best toasties, but considering the dull taste in her mouth, she doubted she was going to enjoy either as much as she might have liked.

She carried the warm sandwich and her mug back to the toastie trailer and leaned against the side, where it was hitched to the Land Rover and she was out of sight of the window. She could hear the sizzle of the hotplate and the clatter of utensils, but not so much as a raised voice from inside. Apparently London's best toasties didn't require shouting. There was the occasional yell from the market, or from waiting customers, but not from the van itself. Just the scent of faintly burnt cheese and toasting bread and caramelised butter, and she set her mug on the tow bar so that she could unwrap her dinner.

"I wouldn't," someone said, and she almost dropped the sandwich. She looked up at Jack, luminous in his ski suit, his feet still bare but a large red tartan shawl draped over his shoulders in deference to the light rain that had started.

"There you are," she said. "Where did you go last night?"

He shrugged. "Away."

"Got that." She looked at the sandwich, then at him, and said, "You want half?"

"No. I don't eat them."

"London's best, I hear."

"Got to be careful if you want to *see*," he said, and peeked at the bridge.

Adams shook the toastie back into the bag with a sigh. She could hardly eat it in front of him. "You want something else? A coffee?"

"Doughnuts?" he suggested, grinning at her. It made him look even younger than he probably was, and she wondered how long he'd been out here, in the cracks of the world.

"Sure. Those are okay for *seeing*, then?"

"Of course. They're *doughnuts*," he said, as if that should be obvious, and led the way to the stall that was laying rich scents of cinnamon and sugar across the night. Adams' stomach growled as she followed him, coffee in hand. Her sandwich was already getting cold. It was going to be awful now. Cold toasties were bad enough, but cold parathas were even worse, and the combination didn't bear thinking about. She dropped it in the bin next to the doughnut stall and ordered a mocha with whipped cream and sprinkles for Jack, as well as three doughnuts with pink icing and even more sprinkles. After a moment's thought she added six mini doughnuts caked in cinnamon sugar for herself.

"Good choice," Jack said approvingly. He already had cream smeared in his ginger moustache.

"Glad you approve." She popped one of the mini doughnuts into her mouth whole, the taste a hard hit of caramel sweetness that momentarily pushed back the dark and sharpened the lights around her. "I checked in with the station," she managed, a little indistinctly. "The one a few blocks away? That was where you went, right?"

Jack took a rather more circumspect bite of his first doughnut. "Yeah. I don't like the sergeant there. She wouldn't see even if she could."

Adams made a non-committal sound and washed the last of the doughnut down with a swig of coffee, then inclined her head for him to follow her. She led the way out of the worst press of the crowd and to a spot where she could keep an eye on the toastie van. "She said that you couldn't give her any names, and that they couldn't find anyone missing who matched your descriptions." *Descriptions* being a generous term.

"I gave her names," he insisted. "But she didn't listen. Not properly."

"I'm listening," Adams said. "But we're going to help each other, okay?"

He gave her a flat, unimpressed look. "You don't care about my friends."

"I care about the fact that people are going missing, and that *kids* are going missing. And I care very much that you might be the only person to have seen something."

He drew away from her. "I didn't do anything. Don't think you can blame this on me."

"I'm not trying to—"

"I know how you work!" His voice was rising, and a couple passing sped up their pace. "You just need someone who looks right! Fill the forms, dot the i's, close the case!" He took a step back, away from her, clutching his paper cup so tightly that the sides were starting to cave in, cream swelling over the top like an eruption.

"I'm not doing that," Adams said. "But if you don't help me with this case, how can I help you with yours?" It was a cheap shot, and it felt mean, but for all she knew the kidnapper was strolling around the market right now, while she argued with a man who believed in carnivorous bins.

"There's been five of them," he said, glaring at her. "Five of my friends. *Five* in the past three months, and no one cares. I tried to tell a police officer on the street the first time, and he told me to sleep it off. I went to the station, and they threw me out. Who cares about some smelly homeless people, right? They're all crazy anyway. Better off without them."

Adams just sipped her coffee and looked at him. She wasn't going to speculate on his mental state when she was the one asking him for help.

"It's not fair," he muttered, and licked cream off his fingers. "People are people."

"I know," she said. "But these are kids. And I will help you if I can."

He examined her for a moment, then tucked his bag of doughnuts into the front of his ski suit. "You already think you didn't see what you saw."

"Does it matter what I think?"

"It matters what you see. I can't help if you won't see."

She changed tactics. "You said it was something new that got your friends. New people? A new gang?"

"New *things. Snap-snap-snap.*"

Adams shivered despite the sugar rush and the warmth of her coffee. The word seemed to echo on the edges of sound, and she glanced at the bridge without thinking about it.

"Yes," Jack said.

"Yes what?" She turned to look at him.

"That's where I've seen them. They come with the fog and the mist and the dark. Maybe they're part of the bridge, or maybe they hide up there." He hesitated. "I tried to follow them once. I tried to see what they were. But they're good at hiding. Too good. That's the problem."

"We searched the bridge. There was nothing there."

"Nothing you could see."

Adams considered it. It wasn't like they'd been that quick off the mark with the bridge thing. Maybe someone really had been using it, whether to get across the river or to get *onto* it, a boat or a dinghy moored at the base somewhere, perhaps. Even Alfie could've been dragged up there and away again before they had eyes on it. They'd all been looking at the crowd or along the shore, after all. "And what did you see last night?" she asked. "When I followed you?"

"When you *chased* me."

"You were running. I'm a police officer."

"You make us sound like a dog and a squirrel."

She snorted, surprising herself, and he eyed her over his hot chocolate, then continued. "I didn't see a kid. I was looking for Jonesy. I can't find Jonesy. I hoped he'd be here last night, getting the sandwiches, but he wasn't. And then I heard the shouts, and saw all the police, and then there was mist. I don't stay if there's mist."

Adams frowned at him. "There wasn't any mist."

"Was." He looked around uneasily. "I have to go."

"You haven't given me anything," Adams said. "I can't help you if you don't at least talk to me."

Jack shook his head. "Not here. Not in the dark." He turned and scurried into the crowd, weaving his way out of sight, and Adams wondered if she should drag him back to the station, force him to talk to her. But there was no point. She wouldn't get any sort of truth there, only what he thought would get him released. So she just tucked her hands into her pockets and wandered back to lean on the toastie trailer, out of the wind, and watched the well-wrapped nighttime perambulators come and go, woolly hats low over their ears and scarves blooming out of collars to meet them. The night held the sort of chill that should have promised snow, but instead just burned the insides of noses and made toes ache even inside socks and boots. Adams allowed herself one longing thought of her hot shower and snuggly bed – with the hot water bottle her mother had forced on her when she'd moved out at eighteen, and which she'd insisted she didn't want, need, or like, but which she used for at least half the year – pulled her phone out, and resigned herself to wait.

She didn't have to wait as long as she'd feared. The Christmas market emptied early on a work night, and it was only about eight when the continuous wash of people started to look very one-way, more people leaving than arriving. She heard the first of the shutters coming down on the stalls not long after, and before half an hour had passed she caught the rattle of the hatch being lowered on the far side of the trailer. She straightened up, shuffling her feet to get some warmth back into them, and a moment later the young man appeared, shrugging into a big jacket and heading for the locker DS Adams had been leaning against. It had a bright yellow LPG sticker on the door.

The young man stopped when he saw her and took a step back, as if afraid she might rush him. "What're you doing?" he asked.

"Just waiting for you to finish up. Wanted another word when you weren't so busy."

It was shadowy on this side of the van, the market lights

blocked by the bulk of it, and it made the young man's eyes seem oddly bright. "What about?"

"If you've noticed anything unusual. People acting strangely. Children who look like they don't belong with the adults they're with."

He took another step back. "I don't know anything about that."

"What about the homeless population around here? Have you noticed anything about them?"

Instead of replying, he just shouted, "*Mirabelle!*"

"Calm down. You'll do my eardrums in." The woman stepped around the van, an oversized hoodie pulled over her baggy trousers. She was lost in the clothing, rendered tiny, but she nodded at the young man. "Finish packing up, will you?"

"She's asking—"

"Theo. Pack up."

He subsided, shot Adams a look she couldn't quite read, then hurried around the van, his ponytail bobbing.

"Think he'd give you a different answer, did you?" Mirabelle asked, smiling at Adams.

It was an easy sort of smile, and Adams found herself smiling back. "How come you haven't been interviewed?"

"I suppose no one thought to."

"Someone should have."

"It's always someone *else,* though, isn't it?" Mirabelle took a roll of mints from her pocket and offered them to Adams. "Want one?"

"No. Shall we do an interview now, then?"

"I'm tired. I've been on my feet all day, and I want to go home."

Adams nodded. "Of course. In that case, how about would you like to cooperate with a police officer, or would you prefer me to pull you in for a *formal* interview?"

Mirabelle gave her an amused look. "I don't think you've grounds for that."

"There's five kids missing. I've grounds for pretty much anything at this point."

"Five. That's not good."

"It's not. So will you cooperate?"

The woman spread her fingers, the nails short-cropped and the knuckles raw and painful-looking from heavy hand-washing and scrapes. "What do you expect me to do?"

"Tell me what you've seen. You're here every night. One of the boys even bought a sandwich from you just before he vanished."

Mirabelle met Adams' gaze, and the DS expected to see something familiar in her expression. The usual worry at being accosted by a police officer, and the resentment of it as well. Perhaps a distaste for authority in general, or, depending on the person, a squirming, ingratiating desire to prove themselves innocent. She doubted Mirabelle would subscribe to the last one, though.

She hadn't expected to feel like the one being evaluated. Being examined. She lifted her chin almost unconsciously, squaring her shoulders under the heavy weight of the coat. She returned the woman's gaze with her own, and after a moment Mirabelle smiled.

"I can't help," she said.

"Can't or won't?" Adams' tone was sharper than she intended, but Mirabelle just shrugged.

"I don't know what happened to the kids. I haven't seen anything. It's busy. We serve hundreds of sandwiches. Thousands, even."

Adams looked at the sky, biting the inside of her cheek, then took her phone out and waved it at Mirabelle. "I looked up your van. Nothing on the market permits that I can see."

"We'll just move on."

"Sure. But it'd be a shame to lose such a nice spot, I imagine."

Mirabelle sighed. "What do you want me to say?"

"Tell me why you were never interviewed, for a start. We might be useless, but we're not *that* useless." Well, Harry might be, but she wasn't going to admit it.

"No one asked."

Adams blinked. "*How?* You were right here. I've seen you here every night I've been around."

"Observant."

Adams had a sudden and very unprofessional urge to throw her arms in the air and shout, "Well, *don't* tell me then!" Instead she said, "Let's start with the easy bits. Back to Edith. She came to get leftovers a lot, apparently."

"Yes."

"When did you last see her?"

Mirabelle tucked her hands into the front pocket of the hoody and rocked on her heels. "A month ago, maybe."

"Did you see anyone with her? Did she seem scared?"

"Everyone's a little scared at the moment."

"Why?"

The other woman didn't answer for a long moment, her gaze drifting to the bridge. It stood stolid and unmoved, and Adams thought there might be mist collecting at its base, but from here it was hard to be sure. It was probably just Jack getting in her head. She shivered, and Mirabelle shot her a sideways look.

"Cat walk over your grave?"

"Something like it. Why do you think everyone's afraid at the moment?"

"You can see it." Mirabelle stepped to the edge of the trailer and inclined her head at the thinning crowd. Theo was handing paper bags out to a handful of people who at first glance didn't look that different from the rest of the shoppers, all bundled into heavy coats and woolly hats. It was only their posture that gave them away, the way they curled in on themselves as they took the sandwiches and scurried away again, hiding themselves from a hostile world that was doing its best not to see them anyway.

Adams watched them for a moment, then said, "But what are they afraid of?"

"Why don't you ask them directly?"

"I tried. Apparently it's hungry bins." She tried to sound mocking, but she could hear the flatness of her own words, and she found herself looking for Jack's bright green ski suit. She couldn't see it. He had said he didn't eat the sandwiches, after all.

"Ask again," Mirabelle said.

"I'm asking *you* what you know."

Mirabelle nodded. "Why? Because you think I'll give you a more palatable answer? Because I look like you? Because I *act* like you?"

"What? You don't—"

"I'm *not* like you," the other woman continued. "And the world's not like you think. But it doesn't matter." She strode across to Theo and snatched a sandwich off him, then turned back to Adams. "Take a bloody sandwich and stop asking questions you don't really want the answers to, just like you lot usually do."

"I don't want a sandwich," Adams snapped. "I want you to answer my questions."

Mirabelle gave her a disbelieving look. "I've told you all I can. You want to dig, be my guest." She pointed at the little crowd, melting away as fast as Jack had earlier. "See what you can get out of them."

Adams scowled, rubbing the back of her neck. "If you're not going to talk to me, I *will* pull you in."

Mirabelle shot her a half smile and turned to the Land

Rover. "You won't. But if you want another toastie, come on by."

"I didn't even eat the first one," Adams said, and immediately felt like a petulant child shouting, *I don't like it!*

Mirabelle stopped and looked back at her. "Why not?"

"It was cold."

"It was not."

"It was by the time I got to eat it." She shook her head, still rubbing the back of her neck. It itched. "Look, I'm sure it was lovely, but I didn't want it."

"Everyone wants a toastie." Mirabelle took a step toward her, her eyes narrowed. "What's wrong with your neck?"

"I don't know. I think something bit me."

"Let me see." The other woman was next to her before Adams could protest, tugging at her scarf, and she made a little *hmm* noise.

"What? What is it?"

Mirabelle patted the scarf back into place and stepped back, her face unreadable. "Probably nothing." She shoved the sandwich at Adams again. "Just have it, will you? You can heat it up in a pan at home."

Adams took the toastie with a sigh, wanting to push, insist, to force the woman in for a formal interview, but somehow the idea of it was ridiculous. Mirabelle hadn't *done* anything. Not really. So instead she just watched her walk to the battered Land Rover and open the driver's side door. She hesitated there and looked back at Adams. "Keep an eye on that bite," she said, and climbed into the driver's seat. A moment later the engine coughed into life, and Adams shivered. It was cold, and she was tired, and she was getting nowhere. She was just asking the same questions and getting the same nonsensical answers.

"I feel like Alice in sodding Wonderland," she muttered.

"Eat something and see if it feels better," Theo said,

appearing in front of her and holding out a paper bag. He took the one she was holding off her at the same time, a smooth transition.

"I don't—"

"They're brownies," he said. "I make them myself. Good ones." His eyes widened suddenly. "I mean, not *good*. Not like … good as in chocolate, not good as in … stuff. I don't … I mean, not to *sell*." His eyes got even wider, if it was possible. "Or at all! Not at all!"

Adams took the bag, as much to put the poor lad out of his misery as for any other reason. "Right. Ta."

Theo started to head for the car, and she said, "You've not seen anything out of the ordinary, then?"

He hesitated, giving her the wide-eyed look again. "Not … not as such."

"What does that mean?"

"I mean … some stuff is ordinarily out of the ordinary, you know? I mean, you don't want it happening, but there it is. It *has* to happen."

"What?"

He licked his lips. "Like freak waves. They're out of the ordinary, but they happen, so they're ordinary, too. They come and go. Cycles, like."

"Right." She thought about it. "Why does that make sense?"

"Because it's true. It's ordinary for the world – for *life* – to be full of the extraordinary. People, too."

Adams looked at him for a long moment, his face pale and pinched in the cold, his nose pink and a desultory stubble decorating his chin, then looked at the paper bag of brownies. "I think I will eat this," she said.

"You should," Theo said.

"Is it extraordinary?"

"Kind of," he said, and grinned, then trotted for the car.

Adams stood on the pavement as the last of the Christmas market packed up behind her, and watched the Land Rover and trailer pull away, bumping out of the market onto the drive and heading up to join the flow of nighttime traffic. "Alice in bloody Wonderland," she muttered.

7

NEVER GOOGLE THE SYMPTOMS

Her flat was silent and vaguely stuffy when she let herself in, dropping the brownies in her tiny kitchen before heading for the bedroom. She'd shower, just to get rid of the grime of the day and the lingering, unsettled feeling of the river's scent clinging to her skin and hair, then she'd sleep. She *had* to sleep. She was so tired it scraped at her bones.

Putting a decent shower in was the one thing she'd done after buying the flat. The cooker was the same rusting white monster that had been there when she moved in, with its broken hinge on the oven door, one burner that didn't work at all and two others that only worked patchily, plus a missing foot that meant it lurched unpredictably under the weight of any pan Adams bothered to put on it. The flooring was a delightful orange '70s shag with scorch marks in it from old cigarettes, the wallpaper a tasty clash of green paisley with purple accents, and the bathroom itself tended toward dusky pink and dark-stained wood, but her shower had one large waterfall head and a second one that could take a layer of skin off if you weren't careful. It had cost far too much to both buy and install, and she had zero regrets.

By the time she stepped out, the bathroom felt a lot like the tropical conservatory at Kew Gardens, and the knots in Adams' shoulders had shrunk to a manageable size. She put pyjamas on, looked at her bed, and gave a small, irritated growl. She might feel cleaner – she *definitely* felt cleaner – but there was no chance she was sleeping. Again. She walked into the little living area and looked from the TV to her laptop, and finally at the brownies sitting on the bench and the coffeemaker next to them. She probably should have kept the toastie. Brownies weren't exactly the ideal chaser after a dinner of coffee and doughnuts.

"But they are extraordinary brownies," she muttered, and went to switch the coffeemaker on.

IT WAS LATE ENOUGH – or early enough – that the ever-present traffic on the road outside had slowed to nothing more than the occasional delivery truck rumbling past, or something overpowered and thrumming with bass that made her register the time automatically. The brownies – which had definitely been better than average, although she wasn't sure if that made them *extraordinary* – were both gone, as were two cups of coffee. Something was playing on the TV, one of those shows where people insist they only have about a hundred quid yet want a five-bed mansion on the Spanish waterfront as a holiday home, but she'd lost track of it almost as soon as she put it on. They might be renovating hotels in Siberia now, for all she knew. Her laptop was on the coffee table with far too many tabs open, and around it was a spray of paper, each sheet scribbled with a brusque heading in permanent marker, and notes scrawled beneath in Adams' straggly hand.

Aliens, one sheet said. *River monsters* topped another, and

Hauntings was on a third. There were also ones for unexplained disappearances, urban legends, and *WTF*. That one was quite full, and a lot of the items on the other lists also appeared on that one. Adams leaned back in the sofa and rubbed her hands over her face. She'd been scratching through the archives of some fairly legitimate publications, but there were also others that seemed mostly concerned about Elvis' alien babies setting up pizza takeaways in Greenwich village, as well as mermen swimming up drains and appearing in the bathrooms of unsuspecting residents in Chelsea. Adams thought that was one of the best excuses for finding half-naked men in the marital bedroom that she'd ever heard.

She'd also managed to track down a few sites that wrote articles with footnotes that were longer than the text itself, and had printed out a few pieces about the science of perception and the medical causes of hallucinations. She was a bit wary of those. She'd already Googled *symptoms of Weil's disease,* because one of the articles mentioned they included hallucinations and headaches. She also vaguely recalled from somewhere (correctly, as it turned out), that the bacteria responsible were mostly picked up through contact with rat urine, or with water contaminated by it – such as the Thames.

Which, she thought as she smeared a generous amount of out-of-date antiseptic cream on the itchy spot at the back of her neck, could be possible. But the timing made no sense. If she'd scraped herself on the bricks in the alley, perhaps she could have picked it up there, but she'd been … maybe not *hallucinating,* but certainly things had been a bit wonky already at that stage. And she certainly hadn't fallen in the Thames or any other murky body of water, so it really made no sense for it to be Weil's disease, but still. If she wanted to get any sleep at all in the next month she was going to have to stop looking at self-diagnosis websites.

Now she got up, stretched, and took her mug through to the kitchen, giving the coffeemaker a longing look. None of the articles she'd read suggested too much caffeine could lead to hallucinations, but it was well after midnight, so if she wanted sleep to be a possibility any more coffee was probably contraindicated. She put the mug in the sink and filled a pint glass with water instead, staring through the window at the orange-lit street. Slumbering cars lined it, and the houses were dark except for one dimly lit window three houses down on the other side of the street. Adams raised her glass to it. It was often lit when she was up late, and sometimes she saw a woman with long white braids staring out at the street just as she was, a cat sitting next to her as they watched the night together. She'd waved once, on a summer night when the windows were open and she could smell the lingering heat on the tarmac and the metallic scent of the cooling city, and the woman and the cat had stared at her for a moment before the woman had raised her hand in acknowledgement.

There was no one at the window now, though, and she was about to turn away when the dog emerged from the shelter of a parked car below. He seemed larger than he had last night, more like the size of a Labrador. The perspective of him perched on the fence must have thrown her perception off. He looked up at her, his floppy ears quirked upward and his eyes still hidden behind the heavy curtain of matted hair. She didn't know how he could see anything at all through that, but he was definitely looking at her. She stared back, then lifted her glass, much as she had to the empty window. The dog's mouth dropped open into something that was unsettlingly close to a grin, and he dipped one shoulder, as if in imitation of some courtly bow. Adams barely stopped herself jumping back from the window, her heart suddenly too loud. She was being silly. He – *it* – just had a gammy leg, or an itch, something like that.

The dog looked over his shoulder, as if his attention had been called by something she couldn't see, then broke into an easy, surprisingly graceful run, loping down the street with his hair flopping softly around him, rendering him indistinct as a shadow. Adams stayed where she was, not sure what she was waiting for, only sure, *sure* that something was going to emerge from the end of the street, something big and sleek and soft-footed, following the dog's scent with its head low and its teeth hungry, its coat dappled by the lights and its eyes huge and dark and filled with the secrets of the city.

She didn't realise she was holding her breath until her laptop gave a sudden, *battery's dying* ding, and she jumped, biting down on a yelp and almost dropping the glass. She set it down in the sink and flicked spilled water off her hand, then jerked the curtains closed over the windows. Too much coffee, not enough sleep. That was all it was.

She picked up the glass again and went back into the living room, looking at the other sheets of paper on the coffee table. *Missing persons. Cults. Monster religions. What people saw.* That one was underlined twice, and she stared at her own brusque notes.

Took dog. Tentacles.

Grabbed kid in stroller. Woman, but had horns and wings and teeth.

Cat brought it in. Too many limbs.

Watching from basement flat. Strange smells. Raining fish.

The sort of things desk sergeants took down not to be reported, but to be stuck on bulletin boards or sent around in highly unofficial newsletters. The sort of things interested internet parties clung to as evidence that the police were ignoring the threat in their midst. She looked at the last line finally.

It was under the bridge. It was hungry.

She pushed the laptop closed and headed into the tiny bedroom. She might not sleep, but she could at least pretend to.

"ROUGH NIGHT, ADAMS?" Zahid asked, as she walked into the briefing room clutching her coffee.

She grunted at him and sat down, eyeing the yellow foam on his moustache. "Turmeric latte today, is it?"

"Better than that poison you keep gulping down."

"I hate to think what colour your insides are. Fluorescent, likely."

"Whereas yours would be sludge." He nodded at the folder she was clutching. "What's that?"

"Nothing yet, I don't think."

"It's not going to be another junkie chase, is it?"

She took a sip of coffee to hide the twitch at the corner of her mouth. "He's a homeless person. No idea if he's an addict as well."

"It's an educated guess."

She sighed. "You forget that they're *there.* They see a lot more than anyone gives them credit for."

"They see bloody dancing pink elephants and all."

"So what've you got, then?" She raised her eyebrows at him.

Zahid was saved from having to answer by the DCI striding into the room, her heels muted on the worn carpet tiles, her back dangerously straight as she turned to face them. She placed her fingertips on the nearest table, the nails blunt and polished, and said, "Anything?"

No one answered, and she took a deep breath. Her hair was press-conference ready, pulled back in a neat sweep of grey-streaked brown, and her suit had the sort of creases one felt had been threatened into it and were too terrified to come out, possibly ever.

"Nothing?"

Still no one answered, and she pointed at Zahid. "DI Mirza. At least tell me what the hell you've been doing, since I came out of my office at eight last night and the entire damn place was empty."

"Following what leads we can, boss."

She raised a perfectly shaped eyebrow. "As, somehow, no report of these fascinating leads has crossed the pristinely empty expanse of my desk, please enlighten me."

Zahid kicked Adams, but she didn't even flinch.

"DI Mirza?"

"It didn't come to much. We spent yesterday running down any possible knowns, and will get started door-knocking once the briefing's over."

"That's it?"

Zahid tried standing on Adams' foot, but she moved too quickly, keeping the folder out of sight under the desk. She didn't have anything. Not yet. She had an itching at the back of her mind, a sense of connections striving to meet, like spiderweb spinning into the void (an image she tried to shake immediately), waiting to find a place to connect, but that was it. She certainly wasn't going to stand up and tell DCI Halloran that a dog had bowed to her and she'd had an extraordinary brownie, and that somehow those things were both connected and important.

"We have five missing children. *Five.* And all we have to go on is the possibility of some door-knocking, but nothing else." No one answered, and she added, "That was a question, DI Mirza."

"Sorry, boss. Yes, that seems to be about the extent of it."

"About the extent of it. You need to spend less time in the

gym, Zahid. All your brainpower's going to your muscles." There was a little titter of laughter in the room at that, and the DCI glared around. "The rest of you don't even have that excuse."

The titter less died than collapsed like a black hole, and into the silence Harry said, "DS Adams has a theory."

Adams wished she were close enough to kick Harry's leg. Leg, or preferably something more incapacitating.

"Adams?" the DCI asked. "Tell me that's true."

"Not exactly, boss, no."

"Not exactly seems closer than nothing, so let's hear it."

Adams pressed her hands against the folder, as if to ensure nothing rushed out and started shouting about tentacles. Or carnivorous bins. "Um ..."

"She's going for the Fox Mulder angle," Harry said, earning a round of smothered laughter, particularly from some of the older detectives. "Chasing up missing persons that don't exist." There was more laughter at that, and Harry grinned. It faded fast when the DCI scowled at him.

"I don't think I asked for your input, DC McMartin."

"No marm," he muttered.

"Adams?"

Adams sighed. "While at the scene the night before last, I spotted someone near the bridge at the time that Alfie Penn went missing. When I attempted to approach them, they ran, but I was able to catch up. I don't have a last name—"

"Junkie Jack, I think the desk sergeant called him," Harry said helpfully, to another round of muted laughter.

"Yes, thus using discriminatory, outdated, and offensive language all at once," Adams replied, and immediately wished she hadn't used *thus* in an actual sentence, out loud, in public. The folk in the cheap seats were grinning even more widely. "Anything else you want to add, Detective Constable?"

He gave her a look that was more hurt than chastised. "I was just having a laugh."

"Missing kids *are* hilarious," the DCI said, and Harry brightened for a moment, then slouched into his chair as she glared at him. "Carry on, Adams."

"Right. Well. This individual told me that other members of the unhoused population have been going missing. He said that he had tried to report it, but no one at the local station would take him seriously." She decided to leave out the bit about chasing Jack into dark alleys, and she *certainly* wasn't going to mention hungry bins or mist-spinning bridges, and she just hoped Zahid didn't decide to remind her she'd been running about alone and unauthorised. She could feel him watching her, but he didn't speak up, and she continued. "I attempted to clarify the situation with the station by phone yesterday, but they just told me they didn't have any reports in the system. DC McMartin and I went down there to see if we had any more luck face to face."

"Did you?"

"Not really," she admitted. "Desk Sergeant Murphy did say that this particular member of the public had tried to file several reports, but they couldn't positively identify any of the people he claimed were missing, and thought it was just attention-seeking."

"You don't agree."

"I ..." Adams hesitated, the edges of the folder rough under her fingers. "I did a bit of research, and I found that there have historically been rashes of missing people in areas adjacent to the river. Seven adults, usually unhoused or otherwise vulnerable, and seven children."

The pause that followed was electric, and Zahid shifted next to her. She could actually hear him in her head, shouting at her for not bringing it to him first. That wasn't going to last long, though.

"Are we talking a serial killer?" the DCI asked, then glared around the room. "How the hell did we miss that for so long?"

No one replied, everyone suddenly very interested in their hands or the floor, and Adams scratched her jaw. "The spacing is … wide."

"How wide?"

"Um. About fifty years. Forty-nine, to be precise."

"*Forty-nine?* How many have there been?"

Adams took a deep breath. "As far back as I can find records, boss."

There was dead silence. Someone gave a cough that sounded very like they were swallowing a laugh, then the DCI said in a very flat, very clear voice, "Just how old is our serial killer, then, Adams? Or do you think it's a family business? Hannibal junior, senior, and Gramps?"

Adams' face was so hot her lips felt numb. "I was wondering about a cult angle, boss."

There was no mistaking the laugh this time, a snicker that spread rapidly around the room until it seemed everyone but her was shaking with barely restrained hilarity. She bore it expressionlessly, not letting her shoulders hunch or her chin dip, just waiting it out. She'd waited out worse.

The DCI let it run for a bit, grinning slightly herself, then clapped her hands. "Alright, alright. We all needed a bit of a laugh." She examined Adams, who returned her gaze as calmly as she could. "I know this is a tough case, and it's getting to all of us. But I suggest more sleep and less midnight research. You're the only one in here who looks like they're getting less rest than me, Adams, and it doesn't suit you."

"Understood," Adams said.

"Good. You'll be telling me it was aliens next." That got a round of laughter, and Adams smiled briefly. The DCI looked around the room. "That was all fun and games, but it stays in the room, got it? If so much as a *whisper* of this gets to the press, you'll wish the damn river cult had got to you. There'll be unpaid overtime for every bloody one of you."

"How's that different to normal?" Abdul asked, apparently in perfect seriousness, and another chuckle went around the room.

"You'll be doing it under my personal supervision, which means *I'll* be on unpaid overtime, and you do not want to see that," the DCI said. Abdul nodded, apparently satisfied, and she added, "No conspiracy theories, no aliens, no bloody cults or serial killers. Anyone got anything constructive to add?"

"Traffic stops," an older woman said, her hair cropped so short Adams could see the outline of her scalp.

"Yes? And?"

"Well, are we doing them?"

"Where? When? Can you be a bit more bloody specific, DI Dankworth?" The DCI snapped, and the DI rolled her eyes.

"That went well," Zahid said in a low voice, grinning at Adams as she sat down again.

"Bloody Harry. He stitched me up."

"You know Harry. He wouldn't have meant it."

Adams looked at Harry, leaning back in his chair next to a big DS called Wilson and a couple of younger DCs. It was the same everywhere. There was always an inner circle, and sometimes being promoted was a sure way to ensure you weren't in it. Not that she would've been anyway. She was lacking at least a couple of key attributes.

"Probably wasn't even his idea to say it," she said.

"Yeah, well. That's what you get for thinking for yourself." He pushed his chair back and got up as the DCI dismissed them with an impatient wave. "Come on. We've got doors to knock. Maybe we can find some aliens out there."

"We should be so lucky." She got up and turned to lead the way out of the room, and Zahid whistled.

"Bloody hell, Adams. And here I thought you were just tired from working late."

"What?"

He pointed at the nape of his own neck. "Get your night-time buddy to cut their nails. Looks like a bloody cat's been at you." He headed for his desk as Adams clapped a hand over the back of her neck, feeling the sting of raised welts with something close to horror and thinking, for some reason, not of Weil's disease, but of the dog staring back at her in the night.

8

PLAYS WELL WITH OTHERS

THE DAY WAS AS FRUITLESS AND GRINDING AS THE PREVIOUS one had been. The only good thing that could be said of it was that at least they weren't at their desks, poking at phone numbers and sifting through horrors couched in detached, technical terms on page after page of reports. Out here, at least, one could imagine that perhaps all of humanity wasn't a glooping cesspit of ugliness, but Adams had to admit that it got harder with every house call. Plus it was raining, an icy slurry that collected in her hair, slid down her collar, and made the scratches on her neck burn. She should have covered them. She didn't trust the rain not to be carrying something nasty. Nastier than anything she might already have, anyway.

"I told you, I was home," a short man in very small red shorts told them. He was wearing an oversized white singlet over the shorts, and when he'd opened the door to them she'd thought for a moment he'd forgotten to put anything on his bottom half. He had let them in affably enough, though, into a tiny front room stuffed with a claustrophobic amount of intensely floral furniture and large display cabinets full of china figurines. He left them perched uncomfortably close together on the two-seater sofa and went to produce two large mugs of tea, one of which had an upside-down pineapple on it, and the other of which read, *Plays well with others.*

Adams was less bothered by her mug than by the contents, which she peered at suspiciously. She didn't like tea at the best of times, and this one had a dubious, oily scum drifting on the surface. She put it down and regarded the man as he sank into a big armchair, his feet not quite reaching the floor. He swung them nervously and said, "I'm sorry I don't have any biscuits. I'm trying to cut down." He patted his belly, and Adams shivered. She hadn't even undone her coat, and there he was in his teeny shorts and enormous singlet. She wanted to tell him to put a jumper on, which was horrifying. She was a DS in the Met Police, not her mother.

"We haven't told you the dates yet," Zahid said, setting his own tea down untouched.

"You did on the phone," the man said, and nodded at Adams. "Detective Sergeant Adams? You're the one I spoke to, right?"

"That's right," she said. "But we need to go over it again. You say you're home *every* night? That seems like quite a sweeping statement."

"I am, though. I don't like going out at night these days. Bad night vision, see." He tapped his temple.

"Right. And can anyone vouch for that?"

"Well, it depends on the night, but probably about thirty-six people. More on Sundays."

Adams and Zahid looked at each other, then around the room. "Sorry?" she said.

The little man smiled. "Little Man Sixty-three."

Neither of them said anything for a moment, then Adams said, "Is that maybe a podcast …?"

"Oh, no. Livestream."

"Of course it is," she said, and tried for a smile. "Are you a gamer?"

He shook his head. "Oh, no. And it's nothing perverted or anything, either."

"You *are* on the sex offender's register," Zahid pointed out.

"For a completely consensual act, filmed with the permission of all parties."

"In a public place," Adams said. "A *very* public place. I don't think the groundskeeper's got over the shock yet."

"Yes, well." The little man straightened in his chair. "Some people are very narrow-minded. I livestream from home now. There's no one to get offended by that."

"We'll have to verify you were here," Zahid said.

"Of course. I record the sessions for premium subscribers. They're all time-stamped, so just tell me where to send a link." He looked at them expectantly.

"Adams," Zahid said, not moving to take his phone out, and Adams sighed, scribbling her work email on a blank page in her notebook and tearing it out.

She handed it across to the small man in his big chair. "You better not give me a bloody virus."

He took the paper, frowning at her. "Now what sort of reputation would *that* get me?"

By late afternoon the day was dark and wet and cold with the sort of chill that nags at the bones and pinches the toes even through heavy socks and thermal layers. The sun hadn't even bothered to put an appearance in. Adams dropped into the seat of Zahid's car, leaned her head back against the seat and closed her eyes for a moment. They felt rimed with grit from the day and the interviews and the sleepless nights before, but there wasn't a lot of rest to be had behind the lids. She opened them again as Zahid started the engine and turned the heater up.

"Head back and start looking at these alibis?" she said, trying to sound, if not enthusiastic, at least not entirely unwilling.

"Send the details through to Harry," Zahid said, pulling into a skinny one-way street. It was lined with cars on both sides, and there seemed barely enough room even for the squat Mini to pass between them. A couple of kids with their hoods pulled up against the drizzle, wafts of vape smoke rising from the shadows inside, watched them go, but otherwise the road was empty.

"Gladly," Adams said, pulling her phone out. She'd sneaked a peek at the site for LittleMan63, and had closed it as soon as lotion was mentioned, feeling that she should update her antivirus no matter what he'd said. "What're we up to?"

"Walking," Zahid said. "I don't know where you're getting your cult angle from, but it's not as far outside the realms of possibility as the DCI seems to think."

"No?"

"No. Or maybe no. I'm not sure. But let's head down to the river anyway. Have a walk, then if nothing jumps out at us we'll call it a day."

Like bridge monsters, Adams thought, but aloud she just said, "Sounds good," and busied herself with handing everything off to Harry. This was the sort of thing you had detective constables for, after all.

The Christmas lights framing the wooden huts of the market gave a mellow, golden glow to the crowd, suggesting wood fires in ski lodges and more exotic backdrops than the cold, hungry stretch of the Thames and its rain-shrouded buildings. The scent of mulled wine and hot chocolate and the astringent whiff of cooking onions wafted toward the detectives as they walked down from the street, a siren call that made Adams think uneasily of predators following scents in the night. Her hand went to her neck, and she found herself looking for the toastie trailer, but it wasn't there. Maybe it was still too early.

They bought drinks from a black and silver coffee van, the man working the machine with hands reddened by cold and a scarf bundled around his neck. He filled Adams' insulated mug and handed it back to her with a grin, and for a moment, in the low gold light, his eyes looked too yellow and the pupil the wrong shape, and his grin faded as he turned abruptly back to the machine. "Enjoy," he said, not looking at her.

"Thanks," she said, giving Zahid a frown as they headed into the crowd.

"There you go, Adams. Making friends everywhere you go."

"I didn't even *say* anything!"

"It's your general demeanour."

She snorted, and they found a quieter spot near a stall selling crystal ornaments and dreamcatchers, where the crowd thinned and the huts opened toward the water. Adams turned her back to the bridge, the scratches on her neck itching, and surveyed the milling mass of people, clustering into couples and groups and families.

"Missing kids don't seem to have put anyone off too much," Zahid said, taking the top off his paper cup to slurp at what looked a lot like pea soup.

"Not much, no," Adams agreed, although she thought that the parents might be holding their children's hands a little tighter, calling to them a little more sharply, especially with older kids they might have been more casual about a week ago. Or even a few days ago. But it was London. Nothing stopped. No one was going to give up their festive fixes just because something *might* happen. That wasn't how things worked.

Adams and Zahid stayed where they were rather than walking, letting the crowds wash past and around them, the movement of others substituting for their lack of the same. They tucked their hands into their pockets against the cold once their drinks were gone, and shuffled their feet, but their eyes never drifted from the crowd, except when Adams looked back at the bridge from time to time. She wasn't sure what she expected to see. That same strange *shift* as the night before? Something swinging down off the structure, some Spiderman kidnapper? The bridge itself creeping closer?

None of it made sense, and in the fading afternoon, with the crowds and Zahid hulking next to her, and the day full of reminders that humans are monstrous enough without needing anything else, it seemed unlikely. So she focused on the people instead, looking for something wrong. Something *off.* Someone smiling too widely at other people's children, following too close behind other families, someone that set the hair at the back of her neck to twitching attention. Even (and wouldn't *that* be a gift) a face that matched a mugshot. Which was unlikely, but not impossible. If people only knew how often a coincidence – and a wanted person's ego – actually solved a case they'd lose what minimal amount of respect for the police they actually had.

But they weren't that lucky. Amid all the hoods and hats and scarves and coats, they were back to the same problem of finding it virtually impossible to tell anyone apart. So mostly they saw kids pleading for doughnuts, office workers getting a little too much into the post-work Christmas spirit, and tourists looking dissatisfied by their bratwursts. There was also one entertaining moment when a very unprofessional pickpocket mistook a slightly rotund detective in a bright pink coat and flower-bedecked crocheted hat for an easy mark. By the time she'd very nearly broken his arm, loudly berated him in tones that suggested she was Very Disappointed in him and was possibly going to tell his mother, and finally arrested him, Adams was fairly sure he was rethinking his career choice.

Zahid nodded at the detective as she handed the man off to one of the uniformed officers patrolling the crowd, and said, "We may as well go. More bloody coppers here than punters."

Adams sniffled against the cold. "Gym, is it?"

"No – if we head off now I can make it home for pizza night, and you can follow DCI's orders and get some sleep."

"Wednesday's pizza night?" she asked, ignoring the bit about sleep. She wasn't sure she had much choice in the matter anyway.

"Yeah. We buy the bases, then the kids get to do their own toppings and stuff. It's fun."

"Sure." She looked along the riverwalk toward the bridge.

"It's good for families to do stuff together. Don't you do Sunday dinner with yours, that sort of thing?"

"Only if I can't get out of it. And that's strictly Mum's thing, anyway. She doesn't even trust me with the gravy."

"Yeah, well, gravy's like the fabric that binds the universe together. I wouldn't trust you with it either."

"I'm not *that* bad. I make bloody good noodles."

"Two minute?" he asked.

"Pot."

Zahid snorted laughter and followed her gaze toward the bridge. The water beneath it was black and opaque, the reflection of the lights stuttering across the broken surface like messages in a morse code Adams couldn't decipher. The bridge loomed above, steady and disinterested, nothing more or less than a monument to construction and expansion, groaning with the passage of traffic over it.

"See something?" he asked.

"No," she said. She could *feel* something, though. A current of unease running off the river like cold water, making laughs too bright and teeth too sharp. She glanced back toward the coffee truck and saw the man looking back at her, his face drawn and pointed. He reminded her of the dog, for some reason, and she touched her neck again, the scratches hot under her collar. "No, let's go."

"At least there weren't any aliens," Zahid said, leading the way to the car, and DS Adams gave a half smile.

There was that.

ADAMS DID SLEEP, in the end. Not well, and she got up to check for the dog twice, but the back gardens were empty, leaving her feeling oddly bereft but also faintly relieved. The bridge had been a bridge, the bin no more than a bin. The dog was gone, back inside with its humans or off exploring other streets. Even her neck wasn't stinging so much. Perhaps things would be normal now, and she could just get on with arresting people and not worrying about inanimate objects being up to mischief. Maybe it had been nothing more than exhaustion and a bad egg sandwich. It made more sense that way.

She ran in the heavy early morning darkness, her footsteps dull under a sulky mist that refused to lift. It rendered buildings shadowy and indistinct, and splintered the headlights of cars, and on the track that ran around the sports field dog walkers and other runners loomed into existence then vanished like ghosts. It was damp and cold and, when she stopped at the far end of her loop, letting her breathing come down a little so that she could push it back up again, she heard *We Wish You a Merry Christmas* playing on a loop from someone's phone, accompanied by small, shouted voices.

She wrinkled her nose and checked her watch. Two weeks to go. She should be calling her mother – or at least taking her mother's calls – so that she could listen to the plans for the day as if they weren't the same every year. She should be making her usual offer to bring a dish only to have her mother tell her not to with something close to alarm in her voice. She should be insisting that at least she could buy a veggie roast, so that her mum could say that no one was bringing ready meals into her house for Christmas dinner, and that she was perfectly capable of making something much nicer. Which was true.

Adams knew she should be doing all these things, fulfilling her side of the unspoken Christmas contract, but she didn't want to. Didn't want to plan for a day in front of the telly and the gas fire, stuffed with food and arguing with her brothers over which of the ancient board games they should play, only to find that it was missing pieces (they were *all* missing pieces, yet somehow no one ever thought to replace them) and have to start again, and then argue over the game itself, or who put a bloody pig in blanket under her cabbage when she'd been a veggie for *forever,* and how many girlfriends had her little brother been through this year, and were those *Gucci* shoes her older brother was wearing, the posh git?

She could feel the warmth of it from here, and it made her skin creep with unease. How could she even imagine it, when there were five kids still out there, lost in the city somewhere – or hopefully so, anyway. How could she be warm by the fire when there were stalkers under bridges and lurking, faceless threats just waiting to snatch another kid away? It made arguing over the Brussels sprouts seem worse than petty. It felt insulting.

She turned for home, breaking into a jog again and leaving the screeching carol behind her. She pushed into a run and then a sprint, holding her pace until her lungs were screaming, trying to turn her mind away from the missing kids, give it a break from picking and plucking and prodding and turning the problem, gnawing at it from every angle. Gone. Just *gone.* No dropped gloves, no half-heard scream, no glimpse on CCTV or shaky witness statement. Just *gone.* She grunted in frustration, pushing harder as the road on the other side of the field came into murky sight, streetlights swimming in the gloom.

Stallholders had seen nothing, parents had barely turned away, divers found nothing in the river, no persons of interest in the area, no witnesses, no ransom notes, *nothing*—she gave something that wasn't far from a scream herself, stumbling to a halt and dropping her hands onto her thighs, heaving great whooping gasps of air, her fingers digging into her legs so hard she'd have tender spots there when she showered.

"God*dammit,*" she hissed, the word phlegmy and caught at the back of her throat. A soft huff interrupted her, and she glared around.

The dog sat a couple of metres away, his hair hanging heavy over his eyes and his matted coat giving the impression of a large woollen blanket draped over a stool. Now that she was closer, he seemed to be more of a spaniel size, but it was hard to be sure. In the mist and the low light he seemed more than ever to be cut from shadows, indistinct and fuzzy at the edges. Adams stared at him, and he stared back, then his mouth dropped open slightly, giving her that strangely humorous expression again.

"What do *you* want?" she asked him, and he jumped up, moving with a startling fluidity that made Adams vaguely embarrassed by her own pounding progress around the park. He vanished into the mist, not looking back, and she sighed, but not at his disappearance.

It was because she'd half expected him to answer back.

SHE LEFT HOME EARLY, her hair scraped fiercely back and her heavy wool jacket swamping the suit underneath, and she was halfway to the station when her phone rang through the handsfree. The display lit up with Zahid's number, and she hit answer. "I've brought coffee from home," she said. "I'm not stopping just to get you an almond milk matcha with a bloody protein shot."

"Bollocks to that. Meet me at the bridge." She could hear the rumble of the Mini's engine, growling with urgency, and her throat was suddenly tight.

"Another?"

"Another. Move yourself." He hung up, and Adams swerved across two lanes, blipping her horn as she went, shot through a light just as it turned red, and accelerated through the snarls of London traffic as well as she could, her heart roaring in her ears like an echo of the Thames.

Another.

9

AND THEN THERE WERE SIX

THERE WERE MARKED CARS AND CORDONS AND TAPE ALL ALONG the road by the Christmas market, and Adams parked as close as she could, which wasn't particularly close at all, given all the other cars with police permits in their windows crowding the place. Mist rose from the river and wound thin fingers around the shuttered market stalls, making the lights of the tree diffuse and uncertain. She hurried to the cordon and flashed her ID to a uniformed officer as she ducked under the tape, spotting Zahid talking to a slim woman with a blanket slung around her shoulders. The woman's face was blotchy with tears and cold, Adams saw as she got closer, and her hair was the sort of dishevelled that came from clutching at it, not from careful styling.

"DS Adams," Zahid said. "This is Annalise Marsh."

"What happened?" Adams asked, and Zahid gave her a little grimace as the woman turned to her. "Sorry. Can you tell me what happened, Ms Marsh? I know you'll have already told—"

"It's fine," the woman said, her voice tight. She tidied hair out of her face with shaking fingers and lifted her chin. She was wearing leggings and fluffy boots topped by layers of flowing tops and scarves, and a giant wool cardigan that was serving as a jacket. Adams was quite sure that if she'd tried to wear anything like it she'd have looked as if she'd lost a fight with an aggressive fabric shop, but it worked. Even the tatty old blanket somehow looked like a fashion choice rather than an emergency measure.

"He was just here," Annalise said, then took a careful breath. "I didn't … he had his scooter, and it goes so *fast.* I was always worried about him knocking someone over with it, you know?"

"Of course," Zahid said. "Great fun, but worrying, right?"

"Yes, *exactly.* I told my husband he was too young—" She stopped, pressing the fingertips of one hand under her eye. "That doesn't matter. We were … we were just coming down the path, and I was *watching,* of course I was, but it's daylight, and I had posts to catch up on, you know, so I had my phone, and he was zipping up and down, and I kept telling him to stay close, and he would for a bit, and he was never out of *sight,* not really, not so I'd worry, especially as it's so quiet here this early, and then he was behind me and I called him, I said … I said Briar, catch up—" She stopped again, and this time the fingertips couldn't stop the tears. "He didn't answer, and he didn't come, and he was just *gone.*"

"And where was this exactly?" Adams asked. "Near the bridge?"

"Just past it. I mean, I was just past it. I looked back, and he was staring all about the place, like he'd never seen a bridge before, and I said, Briar, catch up, and I kept going, and I said it again when he didn't come past me, and then …" She trailed off, staring from one detective to the other. "Where did he go? Where *could* he go?" She reached out and grabbed Adams' arm. "You have to find him. *You have to find my son!*"

Adams managed not to pull away, and patted the woman's arm instead, having a moment of awkwardness when she almost missed it through the many layers. "We're going to do everything we can."

"Annalise! *Annalise!*" A barefoot man in eye-wateringly well-cut suit trousers and a fluffy jumper that Adams had an idea probably belonged to his wife, given how short it was on the arms and at the waist, was sprinting down the path toward them. A uniformed officer stepped forward to intercept him, but Zahid called, "Let him through."

Annalise released Adams – who barely resisted the urge to wipe her arm on her coat, as if it might be smeared with desperation – and rushed to meet her husband. They collided in a mess of overpriced clothing and grief. "*Where is he?*" the man kept shouting. "*Who did this?*"

Adams looked at the bridge, rising out of the mist like an alien mountain range on a metallic world, then back at Zahid. "Nothing?"

"Nothing," he said. There was toothpaste in his beard, and he took a woolly hat from his pocket and pulled it down over his hair. "I've already got CCTV being pulled on all the streets nearby to see if we can get anything. *Again.* This bloody mist isn't helping, though."

Adams looked along the river walk, the streetlights still lit and reflecting on the scraps of fog and murk. "Divers?" she asked.

"I've put the call in."

"This is a change. All the rest were at night, in crowds. Are we sure it's the same?"

"Same area. Same target. Could be they're adapting, since we've had such a heavy presence at the market at night. Or it could even be a copycat. Hardly bloody matters, though, does it?"

"No," she said, watching the bridge. She could hear the

rumble of traffic on it growing heavier as the morning drew on. "It doesn't."

But it did make six.

IT WAS mid-morning by the time DS Adams was able to extricate herself from the search of the Christmas market stalls, from the door-knocking and scouring of the bushes and streets. Uniformed officers were creeping slowly along the riverside path, looking for dropped buttons or torn scraps of clothing or anything to show a small boy had even been there at all, while police boats held a cordon into the river, and flattened, circular swirls on the surface showed where the divers prowled beneath. Detectives were hunting out the owners of nearby buildings, looking for eyewitnesses or security camera footage to add to the council CCTV. There had been a helicopter around for a bit, too, but Adams had a sneaking suspicion that was more for the benefit of the media clustered around the edge of the cordon. A *we're pulling out all the stops* gesture, while the rest of them grovelled around beneath doing the only work that was likely to help.

Not that anything had shown up. There was just the scooter, lying on its side forlornly, and that had been bundled into a giant Ziplock bag and carted away by the scene of crime officers. The parents had been sent home with Zahid, a DC, and a support officer, both in case of ransom calls, and also in case the kid was actually stashed in a cupboard somewhere. It was possible.

It was *all* possible, but Adams didn't think it was likely. Not the kid being stashed, not an eyewitness turning up, not the police divers finding something, and definitely not a security camera giving them a break. And she didn't actually think she was going to have much luck either, but she wrapped her scarf around her neck more firmly, pulling it up over her ears, and hurried under the bridge, giving it one baleful look as she went. It gave her nothing back. Of course it didn't. It was a *bridge,* and she was making something out of nothing.

But at least it was something.

She headed into the bushes where she'd seen Jack standing the other day. He wasn't there now, of course, not with all the police stomping through them, kicking at the undergrowth and swearing as they picked through rubbish with varying degrees of relation to hazardous waste.

"Bloody *hell,*" a young constable complained as she went past. He held half a set of false teeth out to her. "I mean – *how?*"

"Tooth fairy," Adams said, and was rewarded with a laugh. "Bag it, though, yeah? You never know."

"Sure. I bet a lot of serial kidnappers drop their teeth at the scene of the crime," the constable said, but he shook an evidence bag out of his vest. "Gross."

"I'd rather teeth than what I just found," another constable called, but Adams didn't linger to find out the specifics. The teeth made her uneasy, though, and she wondered if any of Jack's friends had had a bit of dental work done. And how many of them had vanished now. He'd told her five, but he'd been looking for another, too, hadn't he? Jonesy, hadn't he said? And what if there were others he didn't know of?

Because it was seven vulnerable adults and seven kids. That was the pattern, as far as she'd been able to see. Maybe a bit of overlap between the last of the adults and the first of the kids, but those were the numbers. Seven, seven, then quiet for fifty-odd years. She couldn't shake the feeling that it really could be a cult, some sort of weird old tradition whose roots went as deep as the city, passed down through families or communities or whatever.

She emerged by the bike lane, and had to wait for someone in neon yellow and black Lycra, coordinated arm and leg protectors, and a matching helmet with spikes on the top to sail past on an electric unicycle. They had a wireless speaker throbbing with bass held on their shoulder like an old-school boombox, and she felt the pound of it in her chest for a brief moment, stealing her breath. She wondered where he'd found the unicycle. They weren't legal here, but that was someone else's issue. She had bigger, bin-size things to worry about. Although the idea of arresting a unicyclist was oddly appealing. She shook her head, thinking, *focus, Adams,* and crossed the street beyond. Everything was getting to her too much, her nerves raw, and the scratch on her neck was itching against her scarf again.

It still felt like it was just after dawn, the light dim and diffuse, even as Adams' stomach assured her it was getting on for lunchtime. She hesitated on the pavement on the far side of the street, looking back at the bridge, but from this angle it looked like every other bridge in the city, grey and beleaguered with cars, even if the lingering mist meant that everything faded out about halfway across the river.

She turned instead to the alley, following it to the intersection at the end, her heart suddenly too fast. She peered around the corner slowly, and saw the bin crouching at the end, just as it had two nights ago. It didn't move. She couldn't smell curry, and the city roared on beyond the alley just as it should. She wasn't even sure why she was here. What did she think she was going to accomplish? Jack wouldn't be hanging out here, not with his hungry bin, and what else was she hoping to find – that the bin had stolen Briar Marsh? Tempted him away with hot chocolates and she'd just be able to snatch him back?

She was momentarily distracted, wondering why anyone would name a child Briar when they already had the last name Marsh, and it shook the last of the lingering trepidation from her. It was just a bin. This was just an alley. She took her baton from her coat and snapped it out, then marched up to the hulk of grey plastic (being careful not to look too closely at the stickers in case they started to look *off* again), and wrenched the lid open.

There was one small part of her that had apparently been expecting to find half-digested children, or rows of serrated teeth, or maybe a small, portable void inside the bin, because when all that looked back at her were piles of greasy black bin bags and some loose bits of polystyrene, she sagged against the side of the thing, blowing air over her bottom lip. She looked around, then reached inside (not without a quick shiver running down her spine) and poked a few of the bags with the baton. Nothing moved other than a rat that surged over the side and took off down the alley, squealing in panic.

"You're welcome," she called after it, and dropped the lid back into place, searching her pockets for some hand sanitiser. Good. So the bin hadn't eaten the kids (*unless it's digested them already,* her mind pointed out unhelpfully), which made sense. The bin couldn't have got all the way to the bridge and back— She stopped herself. No. It made sense because bins don't eat people.

She sighed slightly, rubbing some sanitiser into her hands and dropping the bottle back into her coat pocket. She needed to go back, and drop all the weirdness about the cult and the bin and Jack. She might have nothing else to go on with the kids, but his missing people didn't even seem to exist. All chasing it was going to get her was the label of Fox Mulder for the rest of her career, and she had no intentions of letting that happen. The Fox Mulders of the Met never made superintendent.

As she turned to leave there was a flicker of movement down the alley, well past the T-junction she'd arrived at, and she stopped short, almost stumbling. The light was that same dull, diffuse yellow she remembered from the other night, and she looked for streetlights again. She still couldn't see any, and she couldn't see the movement again, either. It was probably just the rat. Or a cat out chasing it. She walked back to the T-junction and hesitated, looking at the way she'd come in and the slice of dull grey day beyond the alleys. She could taste the mist as a thick, heavy slick at the back of her throat.

"Well, dammit," she muttered, and instead of turning to leave she kept going straight down the alley, away from the bin and the junction and the weak suggestion of daylight.

THE ALLEY WAS WEIRDLY FEATURELESS. No doorways gave onto it, and the windows were merely the suggestion of shapes in the high walls of the buildings, brick filling them seamlessly. There were no more bins, and no turnings, just a straight line leading on and on, the cobbles gleaming dully in the strange light. Adams kept glancing back. She didn't think the bin would be sneaking up on her, not really, and she wasn't quite sure what she was expecting. Dimensions felt strange, the buildings too high for her to see the top of them, even when she craned her neck, and the alley far too long to fit in any city block. She stopped, wondering if she should just go back, and was abruptly seized by the conviction that she wouldn't be *able* to go back, that she'd turn around and start walking and would just never stop, the alley an infinite loop that she could never reach the end of.

"Stop. Think," she told herself, squeezing her eyes closed for a moment. It was just an alley. All she had to do was turn around and walk out. She opened her eyes again and spied a gap in the wall to her left, not even big enough to be called an alley. It hadn't been there a moment ago. She was … well, *almost* sure. Maybe she hadn't been looking properly. She padded over and peered down it. It seemed like a pointless thing, not big enough for a vehicle, or a bin, or even to walk down, really. Zahid certainly wouldn't fit down it, not with his shoulders. She would, though.

She frowned. Not that she'd want to, obviously. There was a gunky conglomeration of rubbish in the bottom of the passage, sedimentary layers of crisp packets and brown bottles and takeaway bags and crushed cans and less savoury things, and the walls were slick and damp with winter cold and London grime. And all it led to, by the looks, was another alley further on, the glimpse nothing more than a frame full of lighter grey with the nodding head of a dandelion growing out of the wall into it. *Plus* it was heading away from the river, and she needed to get back.

And then the flash of movement again. Unmistakeable this time, a deep swirl of dark grey that was like a shadow passing the sun. Adams jerked back, startled, then caught herself. It couldn't be her dog. *Her* dog. Listen to her. It couldn't be the dog that had been around her place, obviously. That was miles away, and she was pretty sure that even if it *could* have travelled that far, it wouldn't, because even strays stick to their own territory, don't they? She had no idea, actually, but it made sense. And why would it be here, anyway? She was searching for connections where they didn't exist, just because this damn case was giving her nothing to latch onto.

She looked down at the build-up of debris in the gap between the walls, then at her suit trousers. They were just from H&M, but they *were* new. Reasonably, anyway. She bent and tucked them into her boots, then peered through the gap again.

"I should probably be talking to someone about this," she muttered, picking her way in. If she angled herself a little, her shoulders didn't rub the sides. "Someone professional. It's not right. Chasing men down dark alleys. Talking to dogs. Following dogs through walls—" She broke off with a hiss of irritation as her boot slipped and she lurched into the brick. "Worrying about hungry bins."

Also worrying about narrowing passageways. Her shoulders were rubbing against the sides now, even when she angled herself, and she turned to shuffle on sideways. It hadn't *looked* like it narrowed from the other side. Surely she'd have noticed that? Her throat clicked as she swallowed, her mouth dry, and she tried to go faster, her feet slipping and catching on the muck, slowing her.

"This is ridiculous," she muttered, but the words came out with jagged edges, and she gave a little, startled cough as something clattered at the end of the passage behind her. She craned her neck to look back, and her bun brushed the wall behind her. It *was* narrower. And dark back the way she'd come. Although it couldn't be. There was the yellow light for a start, and it was almost lunch, she knew that, and—movement.

She strained to see, but it really did seem to be suddenly *dark* back there— No, not dark. Something small and animal in her chest realised it before her brain caught up. *Full.* The passageway wasn't dark, it was *full.* Someone (*thing,* the animal part of her put in) was following her. She could hear their breathing, eager but measured, the squish and crunch of their feet on the rubbish, the scrape of their fingernails (*claws*) against the brickwork to either side. She opened her mouth to say, *DS Adams, Met Police, identify yourself,* and the small animal jumped in first. She could *smell* her pursuer.

Dank river and rusting metal and old, cold patience, deep and slow as the Thames, and she thought, *Jack lost five so far. Maybe six. There's still more to go.*

She launched herself forward, kicking her way through the debris that grabbed at her boots, using her hands to force herself along the walls, aware of the baton in her pocket and knowing she had no way to swing it in here. In here, she was prey. And prey has to run.

Or at least wriggle faster.

10

A CANINE FIXATION

TIME STRETCHED THIN AND ACHINGLY FRAGILE AS ADAMS scrabbled her way grimly along the passageway. She didn't bother to wonder why she'd come in here in the first place. She was here now, and behind her she could smell her pursuer. She could feel their movement in the shift of the ground beneath her, in the wash of air they pushed ahead of them in the narrow space, tangled up in that terrible cold scent, and she knew she had to stay ahead of them. In the alley, she could regroup. She could use her baton. She could sprint. She could bloody well arrest them. She had options. Here, there was nothing but the scrape of brick under her palms and against her back, and the pluck of fright when the passage narrowed enough to press her nose almost to the wall. It was widening ahead, she could see it, but here her coat was catching, slowing her down, and she had no way of getting out except straight on, and the scratching of her pursuer was closer, and she could barely breathe between the scramble to escape and the pressure of the walls.

For one breath-stealing moment she was wedged, her heart screaming in her ears as her jacket bunched, pulling painfully at her neck and armpit as she strained to haul herself through the tight spot, her legs shaking as she pushed into the untrustworthy ground, and she squeezed her eyes shut, exhaling hard, trying to shrink herself as much as she could. Behind her, she sensed more than heard a whuff of triumph, like a hound cornering a fox, and something touched her outstretched hand, cold and hard and unfamiliar. She lurched forward with the sound of a seam ripping somewhere, and then she was moving again, scrambling as fast as she could manage, the passage widening and the opening onto the alley suddenly close enough to all but touch.

She broke into a stumbling, sideways run, using her hands to keep herself off the walls, and a moment later she burst into what felt like a cathedral's worth of open air, the steady drizzle pattering down around her and soaking the tarmac of the alley, empty except for a man in chef's whites leaning against a wall, smoking a cigarette. He gave her an appraising look as she spun back to face the passageway, baton already in her hand. She snapped it out and lifted her gaze to meet her pursuer.

The passage was empty. Of course it was empty. She could see all the way back to the alley on the other side. There was no darkness, not even any more shadows than there should be on a grey December day in London. Even the yellow light had given way to thinner, more familiar tones. Adams rubbed a hand over her face, aware she was panting, and looked each way down the alley carefully.

"Alright?" the chef asked, and she turned to face him. He was standing far enough away that he didn't back up at the sight of her raised baton, but he nodded thoughtfully as he took a drag on the cigarette. "No, then, I take it."

"Did you … did you see a dog?" she asked him.

He considered it, flicking ash onto the ground. “Can’t say as I did. Some bloody big rats around here, though.”

She blinked at him, then checked the passageway again. It was still empty. She lowered the baton and pressed one hand to the back of her neck. Maybe she’d caught an infection from those bloody scratches after all. She should see the GP.

“Want a drink?” the chef asked. “Look like you could use one.”

“No,” she said. “Has anyone been down here?”

“Not while I’ve been out here,” he said, and raised the half-finished cigarette. “Only been here this long, though.”

“Right,” she said, examining him. He had dark circles under his eyes, and he’d missed a patch on his chin when he was shaving. He didn’t *look* like he might be hiding stray dogs, or inducing hallucinations in unsuspecting detectives, or … she didn’t know. “Seen a kid come through? Ten, white, brown hair, blue eyes, corduroy jacket?”

“No kids here.”

Of course not. “Any strangers hanging about?”

“Not exactly a busy spot,” the chef said. “Even the delivery drivers don’t come round the back here. Too narrow.”

“Right.” She had one last try. “Ever see a young homeless man who goes by Jack?”

“Sure,” the chef said, surprising her. “He comes by for left-overs now and then.”

“Have you seen him recently?”

The chef finished his cigarette while he thought about it, then finally said, “Been a few days, I guess.”

“Has he been acting weird? Different?”

The chef snorted. “Define weird.” Then he gave her that same appraising look. “I mean, are we talking bursting out of holes in the wall looking like he’s about to beat the crap out of someone? Because if so, no. If you mean more twitchy than usual, yeah. He came by around lunch a few days ago, and I had to tell him to come back after dinner, because I can't be handing stuff out that we might use in service. He said he didn't want to be out after dark."

Adams nodded. "Do you know where he goes when he's not here?"

The chef shrugged. "I tried to send him to a shelter up the road a couple of times, but he wasn't a fan of being locked in at night. They might know more, though. I think he went there for a shower now and then."

Adams pocketed her baton and straightened the front of her coat. "Right. Thanks."

"Sure." He looked at her for a moment longer, and she thought he was going to ask her if she wanted a drink again, but instead he just pointed at her hand. "You should get that seen to," he said. "I've got a first aid kit inside, if you want."

Adams looked at her left hand, suddenly aware that it was burning. Burning, and bleeding softly. A purple welt lay across the knuckles, angry and bruised-looking, and the skin around it was red and puffy, as if some giant jellyfish had wrapped around her hand and squeezed enthusiastically. She closed it into a fist and opened it again gently, and as she did so the welt split open and started to bleed with a little more intent.

"Yeah," the chef said. "I'll get you something."

"Thanks," she said, and stood in the alley looking at the passageway while cars roared past unseen, and the smell of the city filled her nostrils, dank and salty and grimy.

"NOTHING?" the DCI demanded. "*Nothing?*"

No one in the briefing room replied. Adams sipped tepid coffee, her tongue numb with the cups that had gone before. Not that it mattered much – she'd had to get it from the staffroom machine, where it had likely been sitting since the morning, getting bleaker and more bitter with every hour, like a certain demographic of dater waiting on a reply to a message. It was better she couldn't taste it. It was so late in the afternoon they may as well call it evening, and they'd been at the river all day.

Her fingers and toes were as numb as her tongue, and her forehead still felt pinched by the cold. They'd searched, and interviewed, and liaised with the marine policing unit, and watched divers come up empty-handed, and the feeling in the room was as bleak as her coffee. There had been nothing. Well, nothing except for the diver who'd leaned on the bow of the boat as she briefed Adams and Zahid, her features pinched into a doll's face by the tightness of her neoprene hood. She'd had nothing helpful, but as Zahid turned away she'd held her closed fist out to Adams, her eyes tawny in the dusk.

"Here," she'd said, and for one embarrassing moment Adams had thought the other woman was trying to fist-bump her, which seemed tasteless, then she'd realised the diver had something clenched in her fist. She opened her right hand instead, and the woman pressed something small and hard into it, latching her fingers briefly over Adams'. They were so cold it was like the water itself wrapping around her.

"What is that?" she asked, examining a little, mud-encrusted object. It looked an awful lot like – in fact, exactly like – a rubber duck, but it was heavier than it should be. Brass, or something.

The woman shrugged. "Call it a token."

"Of what? A search with no results?"

The woman cocked her head slightly, and to Adams it seemed as though she angled herself away from the bridge as she answered. "It can be whatever you want." She grinned suddenly. "Besides, just need a few more and you've got a row, right?"

That had startled an answering grin out of Adams, although she had no idea why the woman was giving her a brass rubber duck. Well, a brass thing shaped like a rubber duck. It also had LED eyes that lit up when she clicked its wings down, she discovered when she got back to the station, so it was hardly some sort of antique. But she'd spent the rest of the afternoon carting the thing around in her pocket, and she couldn't really have said why. Maybe because the smile and the touch of the woman's fingers felt like the only real thing that had happened in weeks.

Now she clasped the duck absently in her pocket as she listened to the DIs give their reports. They were all over-explained and embellished, every step taken listed down to the smallest detail, but they all amounted to exactly what the DCI had accused them of. Absolutely nothing.

At the front of the room, DCI Halloran rubbed a hand over her face, looked at her watch, and said, "Well, after that edifying chat, which comes up to you lot finding the square root of bugger all, get back to it. *Find me something.* Any bloody thing. Arrest the damn otters at the park for causing a distraction in the area. Do someone for dodgy ice creams. I don't care what it is, but I've got to talk to the chief in half an hour and at the moment all I can tell him is that my entire department is coming up with precisely dog tits, and then I've got to try and put that to the press in a way that suggests we've almost caught the damn dog itself, when we don't even know if we're looking for a poodle or a terrier."

Adams was momentarily distracted by the thought of dog tits. As far as she knew, all dogs had, if not tits, at least nipples, so if they had *them,* then surely they'd also have the dog, but she doubted the DCI meant it that way. She had an idea that if she were trying to run this investigation on as little sleep as the DCI got she'd be making even less sense, and the very fact that she was being distracted by thoughts of dog tits in the middle of a briefing reminded her that last night had been her best night's sleep since the case started, and she doubted she'd got more than a couple of hours. She was still considering how little sleep one could function on before being distracted by dog tits when the DCI strode past on her way to the door and jabbed one slightly stubby finger at her.

"Adams. With me."

She scrambled up, startled, and hurried after the DCI, shrugging at Zahid when he raised his eyebrows at her. She was almost certain she had nothing to offer, unless the DCI was interested in collecting kitschy ducks of dubious origins.

DCI Halloran led the way into her office, seating herself in the big chair behind her desk with a sigh. "Close the door, Adams."

Adams did, then sat down opposite the older woman, perching on one of the distinctly uncomfortable metal and leather chairs. They were the sort that you either fell into like a deck chair or had to perch on the rim of, and she opted for perching, her stomach twisting nervously. The DCI was digging through her desk drawers, and for one moment Adams thought she might emerge with a bottle of whisky, like they were in some '70s cop show. Instead, she fished out a handful of Freddo the Frogs and offered two to Adams.

"Sugar?"

"Won't say no." Adams took the chocolates, and the DCI leaned back in her chair, tearing the wrapper back from a Freddo and decapitating it in one bite. She sighed again and rubbed her forehead, and Adams noticed her nail polish was chipped at the edges. Adams unwrapped one of her own frogs and took a slightly smaller bite, the chocolate over-sweet and faintly cloying after the acridity of the coffee.

The DCI watched her for a moment, and took another bite before she said, "Have you been looking into those missing people anymore? Your cult victims?"

Adams swallowed, the chocolate sticky at the back of her throat, and said, "I kind of got the impression you felt it was a waste of time."

The DCI shrugged, wiping the corners of her mouth neatly. "Cults always sound like a waste of time. They usually *are* a waste of time. You're probably too young to remember the satanism kick in the '80s. It was bigger in the States than here, but for a bit there it seemed everyone and their standard poodle was convinced the neighbours were making sacrifices to our dark lord of a good time simply because they burned a bit of incense about the place."

Adams wondered briefly if this was the same poodle whose tits they might or might not have, and said, "I heard about it. Lots of wasting police time, and didn't it mess up some cases because even within investigations some officers were looking in the wrong directions?"

"Exactly." The DCI dropped her wrapper in the bin and took two Creme Eggs from the drawer, tossing one to Adams. She caught it reflexively. "Since then, no one even wants to mention the word cult. And, truth be told, even when things look a bit spooky it's usually just some teenagers playing dress-up. But just because it's not *usually* a cult doesn't mean it's *never* one. And you're not exactly prone to attacks of the imagination, Adams. You really think there's something there?"

Adams concentrated on folding Freddo's wrapper carefully, trying not to think of bowing dogs (and their tits) and the throb of her hand and narrowing passageways. She'd always been the one her brothers asked to check under their beds for monsters, and her make-believe had consisted more of wanting to arrest the two of them for crimes they'd invented than fantasy worlds and treasure maps. But she didn't consider herself *un*imaginative. She couldn't be, not if she wanted to put herself in the shoes of others. And there was no other way to work out the tricky stuff. There are many different forms of imagination, after all, each one as powerful and full of potential as the other, but she understood what the DCI meant. She might build on what was there, but she didn't make things up.

"I do think there's *something,*" she said. "I just can't see quite what, exactly. There's a pattern of people disappearing. Not in the same place over time, but in clusters, and all in the same manner. No trace of them left. No warning. It just starts, seven adults and seven kids, sometimes consecutively, sometimes with overlap, and then it stops again just as suddenly. And each cluster is concentrated around a few blocks at most, all near the river." *Near the bridges.*

"How long between them again? Fifty years, you said?"

"Forty-nine, give or take a month. Never more variation than that, and the gaps between the disappearances seem to be wider for the adults, narrower for the kids."

The DCI plucked at the foil on her egg. "How narrow?"

Adams took a breath. "It's hard to be clear how well it holds over time, because I was piecing stuff together off some right dodgy sites, but I think it starts at about a month for the first adult, but by the seventh there's only a week between them. Kids start at a week, and by the seventh it's down to a day or so."

"How far back, exactly?"

"Hard to tell from newspaper records. A few hundred years, at least." *And much, much further when you go down the rabbit hole in the conspiracy sites.*

"How long do we have before the next kiddie, then? Between six and seven?"

"If I'm right about the pattern, a day. Two at the outside."

The DCI took a bite of her egg and chewed slowly, then finally said, "Zahid looped in on this?"

"No. It wasn't an official thing. I only mentioned it because Harry—"

"Is a bit of a muppet, I know." She gave Adams a surprisingly easy smile, more crooked than the polished ones she wore at news conferences, and full of a very different humour to the one she sometimes offered in the briefing room. "Never mind there's always one. There's always a whole bloody pack of them."

Adams smiled back, touching the duck again as if it could ground her. The chocolate wasn't sitting well in her belly, and her ears were full of a faint whispering sound, as if the river had followed her.

The DCI delved back into her bottom drawer and came out with three multi-packs of Yorkie bars. Adams stared at them. She didn't think she'd eaten one since they'd had the "it's not for girls" packaging, and she'd decided to eat them on principle. The DCI threw them to Adams, and she grabbed them clumsily, almost losing her egg. The DCI nodded as if in agreement with something, and said, "I want all your focus on this. We've got enough bodies doing the dog work."

Adams blinked. She was starting to think the DCI had a fixation on dogs. Either that or *she* did, and was simply projecting. "Alright."

"The whole thing may be a crock, but it's more than we've got anywhere else. Talk to your unhoused contacts again. Get someone in records hunting down everything that fits the pattern. Keep it as quiet as you can. Put it together however you want, and if Zahid gets in a snit, send him my way. Just find me *something*. Got it?"

"Got it," Adams said, and raised the Yorkie bars questioningly. "These?"

"Keep them handy. And remember your torch. Long nights and all that."

Adams stared at her blankly, and the DCI inclined her head toward the door, not moving.

"Um, right," Adams said, and got up hurriedly, shoving the creme egg and the Freddo into her coat pocket. "Thanks."

The DCI was already scrolling through her phone, and she didn't look up as Adams let herself out of the office and headed back to her desk. She felt faintly dizzy, as if the sugar had hit too hard, and Zahid looked up as she dropped the pile of Yorkie bars on her desk. The packs slid across each other slickly, and one dived off the edge.

He grabbed it before it could hit the floor. "Dinner of champions."

"Yep." Adams pushed the bars aside and logged onto her computer, clicking through to the records requests.

"What'd Herself want?"

Adams glanced at him, then went back to her form. "For me to follow up the cult angle."

"*Seriously?* She must be getting desperate."

"Six kids gone. What d'you think?" Six kids, and only a day before the seventh, if her pattern was right. And after that it might be too late to find anything. She reached for her water bottle.

Zahid watched her for a second, then said, "You need help?"

She gave him a sideways look. "You're not busy?"

"Not with anything useful. If you've got something, let's run with it."

"I could do with a proper coffee," she said, grinning, and he threw the egg at her.

11

MUST TRY HARDER

Records took as much time over her call as Adams had expected, first asking if she thought they had so little on, and that she herself were so exceptional, that her request was somehow going to shoot to the top of the apparently very extensive list, especially at – she could actually see in her head the officer on the other end of the phone looking at his watch in a theatrical manner – ten to six in the evening? Adams sighed, invoked the name of the DCI, and waited while the officer huffed his way through half a dozen mistakes on the request she'd sent through (including the fact that she should have used semicolons in a list, not commas), then grudgingly agreed to prioritise it. Adams was fairly sure that meant he'd leave a Post-it Note for whoever came on shift tomorrow, but it was as good as she was going to get. Shouting and banging fists on desks might work on TV, but around here it got any request for help pushed so far to the bottom of the heap she'd be lucky to see results before she retired.

She got up, taking her jacket from the back of her chair and shrugging into it as Zahid ambled back into the room with her travel mug in one hand and a bright green thermos mug printed with pirouetting dinosaurs in the other. Adams took her mug and nodded at the other. "Nice to see you bringing a little colour into the place."

"Yeah, well. I dropped a dumbbell on mine and now the lid won't fit."

"Told you all that gym work was dangerous. So your backup option is dinosaurs?"

"It's Aisha's, but she's gone off dinos now." He took a sip, and made a face. "Everything I put in it tastes like tomato soup."

"Amazing the flavour combos they come up with." Adams stared at the pile of Yorkie bars, then gathered them up and shoved them into the bottom drawer of her desk. They wouldn't last five minutes out in the open. "Not sure tomato almond lattes will take off, though, really."

"Chilli and chocolate's still a thing," Zahid said, following her as she headed for the stairs. "Same sort of deal, really."

"It's not right, ruining good chocolate like that. What's Aisha's latest animal love, then?"

"Snakes."

"Snakes?"

"Apparently thinking of all the dead dinosaurs made her sad, and not being able to have one as a pet was the *worst*, so now she likes snakes."

"And wants one as a pet?"

"And wants one as a pet."

They let themselves through the security door into the damp, creeping cold of the parking garage, Adams fishing in her jacket pocket for her car keys. "It'll eat less than a dog, I suppose. And you won't have to take it for walks."

"I'm going to tell her police aren't allowed to have snakes. It worked when she was in the scorpion phase."

"Good luck with that." Adams let them into the car, starting it up and getting the heating going.

"Can I use the same excuse for boyfriends?"

"Police are allowed to have boyfriends. Amira might object, though."

"Oh, ha. No." Zahid considered it for a moment. "Maybe she'll be less enthusiastic about boys than snakes."

"You can only hope," Adams said, pulling out of the parking space.

"Where're we off to, then?" Zahid asked, taking the lid off his mug to peer at the contents.

"Close that thing," Adams said. "You get exorcist juice all over my car and you're paying for the cleaning."

"Matcha, Adams. It's good for you."

"Nothing that colour's good for you."

"But coffee black as Hades is fine?"

"Absolutely." They pulled out onto the street, the evening blurred and pulled down at the edges by the rain. "And we're going to see if we can find Jack. There's a night shelter he goes to sometimes."

"Ugh. Godawful places. They all bloody stink."

"You can stay in the car, then. We're not going to get anywhere with you being a git about it."

"I'm positively delightful. I just don't like junkies and scroungers."

"Wow. Offensive, derogatory, and reinforcing of stereotypes all in one go. Impressive." She shook her head. Along with the coffee run, she'd tasked Zahid with trying the bridge station again, since he was rather better at charming things out of people than she was. "Did you get anywhere with the lovely DS Murphy? Sounds like you have a lot in common."

"Stop being so rude to a senior officer. And no, no further than you did. Our Jack the lad's not been in for a week or so, but when he was, he was spouting off about his missing friends with no evidence that they even existed. I reckon it's just all some big paranoid delusion."

"The missing kids aren't a delusion," Adams pointed out.

"No," Zahid said. "Not even slightly."

"So play nice. Jack might be our only option."

Zahid sighed. "*Fine.* But you owe me a protein shake. A good one."

IT DIDN'T TAKE AS LONG as Adams had expected to get to the shelter, the flow of traffic heavy but steady, and oddly muted as the night deepened. She pulled her car into a loading bay and stuck her police permit on the dashboard, climbing out of the warm cocoon of the car into the dullness of the evening. The shelter was a grubby 1960s' building, squat and grimy, with barred, opaque windows leaking warm light onto the pavement. A small plastic sign by the door named it the Daffodil House, which seemed a little optimistic. Another sign printed on peeling, laminated paper reminded residents that no intoxicants would be permitted inside, and that aggression wasn't tolerated.

Zahid leaned over and pressed the doorbell.

"Thought you were staying in the car," Adams said.

"I can play nicely with others. More than can be said for you half the time." He examined the sign. "Don't know how they do it."

Adams didn't either. An endless fight against a world that was happy to keep the displaced firmly displaced, trying to reattach the lost to some version of reality with skinny budgets and sparse donations and no promise that anything would ever get better. And for the homeless people themselves it was a frayed safety net that cut into the dignity and the soul. Which was no fault of the shelters', but of the world.

These places were only ever meant to help the unlucky survive, and if they did that, then the shelter had succeeded, even if everyone wished they could do more.

Everyone who thought about it, anyway, and wasn't that the problem? The general public tended to want the problem to just go away, so that they didn't *have* to think about it. And what that really meant was that they wanted the *people* to just go away, to not show their dislocation to the world, exposing the gaps in civilisation and how close everyone drifts to them.

The door opened partway, and a tall woman with a thin face and a long, flower-appliqued green dress with patches on the elbows peeked at them through the gap. She peered at Adams and said, "Hello, love. You need some help?"

Adams blinked down at her jacket, thinking that she really did need more sleep, and Zahid snorted. She scowled at him, then turned to the woman. "I do. DS Adams and DI Mirza. We just wanted to ask a few questions."

The woman's face tightened, her lips becoming a hard line, and she closed the door a little. "You need a good reason. You can't just come in here hassling people because they're easy targets."

"I'm not trying to do that," Adams said. "In fact, I might not need to talk to them at all. You might be able to answer the questions for me."

The woman examined her, not relaxing her grip on the door. "Ask away, then. I don't promise I'll answer. My residents deserve privacy too."

Adams rubbed her hands against the cold, but the woman made no move to invite them in, so she just said, "What was your name?"

"Cam," the woman said, not offering a last name. Jack didn't seem to be the only one with name issues around here.

"You run the place?"

"Pretty much."

"And you're here most nights?"

"Six a week. I take Tuesdays off."

Adams offered her a smile. "Rough schedule."

"We're not exactly overburdened with staff."

"So you're familiar with all your …" She hesitated.

"Guests," Cam said, and Zahid made a small, disbelieving sound. Adams kicked her boot into his warningly, and Cam continued, "I prefer *guests.* And yes."

"Right," Adams said. "So have you noticed any of your guests going missing over the past, say, six to eight weeks?"

Cam didn't answer straight away, although she opened the door a little wider, her skinny fingers tapping the wood. Her dress was cut low at the front, a scarf hanging loose around her neck, and Adams could see the bones of her chest outlined against the skin like the exposed skeleton of a bird. She gave Adams another careful look then said, "People come and go. We try to keep an eye on as many as we can, but if people don't want that …" she spread her fingers, giving a shrug that said everything. "It's not ideal here. They've got to move out during the day anyway, and there are plenty who'll just come by now and then, when the weather's too bad or they're not having much luck on food. This isn't a place people *live*. It's a stopgap."

"I understand," Adams said. "So you couldn't say if there was anyone missing, really."

Cam scrutinised her again, and Adams found herself vaguely unnerved by the woman's pale eyes. They had the same steady evaluation she'd seen in the better crime scene officers, and she found her hand closing over the duck in her pocket. "There's at least four we haven't seen in a while," Cam said finally. "Don't know last names. We don't use them here. Lilith, Tommy, Bertie, and Alistair. They're regulars – normally come in a couple of times a week for a hot meal."

"How long's a while?"

Cam considered it. "A month or so for Alistair. Couple of weeks for Lilith. I noticed her particularly, because she likes to get involved. Washes dishes, folds sheets, does what she can to feel useful."

"So does just up and leaving seem out of character?"

"Maybe. Maybe not. Things change."

Adams rubbed her thumb over the duck's head, soothed by the smooth metal. "Do you know where they go when they're not here?"

Cam shook her head. "It's all I can do to keep this place running. I don't have time to go hunting people out." Her eyes kept sliding to Zahid, who was standing with his hands in his coat pocket, listening attentively enough but generally giving off the air that he'd rather be anywhere else than here.

Adams looked at him and said, "I'll meet you in the car."

"You can't interview—"

"I'm not. I'm just asking questions. Give us a moment."

He sighed and turned on his heel, heading back to the car as Adams beeped it open. She looked at Cam. "I get the not having time bit, but do you *hear* of anywhere, maybe?"

Cam kept drumming her fingers on the doorframe, watching Zahid slam the car door. "He's one of *those.*"

"He's a good detective."

"Didn't say he wasn't. But you can always see it. They're one step away from writing *must try harder* on everyone's report card."

Adams snorted. "Yeah, fair."

Cam shifted that sharp gaze to Adams. "So why the interest now, if they've been going missing for two months?"

Adams spread her hands. There was no point denying it. "We think it's linked to the missing kids by the river. I met a lad called Jack – tall, skinny, ginger beard, bit posh maybe?"

Cam frowned. "I can't think of a Jack."

"Maybe he spent time with the others? He was the one told me they were missing."

"He doesn't sound familiar." Cam shrugged. "Not everyone trusts shelters to be safe spaces. Not all shelters *are* safe spaces. He might have known them outside here."

They were both silent for a moment, then Cam sighed and said, "I know there was a bit of a community in an old Tube siding until a few weeks ago. Lilith used to go there during the day, but something happened and they all up and moved."

"Do you know what happened?" Adams asked, thinking of the dark stretches of the Underground. Deeper shadows there than even under bridges.

"Could be anything. Fell out with each other, or it got too crowded. Or someone moved them on," she added, tipping her head.

Adams nodded. "It's possible."

"Lots of things are possible. We're not people's keepers. Some move on by choice. Reconnect with family. Take jobs, sometimes. We had one woman suddenly send us a postcard from the south of France, of all places."

"France?" Adams asked.

"Yes. She hitchhiked down there after reading some book or other, and ended up working in this posh villa as a gardener." Cam smiled. "She even sent us a donation."

Adams had a sneaking suspicion that Lilith, Tommy, Bertie, and Alistair – and Edith, who Jack had mentioned, even if Cam hadn't – were unlikely to have run off to Cannes to prune roses, but she made an appreciative noise and said, "Is it usual for a group to move on so close together?"

"No," Cam said, without hesitating, then sighed. "But nothing's ever usual. They knew each other – friends might be pushing it, but they spent time together. Maybe they all came up with some plan." She glanced behind her. "I have to go. This is going to make the guests nervous."

Adams fished in her phone case and found a card. "Of course. Thank you." She held the card out to Cam. "Can you call me if they turn up? Or if anyone else goes missing?"

Cam took the card, pocketing it without reading it. "Not often the police are interested. It's like the missing going missing, really. Nothing to get excited about." She gave Adams a level look. "Present company somewhat excepted, maybe. Not sure yet."

She nodded. "I get that, and I'm sorry." Sorry that there was never a safety net big enough, sorry that the world seemed to be designed in such a way that there were always cracks for those not firmly secured to fall through. Sorry that she knew she wasn't an exception – she'd never have been here if not for the missing kids.

Cam gave her a tight, tired look. "Everyone's sorry. No one does anything. I'll let you know, though."

"Thank you."

Cam nodded and shut the door, the lock thudding firmly into place, and Adams turned to look back at the street. It was empty and silent, other than a glimpse of the back of a trailer just turning the corner the shelter sat on. She stared after it.

"Adams?" Zahid called, cracking the car door open. "You get something?"

"One sec," she said, and headed around the corner, the misty rain smoothing her cheeks and soaking into her hair.

The old Land Rover was idling at the kerb, the toastie trailer waiting obediently behind it, and the window was already down when she got to the driver's side. She looked in at Mirabelle.

"Evening, detective," the other woman said, smiling slightly.

"What're you doing here?"

"Dropping off leftovers. Our market spot rather unexpectedly fell through for the moment."

"Plus there was mist," Theo added. "No one's out in that."

"And we don't like to waste food," Mirabelle said. "We bring our leftovers here whenever we have any."

"Except when you give them out at the riverside," Adams said.

"Except then. But obviously there's no one about now other than your lot."

"It's very good of you," Adams said. "And do you know where your regulars spend their time when they're not here, then?"

Mirabelle inclined her head slightly. "If we did, would we be dropping food here?"

"Perhaps you do both. Since it's been such a slow night."

They looked at each other, that edge of a smile still on Mirabelle's lips. "People deserve their privacy, detective."

"People deserve safety, too. Do they have that?"

"Do you think you can give them that? Or do you think you'll just draw attention to them?"

"Draw whose attention?"

Mirabelle's mouth twitched, but she didn't reply.

"Should we go?" Theo asked, his voice hushed.

"What do you know about the bridge?" Adams asked, putting one hand on the car window and leaning down so that she could see Theo better.

"Oh dear," Mirabelle said. "Your hand as well? You have been in the wars."

Adams looked at the clumsy bandage and back at the other woman. "As well as what?"

"You had that bite on your neck, too."

"Scratch," Adams said.

"If you say so. You need to be more careful." Mirabelle looked at Theo. "Get the detective a toastie, would you?"

"I don't want a toastie."

"You should have a toastie. Best in London."

Adams shook her head irritably, and put more emphasis on her words. "Do you know where your regulars go when they're not at the riverside or here?"

"Leave them alone," Mirabelle said. "They haven't done anything."

"I don't think they have. But I think something's been done *to* them."

Mirabelle and Theo both stared at her, and she had one of those twisting, sliding moments again, where their eyes were too sharp and too bright and the proportions of their faces were simply *wrong*. Then it was gone.

"I can't help you," Mirabelle said.

"Of course not." Adams shoved her hands in her pockets with a grimace, then without thinking about it, said, "What about the dog? What does the dog mean?"

"I have no idea. Do you mean that song? What does the fox say, wasn't it?"

"You know what I mean."

"I know that we need to drop the food off," Mirabelle said. "We can't use it tomorrow."

"I'll get it," Theo said, reaching for the door handle.

"*Stop,*" Adams said, and the young man jumped, tugging his hand back as if the door might shock him. "Tell me what you know."

"About what?" Mirabelle asked. "About a scratch on your neck and meaningful dogs? Detective, I think you might need more sleep."

Adams had to resist the urge to press a hand to her forehead as she felt the sudden weight of her weariness press down on her, as if it had only been waiting to be acknowledged. "I do. But I'm not getting any anytime soon. Now, *where do your regulars go?*"

Theo looked at the floor as if afraid he might blurt something out if he met her eyes, but Mirabelle smiled slightly, tapping her fingers off the wheel. "Do you care so much?"

"Yes." She said it simply, wearily, and Mirabelle tipped her head.

"Maybe you do. For whatever reason. But we can't help you." She opened her door, forcing Adams to step back. "Some things just happen."

"Like missing kids?"

"Like seasons, and migrations, and forest fires, and floods."

"That's not the same."

"Maybe, maybe not." Mirabelle went to open the trailer. "Now, I have food to unload, then I want to go home and put my feet up and watch *Corrie*. Choose your battles, DS Adams. Not all are to be won. Some shouldn't even be fought."

Adams watched her climb into the trailer, not looking back, and wondered if she should arrest her just for spouting annoying babble.

"Brownies," Theo said, stopping next to her, and she barely managed not to jump. He was alarmingly quiet.

"I don't want—"

"Brownies," he insisted, shoving a paper bag into her coat pocket, and turned hurriedly back to the trailer to take a box from Mirabelle. "I'll take these in."

"That's the general idea," Mirabelle said, ignoring Adams, and vanished back into the trailer. Adams looked down at the bag, feeling the weight of the brownies inside, and spotted ink on the corner. She tucked it further into her pocket, hiding the pen marks.

"Enjoy *Corrie*," she said, and headed back toward the car.

12

IN THE DARK & THE MIST & THE LOST PLACES

ZAHID WAS BEING IRRITATING.

"I'm not staying here," he said, staring at the sagging wooden doors that filled the arched gateway of a derelict warehouse. The address scrawled on the brownie bag had been vague, but clear enough to lead them here, to the harsh, austere lines of a three-storey building that took up most of one block by a small waterway. There were no identifying signs to suggest what it might once have been, but Adams would have put money on a timber yard of sorts, loading milled wood onto barges to be taken down the tributary to the Thames. The windows were small and high, boarded or broken or both, and opportunistic plants were growing out of the roof and chimney stacks.

"I won't be long," she said.

"You're not going in there on your own."

She scowled at him. "Cam didn't even want to talk with you there because you have the air of someone who's going to start spouting things about people just needing to put the effort in. How d'you think that's going to play with Jack? You'll scare him off."

He gave her an unimpressed look. "He's not some delicate bloody forest faun. And you walking into abandoned warehouses alone is so far against SOP it's not even funny."

"You'll be right outside. I can shout if I need to. He's not going to talk if you're there, and this is the only lead we have."

"It's not even to do with the kids!"

"I think it is. And the DCI said I could run this my way—"

"She didn't mean go gallivanting into warehouses with junkies—"

"*Stay here.*" She snapped the last words with the sort of finality that would have impressed her mum, swinging out of the car and slamming the door without waiting to hear his response. A few strides took her to the gates, and she hoped they weren't locked. It'd kind of ruin the grand exit if she had to go back for the bolt cutters, or get Zahid to help her over the top.

But the gates were open, the chain slung through gaps sawn in the wood and the padlock neatly severed, used just to hold them in place. She glanced back at the car as she let herself through, seeing Zahid had climbed out and was standing next to it in that familiar, wide-legged stance she'd used herself so many times, hands tucked into his coat pockets.

He scowled at her. "If you get mugged, I'm saying 'I told you so' at least twice before I help you."

"Only twice? That's positively empathetic." She ducked through the gates and left the world behind.

Inside, the space was cavernous, running away from her in a vast open hall with a high, vaulted roof that was still mostly intact. The loom of streetlights spilled through the few unboarded windows, drawing everything in shadows and strangely hued shades. The light ran across the heavy wooden beams that still cross-hatched the space, then poured through the mysterious metal frames that clung to them, dangling precariously overhead. The smell of scorched metal lingered like a ghost, and Adams revised her guess from timber yard to metalworks as she stepped forward slowly, rubble crunching under her boots. There were more wooden double doors to the far side of the building, three sets of them, and through the ones that gaped open she could see the river whispering past, green and slow and muscular.

The other thing she could see, blossoming against the wall furthest from the river, was a small collection of tents and lean-tos, shored up with broken signs and scraps of wood. There was no movement from any of them, but she could feel herself being observed, and she was almost certain she could catch a whiff of smouldering wood.

"Jack?" she called. "It's Detective Sergeant Adams. I'm here to help with your missing friends."

There was no answer, just that same sense of eyes on her, and she glanced at the river uneasily.

"Jack, I can't help you if you won't talk to me."

Still silence, and she was deciding if she should go and poke into the tents or if that was likely to be counterproductive when there was the scuffle of limbs on canvas, and a small light came on inside one of the tents, turning it into a blue-toned jellyfish with the distorted silhouette of a person cast onto it. The strange proportions sent a shiver down Adams' back, and the welt on her wrist throbbed in time with the scratch on her neck. Her heartbeat, she supposed. Then the light was bobbing toward her, and a moment later Jack pointed it at her face. She raised a hand to protect her eyes.

"Easy with that."

"Sorry." He shone it at his own chin instead, turning his face into a Halloween mask, which wasn't a huge improvement. "Hello, Detective Sergeant."

She tried for a reassuring smile, but judging by the way he flinched and started playing with his hair it didn't work well. He was still in the green ski suit and orange hat, and there was a scratch on his cheek that looked inflamed. She gave up on the smile and held out the brownies instead. "Here. From Theo."

"Oh. Thanks. He makes exceptional brownies."

"He does," she agreed, and he hesitated.

"Have you had one?"

"I'm fine."

He shook his head and opened the bag, holding it out to her. "Have one."

Adams started to protest, then gave up. Maybe he thought she was trying to poison him and needed to see her eat one first. So she took one and had a bite, then watched him turn and wave the bag toward the tents. Someone scurried forward to grab it, then was gone again before she could glimpse them properly, protected behind the glare of Jack's torch.

"You're not having one?"

"Don't need one," he said, and scratched his arm urgently. "Do you believe me now? Are you seeing them?"

Adams took another bite of brownie. They really were very good. "I just wanted to get some more details from you."

"Huh." Jack rubbed one bare foot on top of the other, the toes long and bony. "Another kid went missing, right?"

"Yes." There was no point saying it wasn't to do with that. He wouldn't believe it, and she didn't believe it herself.

"I saw."

"You saw us searching?"

He shook his head and switched off the torch, plunging them into a sudden darkness that made Adams grab for her phone. Her hand closed on the duck instead, and she waited as her eyes adjusted to the dimness. "*I saw,*" Jack repeated, his voice low. "I was there, because ... because of Jonesy. I found him, see, but now he's gone, properly gone, they took him, and I thought maybe I could find him again, you know, since I found him once, so I keep going back, keep going to see if they might let him go, you know? And I saw, and I ran, because I couldn't ... I wanted to, but ... I *couldn't,* if they *saw* me, I—"

"You couldn't have done anything," Adams said, putting as much conviction into the words as she could. *And Jonesy makes six.* "It's not your fault. They'd have taken you too, wouldn't they?"

"Yes," Jack whispered.

"Like they took your friends?"

"Like Lilith. And Edith. Like Jonesy. Like *all* of them."

"Like Tommy and Bertie and Alistair? Is Alistair Weird Al to you?"

He blinked at her, then said, "Yes. You did look."

"I believe you, Jack." *Some of it, anyway.* "Tell me what you saw, and I'll try to help. It's the same people, then, taking the kids and your friends?"

"Yes, yes." He was playing with his hair again, plucking it from under his hat and twisting it in tight spirals around his fingers. "But different, you know? With Jonesy it was all *snap-snap-snap,* all rough and hungry. With the little boy it was softly-softly, gently as a dream. No crying, no screaming. Just gone."

Adams barely managed to suppress a shiver. She couldn't have said which sounded worse. "And they were taken in the same place? By the bridge?"

"No. But close. All of them were close. In the quiet places, the forgotten places. In the quiet streets, in the dark and the mist and the lost places."

There was no stopping the shiver this time, and she shifted her stance to hide it, thinking of the low, hungry mist as she ran through the dark of the sports ground. "It doesn't seem very safe for you here, then."

He shook his head. "Here we can be together. They like us alone. Together is safer. Otherwise … they know our patterns, see? So the shelter, say. That's dangerous. They wait in the alleys, in the side streets, wait for us to come searching for safety alone in the dark. Then *snap-snap-snap.*"

"So you saw them take Jonesy?"

"Yes. Yesterday."

"And the boy the other night."

"Yes." Jack pulled at his hat, tugging it down as far as it would go.

It was too much of a coincidence that he was at both disappearances. Yet she couldn't imagine Jack hurting anyone. It wasn't just the fact that he was skinny enough she felt she could probably break him over one knee. It was in the genuine concern he had for his missing friends, the fact that he was out there searching, even when he was terrified of whatever nightmares he'd peopled the city with.

"Who are *they?*" she asked now. "Is it a gang of some sort?" Because she had to ask that, *had* to, and had to believe it as well, even while she thought of shifting shadows on the bridge, and swirling mists, and *snap-snap-snap* and rough, hungry things. But that way lay more sleepless nights and some very awkward conversations with the police psychologist.

Jack gave her a surprisingly sweet smile. "You know it's not. You can *see,* when you stop looking. Like the bin."

"But it was just a bin." Her headache was starting up again, and she found she was still gripping the duck in her pocket, the shape of its wings oddly comforting as they dug into her fingers. "And it has to be people. Traffickers, perhaps?"

"*People* is a wider term that you think." Jack leaned

forward confidentially, bringing with him a whiff of damp and musty clothing and the sweet scent of jellybeans. "Now you can see, you have to believe, or *snap-snap-snap.*"

Adams recoiled at the last words, hearing an echo of them somewhere in her stomach, and she threw an anxious look at the river, creeping past the warehouse with its belly of secrets. "But … it was a *bin.*"

Jack switched his torch back on, shining it on her bandaged hand. "And that's just a scratch?"

Adams squeezed her hand into a fist, wincing at the sting, and tucked it into her pocket without answering.

"Sometimes crazy is just seeing the world differently," Jack said. "And once you see it differently, you understand that everyone else is crazy for *not* seeing."

Adams was fairly certain that she knew which version she preferred, but instead she just said, "Will you help?" Whatever version of reality he was in, he'd seen *something*, and it was the best she had right now. "Will you show me where the boy was taken?"

Jack switched his torch off again, and used it to scratch his chin. "I don't know …"

"This is how *my* world works, Jack. You help me find the kids, I help you find out what happened to your friends."

"But I know what happened. *Sn—*"

"*Snap-snap-snap.* Yes, I know. But we need to stop it happening again. And I can do that, if you help me."

He gave her an evaluating look. "Only you?"

"And my DI."

He shook his head. "I don't like other police. Even if they *could* see, they wouldn't."

Adams considered this and decided it wasn't worth arguing about. It had a certain ring of truth, anyway. "Well, he's in the car, and I can't leave him here. But once we get to the river you can show me what you need to show me."

"Just you and me?"

"Just you and me," she assured him, wondering how exactly she was going to manage that and just how much her ears were going to hurt by the time Zahid had stopped shouting.

Jack put his torch on again and shone it in her face. She squinted against the light but didn't object, and after a moment he turned it off, apparently satisfied. "Okay. But it has to be just us. We can't keep anyone safe who can't see."

"Fine. Let's go." She couldn't summon a smile. Her stomach was crawling with a cold dread she hadn't felt since her early days, in those first deeply awful brushes with human darkness.

Jack took a pair of slippers from his pockets and put them on. "Alright. Do you have coffee?"

"We'll get some." She turned and led the way back to the car, the weight of the early night pressing its belly to the city above them, fat with secret lives.

JACK WAS SURPRISINGLY unbothered by the presence of Zahid in the car, despite his earlier protests, and offered him a Werther's Original from a tatty pack. Zahid declined without being too rude about it, and Jack sucked on a sweet loudly as Adams wound her way back to the Christmas market via a stop at a coffeeshop, because Jack seemed primarily motivated by sugar and she needed the caffeine.

Harry was standing in the middle of the Christmas market taking selfies of himself in front of the unlit tree as they ducked under the police tape, Jack hanging back and staring at the DC warily. The mist hadn't lifted – if anything, it was thicker than when they'd left, stroking the roofs of the stalls with curious fingers and moving in strange currents on the river, revealing it in sudden flashes of inky black, then smothering it again.

"Evening," Harry said, shoving his phone away hurriedly.

"What're you doing here?" Zahid asked. "Shouldn't there be some uniforms on this?"

"They're around," Harry said, waving vaguely, and Jack tugged Adams' sleeve.

"What?"

"I don't like him, either. He's all wavy lines and cold chips."

Adams looked at Harry and wondered why that description made perfect sense. "It's alright. He won't be coming with us."

"Now what?" Zahid asked, taking a final gulp of beetroot latte and leaving a bright purple froth on his moustache. He made a face. "I can't believe you got me soy, Adams."

"They didn't have almond."

"Almond's bad for the planet anyway," Jack said, taking a large bite of an almond croissant before shoving it back in his pocket. "Oat's a better choice."

Zahid started to say something about lifestyle choices and Adams held up a hand. "It's getting on. Zahid, you stay here with Harry. Jack and I will head up the river a bit."

"Where you off to?" Harry asked, and Zahid talked over him.

"Not bloody again. You've got to stop vanishing into alleys with Jack the bloody lad here."

"We're not going far," Adams said. "Just up to the bridge, probably."

"In this muck that's out of sight," Zahid said, waving at the mist.

"You can't come," Adams said. "Jack seems to have taken against you."

"Nothing personal," Jack said, retrieving his croissant and stuffing the last bite into his mouth.

"Adams—"

"Maybe I could come," Harry suggested. He was smiling, but Jack looked away, shaking his head.

"Seems not," Adams said.

Zahid shook his head. "This is bollocks. What the hell are you going to do if you *do* find something, but you've got no backup and no corroboration of anything?"

"I'll call you. We're literally two minutes' walk away. I know you don't like leg day, but surely you can sprint that in half the time?"

"That's hardly the point—"

"It's not negotiable," Adams said, and looked at Jack. "Let's go."

He crumpled the paper bag that had held his croissant and dropped it in the bin, then looked at her, still clutching a large takeaway cup of something that had sounded eye-wateringly sweet to Adams – caramel mocha with something something and cream and something else. He seemed to be enjoying it though.

"Alright," he said. "I'm ready."

"Five minutes," Zahid said. "Call me every five minutes, or I'll bloody well kick you off the case."

"I think it's my case," Adams said, grinning at him, and turned to walk into the mist, Jack falling into step with her, his mug clutched in both hands like a chalice of poisoned wine.

THE MIST SWALLOWED THE CITY. That was the sense Adams had. Not that they'd been stolen away by the damp, thick air, but that everyone else had. Cars still purred along the approach to the bridge, but they were a distant hum that could've been from a misplaced bumblebee or some monstrous machine. The lights on the riverside path were yellow smudges above them, and Jack's footsteps slowed. He fell behind her, and came to a stop as they approached the bridge itself.

"What is it?" Adams asked, turning back to look at him. Her voice was low, although there was no reason for it. The words hardly carried in this.

"It's not good," he whispered, tucking his cup closer to his chest. "Not like this. We shouldn't be here when it's like this."

"Like what? The mist?"

"It's not mist."

"It is. It was even on the forecast. Foggy patches expected."

He shook his head, a jerky negation. "Back there it's fog. Here it's *them.*"

"We were here before. There was nothing—"

"It's *them,*" he insisted. "It's like a nest. Or camouflage, maybe. You go into the fog alone and you never come out." He looked at her, his face pale and young under the straggly beard. "Never go near the bridge in the fog. *Never.*"

Adams sipped her half-forgotten coffee. For a moment – well, for a moment she'd almost believed him, that some monsters were spinning fog out of river water and turning it to spiderwebs or some sort of airborne quicksand, trapping the unwary. But it hadn't been foggy when the kids were taken. Plus the whole idea was ridiculous, obviously. What wasn't ridiculous was someone using the fog as cover, like some Victorian villain lurking in the pea-soupers with a topcoat and a razor.

"Was it foggy when your friends were taken?"

"Yes. Because we can see, so they can't just grab us. They need to sneak up on us, and wait for us to be alone."

"But Jonesy wasn't alone."

"It must've been hungry. They seem to be hungrier now – they're taking people quicker. And it came even though there were two of us." He took a shaky breath, his eyes abruptly liquid with tears. "I see better than Jonesy and I … I *ducked,* I ducked when it reached for me, and I shouted to Jonesy to run but he was too slow and I … I left him. I left him with that *thing!*" The tears were spilling and he was shaking, sugary liquid sloshing in his mug as his fingers dug into the sides. "It wanted *me* and I let it take him instead!"

Adams walked back to him and patted him on the shoulder, a little awkwardly. "Well. I'm sure he'd have done the same. I mean," she added hurriedly, when Jack stared at her in horror, "I mean he'd understand. You were scared. Anyone would've been."

Jack snuffled, and finally eased his grip on the cup, searching in his pockets until he found a napkin. "I still shouldn't have left him."

"Well, now you can make up for it. Show me where you saw the boy taken."

He looked up at where the bridge loomed unseen in the mist, its presence palpable. "I can't. I'll tell you, but I can't go there in the fog. *We* can't."

Adams bit down on a sigh and considered arguing, but there was no point. His gaze was the haunted look of the hunted, and the mug was at risk of terminal loss of structural integrity. He wasn't going to make any sense here. "Alright. You still hungry? Cause I'm bloody starving. I'll buy you something decent if you stop talking in circles and tell me absolutely everything you know. *Everything,* got it?"

Jack took a shaky breath, then nodded. "Okay."

"Good. Let's go." She started past him, back toward the Christmas market, and he grabbed her arm.

"*Listen.*"

She froze, less from the touch than the naked horror in his voice, and stared into the mist. There seemed to be two levels of sound, the same way that she'd been seeing things on two levels the day she'd seen the bin. At one level was the persistent hum of cars, and the louder rumble of lorries on the bridge, underlined by the distant scream of a siren muted by the mist. Somewhere seagulls were screeching.

But beneath that … Beneath that. Something scraped on the metal of the bridge, something that set her teeth on edge and raised the hairs on her arms. Something like metal sliding over metal, a knife sharpening or the creak of high-tension wire, as if somewhere up there the load was getting too heavy. And something else as well. The whisper of some sort of communication, of wings sliding over hard casings or scaled paws twisting together or even low murmurs in alien throats. A susurrus of sound that was both insectile and hideously intelligent.

"What the hell is that?" she whispered to Jack.

"It's *them,*" he hissed back, as if she hadn't already known, at some deep and terrible level. "They're *here.*"

13

SNAP-SNAP-SNAP

ADAMS TOOK A STEP BACK, THE LOGICAL PART OF HER BRAIN trying to insist that she was just hearing late workers on the bridge, or the girders settling in the damp (although she didn't fancy being on any bridge making those sorts of noises). Maybe it wasn't even the bridge. Maybe it was something on the river, a toiling barge or a tug pressed to the nose of a ship, steel scraping on steel. Maybe it was the dredgers. It could be *any* of those things, and with the fog it was hard to tell where any of the sounds were coming from.

But she took a second step back anyway, in the direction of the Christmas market, as the skittering, scraping noise ran overhead and to the side, as if the noise-makers had slipped down the arch of the bridge to the ground, out of sight in the cloying mist. It had thickened further in the moments since they'd heard the sound, and she'd never seen it this dense. It made her think again of legendary pea-soupers and knife-wielding lurkers, and monsters that should stay hidden.

"Come *on,*" Jack hissed, and she glanced around at him. He'd retreated toward the Christmas market, cringing away from the sounds. "It's not safe. They're *hunting.*"

Adams barely stopped a shudder as he hissed the last word. But that was ridiculous, wasn't it? Nothing could *really* be hunting them. They were in London, for God's sake, not trekking across some alien planet peopled by hostile life forms, or skulking in the alleys of an underworld city.

Some little voice at the back of her head pounced on the idea of aliens, but she pushed it away as firmly as the creeping dread the scratching and clicking noises had awoken in her. She was a detective sergeant with the Met, and she didn't believe in bloody aliens and things that go bump in the night. Not unless she got to bump them over the head herself, anyway.

She straightened her shoulders and said in a firm, clear voice, "DS Adams, Met Police. Show yourself, mate."

There was a sudden silence, so thick that it felt as if her ears were full of cottonwool.

Jack made a noise that trod the no-man's-land between frustration and terror, and hissed, "They're not *people!* You can't arrest them!"

"I'll arrest who I like," she said, peering into the blank wall of the fog. The bridge was all but invisible, even this close up, more a suggestion of darker tones above them than anything concrete. There must be some weird pocket of atmospherics here, gathering the murk close about the pilings and above the river, and shredding on the edges further out to become more normal. More *real.*

There was movement in there. Currents swirled and eddied in the dense grey, shifting and layering. She licked her lips, her mouth suddenly dry, and said, "Stop mucking about in there. I'm not looking to arrest anyone, so don't give me reason to." Although she wouldn't have said no to arresting someone. A nice arrest would be deeply satisfying after all the poking around and trying to avoid talking about monsters.

"Come *on,*" Jack begged. "Come on, come on, *please.*"

She glanced back at him, intending to tell him to go back to the market, when movement in the mist snapped her attention toward the bridge. Something *loomed.* Something tall, all sharp angles and long, sleek lines, like a crane come to strutting, twitching life. It was there, surging out of the murk, then gone, and now she could hear the chittering again, clicks and scrapes that weren't just city noise. They had *meaning.*

She took her phone out, eyes never leaving the mist, and unlocked it, scrolling to Zahid's number as she said, "Come out." The words rang clearly against the night, even though her mouth was almost painfully dry.

Movement again, fast and faint, and she was left with the fleeting impression of multi-jointed limbs lifted high over a smooth back glossed with damp air. What the hell *were* they? Some sort of robotics, like those freaky things on YouTube, running and jumping and making the baser instincts get all twitchy? They could be, right? Remote-controlled, perhaps?

Jack had started moaning, a keening soundtrack of terror, and she looked around at him again. "Go back," she started, and he shrieked, pointing behind her.

Adams dropped into a crouch without thinking, spinning away in the same movement, her hands touching the ground for balance as she dropped the phone. Dirt scraped under her palms, and one knee knocked the ground, and something fast and hard whistled through the space where her head had been. She stayed down, skittering a few metres away before coming to a halt still in a crouch, staring into the darkness.

"You have to see!" Jack screeched. "You have to *see!*"

Adams wondered briefly where Zahid and Harry were, why she couldn't already hear them running down the path after Jack's first shout, then something came jittering out of the mist toward her. It was moving too fast on too many legs, and she bounced to her feet, breaking into a sprint for the river.

"Jack, *run!*" she bellowed, and something hooked her ankle. She stumbled, almost caught her balance as she kicked free, then was jerked backward by a hard grip on her jacket, like finding herself caught on an unexpected hook. A hook which was dragging her away with an inexorable grimness that had her suddenly in mind of the sort of hooks one finds in slaughterhouses. She scrabbled at her coat pockets, fighting to find the collapsible baton. The chittering was rising behind her, and she dug the heels of her boots into the ground, trying to resist whatever – *whoever* – had her, but it was like trying to stop a car with one hand.

"You're assaulting an officer," she managed, her shout half-strangled by the neck of her own coat. "Stand down! Stand down *right now!*"

The chittering seemed to have a distinctly amused tone to it, and she gave up on trying to pull away. She started working on the buttons of her coat instead, wishing they were slightly less well-attached, then the angle of the pull changed. Were they *lifting* her? Her feet left the ground, her jacket doing its absolute best to tear her head off, and she lifted both hands straight overheard like a child being undressed. One quick wriggle, a bit of help from gravity, and some unpleasant pulling on her hair, and she slipped out of the coat and dropped to the ground in a crouch.

She didn't look around, didn't pause, just bolted in what she hoped was the direction of the Christmas market, still lost in the mist. Behind her, something screeched in fury, and she ran harder, the mist swirling around her in tight currents. She swerved as she caught movement in the corner of her vision, a metallic limb slamming into the earth as the scrapings and chittering swelled up around her. The second limb to come down was close enough that the wind of it brushed her face, and then she almost ran into Jack as he emerged from the murk. He was screaming something inarticulate and waving a traffic cone, which he swung at her wildly, and she ducked with a yelp.

"It's me, *it's me* – go back!"

Jack spun around, still waving his traffic cone, and pelted off in the direction he'd come from. Adams hesitated a moment, listening to movement in the mist. Fast, skittering, the sort of noise crabs make on hard surfaces. It was coming from both sides, and she braced herself for those vast limbs to lash out of the fog, but then they were past her, hurtling on unseen.

"Jack, *run!*" she yelled, and sprinted after him, glimpsing movement ahead now, all angles and coiled power. Nothing human, but nothing machine either. Something that was both metal and life, something that had grown out of the city itself. *Not possible,* she thought, and the back of her neck ached from the scratches.

She spotted a flash of fluorescent green in the murk, as Jack screeched and swerved away from something that was more suggestion than form. She wondered again where the hell Zahid and Harry were, and bellowed, "Met Police! *Stand down!*" Not that she thought it would do any good against the … *things,* but protocol was protocol, and surely they'd hear *that*. She reached Jack just as a giant limb emerged from the fog and tried to scoop him up, and she didn't stop running. She hit him in a tackle, taking him to the ground and rolling them both out of the path of the attack. Something grumbled annoyance above, and she slapped her free hand to her trouser pockets as she pushed Jack away, meaning to call Zahid.

She'd dropped her phone. She'd forgotten. Bloody hell, her *phone*— Something flashed toward her, carrying with it a suggestion of hard surfaces like the chitinous shells of praying mantises, or the slick curves of old railway carriages. She was still on the ground, Jack curled in the foetal position next to her, so she just fell to her back, kicking out as hard as she could. She hit the thing's leg, the impact sending shocks jarring into her hip, and she had *something* in her pocket, and now her hand, but it wasn't her phone, it was the silly bloody duck, and as not one but two of those terrible limbs came carving toward her she squeezed the thing like a lifeline. The little LED light came on, pale and fragile, and she swore at the futility of it, but the monsters *screamed.*

The light built. It shattered across the wall of mist, rebounding on every water droplet, refracting and magnifying until Adams had to shield her eyes against it. It was like wielding a searchlight, not a tacky little keyring duck not meant for anything more strenuous than getting in the door at night.

One of the limbs came sweeping toward her again, accompanied by the scream of tearing metal, and she rolled away easily, aiming the duck in the general direction the leg had come from as it withdrew. There was a lot of chatter going on behind it, and she scrambled to her feet, standing over Jack's curled form. She waved the duck meaningfully.

"DS Adams, Met Police," she said again, pleased that her voice still seemed relatively level, even if the rest of her felt decidedly *un*-level. "Back off now. *Now.*"

There was a pause, and she was aware of scrutiny in the mist. Things were watching her with whatever they had that served as eyes, and she could feel the consideration of something not human. She lifted her chin – and the duck – slightly.

"Last chance. Do not make me escalate this." To what? A goose? She swallowed a small laugh that had an unpleasant edge to it. And her handcuffs were in her coat, for all the good they'd do. She wasn't quite sure how one went about arresting bridge monsters. She had a feeling her standard issue cuffs might not quite cut it. Plus the things seemed to have more limbs than were necessary, and *that* was going to make things difficult, too. She bit the inside of her cheek, aware that her thoughts were getting away on her, and said again, "Back off, lads." Not that they were necessarily lads, obviously, but in the absence of evidence to the contrary, the antisocial behaviour seemed to be lending itself in that direction.

And then they were gone. She wasn't sure how she knew – they didn't make any noise as they retreated, which made her think that all the scratching and chittering had been for show. The fog didn't suddenly lift, but it did lose its suffocating grasp on her, and then she was just standing there on the bank of the Thames in the depths of a chilly December night, with one knee aching from hitting the ground and sweat coating her shoulders and the back of her neck. The night was empty. She could feel it, and as if to underline the fact, further down the river a boat horn blew, clear and sharp, and a motorbike went over the bridge with a bellow of exhaust. She took a deep, careful breath and bent over, resting one hand on her knee and keeping the other squeezing the duck. Its light had faded, though, down to the usual barely-bright-enough-to-be-useful of LED keyrings everywhere.

Still bent over, she looked at Jack. He had his hands clamped over his head and his knees drawn up to his chest, but he cautiously opened one eye to stare at her. "Jack?" she asked. "Are you hurt?"

He looked around cautiously, then released his head and sat up. "I don't think so. You?"

She inspected the torn knee of her trousers. "Not really."

"That's awesome," Jack said, nodding at the duck. "How does it work?"

"I have no idea," she said, then offered him a hand and pulled him to his feet. The cold was clamping down on her now that the adrenaline was fading, the mist slipping clammy fingers around the cuffs of her suit jacket despite the fact that she'd managed to keep hold of her scarf. She shivered. "Let's get back."

She turned toward the village, finally loosening her grip on the duck. Its tiny light winked out, making no difference at all against the glow seeping through from the streetlights and the bridge itself. She wondered why they hadn't done that before, why it had seemed so unrelentingly grey, then decided she didn't want to think about it right now. There were lots of things she didn't want to think about right now.

"You believe me now, right?" Jack asked, padding next to her in his slippered feet.

She glanced back. The mist was thinning, the shape of the bridge emerging slowly, and all around she could hear the constant, comforting cacophony of a city at night. "Sure," she said. "As much as I believe anything, anyway."

"Good," Jack said. "Because you have to believe as well as see. One without the other is no good. It's like air without breathing."

She looked at him for a moment as they walked on, the lights of the Christmas market taking shape ahead of them, then said, "Sure. Why not."

ZAHID AND HARRY were arguing about the relative merits of their local football teams, leaning against one of the wooden stalls in the wash of yellow Christmas lights.

"Yeah, but last season was a fluke," Harry was saying. "I mean, the goalie broke his arm, the centre-half broke his leg, and there were so many sprains I lost count. Plus our top striker got concussion from heading an opposition player instead of the ball. How does that even happen? Like a bloody curse, it was."

"Face it," Zahid said, grinning. "Your team just objectively sucks, mate."

"I'd've had an exorcist in if I'd been manager," Harry started, then straightened up as Adams and Jack came hurrying toward them under the light. Adams was trying not to shiver too obviously, but her knee already felt like it was stiffening up in the cold. She wasn't sure how she looked, but given the start of a limp, some torn trousers, and the fact that she was pretty sure half the hairpins had been pulled out of her bun, she doubted it was her finest moment.

"What the hell happened?" Zahid demanded. "Why didn't you call?"

"I was a bit busy," she said.

"Did you get jumped?" Harry asked, one hand pressed to his chest almost theatrically. "Are they still about?"

Jumped by super-sized bridge spiders, Adams thought, and swallowed a laugh. "Yeah," she said. "The fog's bloody thick along there." She waved vaguely at the bridge, which was now clearly visible, lifting above a few vestiges of mist still clinging to the river.

Zahid squinted at her. "And they took your coat?"

"Excellent detecting there, boss." She pointed at Jack. "You stay here. I'm going back to look for it. My phone's still out there too."

"Well, that'll be long gone," Harry said.

"You've not seen her phone," Zahid said. "Captain Technology she is not."

Jack tugged at Adams' sleeve. "They might still be around."

"Well, I'm going with you this time," Zahid said. "And Jack

the lad can stay here with Harry. You sure it wasn't his buddies that jumped you?"

"It wasn't," Adams said, while Jack shook his head vigorously.

"Just because I refuse to be tied to your societal norms doesn't make me a criminal," he said, folding his arms.

"Other than the vagrancy," Zahid said.

"Trespass and squatting," Harry added.

"No one's charging you with anything, Jack," Adams said, and glared at the two officers. "Leave off. He's trying to help, and this was nothing at all to do with him." She nodded at Harry. "Put him in your car to warm up, okay?" She turned and headed back toward the bridge before anyone could answer, trying to ignore the shivers running down her spine like electric shocks. If she didn't go back now, she had a feeling she wouldn't go at all.

Zahid caught up with her in a couple of strides, the lingering mist giving the night soft edges without obscuring anything. "You alright?" he asked her.

"Sure. I just wanted Jack out of the way before I went back for my coat." She kept her eyes on the bridge, watching for movement, for a thickening of the fog.

"Why didn't you shout? We were listening."

"It happened too quickly.," she said, thinking of bellowing, *stand down* into the cottonwool thickness of the fog. "I suppose I just didn't have time."

Zahid stopped, and she slowed, looking back at him.

"What?" she asked.

"Something's not right here. *You're* not right. What the hell d'you mean, you didn't have time? *Of course* you had time. You're bloody police, not some panicked maiden aunt. Did you take a knock to the head or something?"

Adams stopped with a sigh and turned to face him. "No, I didn't get hit in the head. Look, I shouted a bit, but the fog must've messed up the sound. It was really thick along here. I couldn't even see the Christmas lights."

"Really?" Zahid frowned. "I suppose it was pretty thick there for a bit. But we'd have still been able to hear you. We even saw you for most of it."

Adams thought of being dragged backward through the murk and hauled up into the air by her jacket like a leopard's kill, not to mention rugby-tackling Jack to the ground. "Just weird atmospherics, I guess."

"I guess." He looked at her curiously. "You look a bit off. What's going on, Adams?"

"It's just this case. Some of the kids have been gone a long bloody time now." And she doubted the bridge monsters were exactly extending the best hospitality toward them. She started walking again. "Come on. It's freezing, and I want to see if they dropped my jacket."

"Pretty crap muggers if they have."

"It's how I prefer all my muggers to be," she said, and he snorted laughter. It sounded both incongruous and welcome against the night, and she touched the scabs at the back of her neck.

Some things just happen.

But not if she could help it.

14

THEY HIDE IN PLAIN SIGHT

THE COAT WAS LYING AT THE BASE OF THE BRIDGE, CRUMPLED like a shed lizard skin. Adams slowed as they approached the shadowed underside of the structure, aware that Zahid was eyeing her with his eyebrows drawn down. She ignored him, straining to hear that scraping chitter on the edge of her senses, to glimpse the thickening of the mist again. The bridge lay silent above them, devoid of any movement but the passage of cars and the half-seen swoop of gulls, confused by the lights. There was no sudden insectile lurching of some nightmare offspring of metal girders and old consciousness, no stealthy unfolding of limbs from the struts and supports.

Not that there really could have been, of course. Even with only a few minutes' distance she could see that. She'd just been taken aback by the unexpectedness, was all. She didn't believe in monsters. It must have been some sort of robotics, maybe with a smoke machine, or some new technology. *Had* to be.

The memory of that scraping chitter was loud in her ears, and she shivered.

"It's there," Zahid said, pointing at her coat.

"I know," she snapped. "I'm just … assessing the situation."

"Assessing the empty, well-lit path and the complete lack of cover for anyone to jump out, you mean?"

She scowled without looking away from the bridge, as if by keeping her eyes on it she could force it to behave itself. "I just got jumped here. In the fog."

Zahid looked around pointedly at the wisps of mist clinging unassumingly to the heavy stone bases of the bridge support, more decoration than obscuration. "I can see how they managed it. You sure your new buddy didn't slip some illicit substances into your coffee?"

She closed her eyes, thinking, *You have to see without looking.* Or was it *without seeing?* And there had been something about believing instead of … breathing? Or in the same way as breathing? You wouldn't want to stop breathing, after all. It was like all those self-help things – *just breathe!* Of course she was breathing. Stopping wasn't really an option.

She opened her eyes with a sigh, aware that she was wandering again. It happened every time these … happenings, or things, or however you wanted to describe them weren't in front of her. It was like those old 3D pictures she remembered being popular when she was a kid. They looked like a mass of coloured dots unless you crossed your eyes just right, and then suddenly, *bam,* dinosaur. She squinted at the bridge, but she wasn't going to try crossing her eyes with Zahid here. He was about one missed gym session off recommending her for administrative leave as it was.

"Can I pick it up?" he asked now. He was standing over her coat, pointing at it. "I mean, d'you want to photograph it in place, maybe? Or are there any bodily fluids I should be aware of?"

She scowled at him, ignoring the headache tightening

behind one eye, and the little motes that floated in her vision as she strode across to him, her back prickling as she turned it on the bridge. She snatched the jacket up. "Sure, Zahid. I just had a roll around on the ground for the hell of it, tore up my new trousers, and"—she shook the jacket at him—"got a great bloody hole in the back of my one good coat. All as, what? What d'you think I'm doing? Some elaborate prank while there's kids missing? *I'm trying to find them.*"

He stared at her jacket, and she couldn't help doing the same, the flare of anger fading. A jagged tear ran from the middle of the back up to where the seam on the shoulder had stopped it, and not even her mum's clothes repair skills, honed on three children who couldn't see a wall without wanting to climb it, were going to save it.

"Jesus," Zahid said. "Who'd you meet out here? Captain Hook?"

She shrugged into the coat, tear and all. It was cold out here. "I didn't get a good look at them." Her ID was still in her pocket, as was her collapsible baton, and now she scanned the ground for her phone.

"You think this was connected to the disappearances?"

Yes. "I don't know. I'm hardly the target demographic." She spotted her phone, abandoned face down on the path, and hurried to pick it up. She gave a little sigh of relief when she found it undamaged, just with some dirt ground into the corners of the silicone case. She dropped it into her coat pocket, then found her hand going to her trousers, checking for the duck. It was still there, oddly reassuring. "I need to go home and change. I'll drop Jack along the way – can you get yourself back to the station?"

He scowled at her. "You're not telling me something. Is this to do with the whole cult thing? The bridge cult or whatever the hell? You think he's part of it?"

Adams headed for the Christmas market, wrapping her poor abused coat around her as best she could. "I got jumped, Zahid. My knees hurt, my coat's trashed, and whoever did it's gone. I'm going for a shower and some intact clothes, so are you going to sort yourself out or follow me home like a stray cat?"

Zahid made a frustrated noise behind her that she thought would likely be accompanied by him throwing his arms in the air like a theatrically exasperated game show host. "I wouldn't follow you home if I *was* a cat. I know what happens to those house plants your mum keeps giving you. I'd be safer on the streets."

She turned to walk backward, giving him the finger, and he laughed. She did too, but her eyes drifted up to the hulk of the bridge, and she could have sworn that part of it *shifted,* unfolded then eased back, like a beast resettling itself in a nest. Something fluttered down from above, and she watched it fall before she turned away again. Shredded foil, with glimpses of purple. A Freddo wrapper, and she touched her coat pockets as Zahid fell into step with her. The creme egg was still there.

Keep them handy.

HARRY HAD BEEN JOINED by a tall, solid PC with a face pinkened by the cold when they got back. He nodded at Adams and Zahid.

"Evening."

"Evening," Zahid said, and looked around. "Just you, PC …?"

"Alex James," the PC said. "Yeah. I mean, it's not like there's a lot to see." He waved at the bridge, fully emerged from the mist now.

"And there's me," Harry said cheerfully. He'd produced a crumpled paper bag of sugar-encrusted peanuts from somewhere, and now he offered them around.

Zahid took a few and popped them in his mouth. "I mean, I know we've got staff shortages, but bloody hell. Anyone across the water? Or on the far side of the bridge?"

"Of course," Harry said, offering the bag to Adams. "It's all covered."

Adams waved it off and said, "How long you on for, Harry?"

"Oh, you know. Whenever." He took a handful of peanuts and tucked the bag away again, and Adams frowned at him.

"*Whenever?* Aren't you on a rota?"

"Nah. The boss just said to make myself useful, so I figured I'd be backup or something."

Adams and Zahid looked at each other, and he shrugged, then said, "Right, well. You can make yourself useful by running me back to the station so I can get my car. Adams here is off for another jaunt with her favourite junkie."

"Sure," Harry said. "I need a wee break anyway."

"A wee break?" Zahid demanded. "Are you Scottish now?"

"No. A *wee,* as in a break for a wee. I don't like using public toilets."

"Of course you don't," Zahid said, and scowled at Adams. "I'll have a matcha latte tomorrow, and it better be on almond milk. Plus at least four protein balls. And not the packaged ones."

"Fair," she said, and spotted Jack sitting cross-legged below the Christmas tree like a particularly luminous gnome. "Why's he still out here? It's freezing."

"I tried to put him in the car, but he wasn't having it," Alex said. "Probably figured I was going to arrest him. I've run into him before. Had to move him along a few times."

Adams looked at the bulk of the PC and wondered what

that had looked like. "He's helping with the investigation," she said.

"He's completely off his head, though, right?" Harry pointed out.

Zahid snorted. "He's not the only one."

"For God's sake—" Adams swallowed the rest of what she wanted to say, then grabbed Zahid's elbow and pulled him away from the other two. "The DCI told me to poke around the cult angle. She didn't say anything about what *you* had to do. So. Whatever. Go home, get some sleep, make some calls, *whatever,* just stop being such a git, alright?"

"I'm not happy with this. You're putting all your trust in some junkie who probably set you up to get rolled—"

"He's the only one who *might* have seen *something,* and it's more than we've got from anyone else, isn't it? *Isn't it?*" she repeated, when he didn't reply. "I don't want to ask you or anyone else to come off other leads unless I get something solid, but I *am* going to follow what I've got."

"You know running about on your own with him is plain stupid. And dangerous."

She scowled at him. "You can take *stupid* and shove it in your matcha latte, Zahid. Anyway, it's the only way this works. Now are you going to let me go, or will I have to tell the DCI I couldn't follow the leads I wanted because you objected to my *stupid* technique?"

Zahid shook his head, blowing air over his lower lip. "*No.* But be a bit bloody careful, Adams. You getting rolled as soon as you walked off with him was no coincidence. I'd put my Ninja mixer on that."

"You're probably right." She found her car keys and beckoned to Jack, who scrambled up and hurried over, giving the other two men a wide berth. "But it's not him that worries me."

She left them standing in the warm light of the Christmas village, Alex rocking on his heels and watching a late ferry chug past on the river while Harry munched on peanuts and Zahid scowled after her.

As they reached the street, Jack said, "Will he be okay?"

"Who?"

"Your friend. The big beardy one."

"I didn't think you liked him much," she said, beeping the car open.

Jack shrugged. "He's just like everyone. He has walls in his head and nothing can cross them. Doesn't make him bad. Just … walled in."

"He's good sorts, for the most part. He's fine."

Jack looked back at the market, the three men out of sight, and said, "I hope so." Then he clambered into the passenger side and waited until she climbed in the other before adding, "I fancy Indian."

She looked down at her ruined trousers then at his green ski suit. "Yeah. It might have to be takeaway." She started the car up and pulled out of the parking spot and away from the river.

Away from the bridge.

IT WAS TOO cold to eat outside, and Adams wasn't having anyone eating Indian in her car, so they settled on fish 'n' chips from the sort of greasy caff where the staff didn't even glance at Adams' torn trousers or scraped knuckles. She ordered, then left Jack to pick up the food from the counter while she went into the pokey little toilet, cluttered with a bucket and a mop and a broken-doored cupboard stuffed to capacity with cleaning supplies. It smelled clean, at least.

She washed her hands carefully, wincing at the antibacterial soap on her grazes, then tried to scrape her hair back into a bun. She didn't have much luck – she'd lost too many hairpins, and it was always a losing battle by this time of day anyway. She did what she could, then leaned against the sink and stared at her fingers, skin dark against the white porcelain. For some obscure reason she wanted to go home. Not to her home, but *home* home.

Home to the little terraced house where her parents still lived, although they kept threatening to sell up and move to Cornwall. Home to her own tiny bedroom (now ostensibly a craft room for her mum and an exercise room for her dad, but the stationary bike had been covered in swathes of material last time she was there, and her mum was still stacking the dining room table with fabric and random collected twigs and feathers and tubs of buttons). Home to her mum plying her with curry and banana bread, and her dad wanting to know if she'd arrested anyone famous recently. She swallowed hard, her throat clicking. That was ridiculous. She was a grown woman. She didn't need to run home to her parents just because …

"Just because I'm scared of the monsters under the bridge," she said to her reflection, and snorted. Her reflection didn't seem all that impressed, so she checked the paper towel dispenser, sighed as she found it empty, and wiped her hands on her trousers instead. It wasn't going to make matters any worse at this stage.

When she emerged from the toilet Jack immediately jumped up from a table in the corner, waving like a man on a desert island pleading for rescue. She lifted a hand in return and skirted the other tables to join him. No one looked at her twice. It was the sort of place where strange dinner companions and unusual dress standards were studiously not taken note of. She spotted two men huddled over their chips, giggling and trying to catch invisible things in the air, while at the table next to them a large man with a black eye was eating a chip butty. A much smaller man in a top hat talked at him intently about the demise of dog racing, and the big man paid him no attention whatsoever. There was also a couple in his 'n' hers black suits seated in the corner, one serving of chips divided neatly between them, which they were eating with forks in perfect synchronicity. And that was quite besides the various loud post-pub clusters, two women in hair curlers feeding each other spoonfuls of tomato soup, three elderly men in snazzy waistcoats carrying guitar cases, and a woman in a fur coat with a parrot on her shoulder. The parrot was eating a pineapple ring.

Adams shook stray chips off the plastic chair and sat down, poking at her veggie burger. She'd had them here before, and they were usually okay, but once she'd bit into one to find it was definitely not veggie, and another time someone had added half an unsliced onion to the top, presumably for extra flavour. This one looked alright, though.

Jack was emptying most of the contents of a vinegar bottle over his chips. "So, now what?" he asked.

"Now you tell me everything you know," she said. "*Everything.* Where you first saw them. Where you've seen them other than the bridge. How many people have gone missing. What you think they might ... *do* with them."

Jack stabbed a piece of battered fish, dripping with vinegar, and managed to get the whole thing in his mouth. "Mostly at the bridge," he said indistinctly. "Or the alleys nearby. Sometimes, when the fog's out, they go further, but that's their place."

Adams shook a slightly more circumspect amount of vinegar over her own chips. "And what are they?"

Jack shrugged. "They're just one of those things, you

know? Like the bin, or the birds that aren't birds, or the creatures that live in the drains and steal your shadow."

"Your *shadow?*"

"Yeah. And no one ever recovers from that." He sighed, and picked up a couple of sodden chips. "Old Nora lost hers years ago. I've never known her with one at all, and she's completely batty."

Adams stared at him, wondering what the benchmark for batty was in Jack's world. What her own benchmark might currently be, for that matter, because she was definitely getting the feeling that her standards were slipping. "So what other things are there? You know, other than bridge monsters and shadow thieves?" She glanced around, but no one was paying any attention to them. The man with the black eye had gone to sleep with his head on the table, and his companion was leaning forward, still continuing his one-sided conversation. The parrot had finished its pineapple ring and moved on to deep-fried cheese sticks.

"So many things," Jack said. "Even I don't see them all, I know." He considered it, chewing a chip thoughtfully. "I think there are different levels of hiding. Some creatures are so good at it that they look perfectly human, and you only get a glimpse out of the corner of your eye – like suddenly you see hooves, but when you look back they're just really shiny shoes. Only they're *not,* but you just can't see them. Or you think you see horns but when you turn around it's just a woman with a really cool hairstyle. They hide in plain sight, you know."

Adams waved vaguely. "So they're everywhere?"

"Sure," Jack said. "You just have to *see.*"

Adams rubbed her forehead with one greasy finger. Her headache was still there, a low, persistent throb that was making the burger sit heavy in her belly, the chips less comforting than she'd hoped. She opened her can of Tango and took a gulp, trying to wash the dryness from her throat. How much should she believe him? Were there bits that were true and the rest fantasy? Did she get to pick and choose, or was it believe the one thing she'd seen – the one thing that had destroyed her coat – and she had to believe it all? Believe in monsters stealing shadows and hoofed creatures passing as human in the streets? And did she believe any of it at all, for that matter? There was still the possibility, however remote, that the things had a proper, normal, human explanation, like drones or robots. *Something.*

She leaned back in the chair – or as much as she could, given that it felt like it might give way at any moment – and touched the back of her neck. The scab was hard and hot under her fingers. She really should go to the GP. "Alright. So there's lots of things about. But you *saw* the bridge things take Jonesy? And the boy?"

"Yes," Jack said to his fish, his voice low.

"And they're always around the bridge."

He looked up. "No, I told you. If it's foggy they can go a bit further. Jonesy was on one of the canals, and Edith was in an alley. But it's all in the *area,* you know. And all the same. Just *snap-snap-snap* – gone. No blood, not even a scream."

Not even a scream. Just like the kids. And all of them taken near the bridge, the damn thing looming over the river like a haunted bloody castle on a hill. "What do you know about them?"

He shrugged. He'd stopped shovelling the food down and was just using the little wooden fork to break the fish into a soggy mess. "They're fast and strong. And your head hurts when you see them, like nothing can really be like that, so your brain doesn't know how to process it."

"Huh," Adams said, resisting the urge to rub her forehead again.

"That's all I know. Once I saw them, I stopped going near the bridge. They scare me."

"Understandable."

"I was only there the other day because it was the last place Lilith had been."

"You find anything?"

Jack abandoned the fork. "Just her hat." He pointed at the woolly concoction on his own head. "I suppose they took everything else."

They were both silent for a while, staring at their respective meals, then Adams said, "You want me to drop you back at the warehouse?"

"The settlement? Yes."

"Is it safe? I mean – you're right on the water." She wouldn't want to be anywhere near the river. Anywhere near bridges.

"They've never come that far." He gave her a sudden, surprisingly bright smile. "And it's *our* place. Everyone needs their own place."

She nodded. "I see that."

They were both silent again, then Jack said, "You're not going back, are you? To the bridge?"

She bundled up her barely touched burger and chips and got up. "Let's get you home."

Jack followed her as she led the way out of the cafe, dropping the remains of their meal in the bin on the way. Then they were out in the blunt cold of a December night, the air tasting of exhaust fumes and old grease and old lives, and the hard silence of the stars and the whispered memory of the river. Adams looked at Jack. "You need anything?"

"No. I'm not hungry now." He made a face. "Besides, those chips were really vinegary."

She bit down on a laugh and headed for the car, trying not to stare at anyone too much. Partly because staring too much at certain times of night in certain parts of town was a good way to Start Something, and partly because she was afraid of what she might see. Or *see*. And she didn't want to *see* anything right now.

Bridge monsters were enough to deal with.

15

BATON. TORCH. YORKIE BARS. DUCK

ADAMS LET JACK OUT OF THE CAR OUTSIDE THE OLD metalworks with a warning to stay away from the bridge, not that she thought he really needed warning.

"You shouldn't go back either," he said, bending down to peer in the window at her. "They'll be looking for someone else, since they missed out earlier."

"Is that what they do? If they miss someone they keep trying straight away?"

Jack shrugged. "I don't know, really. But it's what you do when you're hungry, right? Keep trying until you get something."

"I suppose," Adams said, and rubbed her eyes, her stomach turning over faintly. *Six of each.*

"Do you … do you need help with something?" Jack asked. "I don't want to go near the bridge but I can come with you if …" He trailed off, sounding like someone offering to help with the Sunday lunch dishes and desperately hoping to be told not to worry.

She shook her head. "Off you go. I might pop by for a word tomorrow though."

"Sure," Jack said. "Make an appointment with my secretary." He grinned at her, slammed the door, then trotted off to slip through the gate into the shadows beyond.

Adams sat there with the car purring softly around her, smelling faintly of coffee and hot chips. She wanted to go home. Her bare knee was both cold and starting to stiffen up, and her right shoulder was tight with strain. She needed a shower and some warm gear if she was going to be hanging around the river for the rest of the night. And she was – Zahid would be gone by now, Harry was next to useless, and the uniformed officers watching the scene had no idea what was out there. Or even less idea than she did, anyway.

She checked the time, sighed, and pulled back onto the street. There was no time to go home. Maybe the monsters wouldn't ordinarily come out till the city got as close to sleep as it could, in the wee small hours, but they'd been out and hunting when she and Jack were there. The station was close enough, and she had workout gear in her locker. Not as professional or warm as her torn suit and jacket, but more comfortable.

And better for climbing.

ZAHID RANG as she swung through the still-busy streets toward the station. He sounded tired and cold and more than a little irritated over the speakerphone.

"Adams? You coming back or off on your hols?"

"I'm coming back. I thought you were going home." She couldn't stop a twist of relief that he hadn't. The thought of the uniformed constable – of anyone – standing alone on the deserted riverbanks while the night poured on toward midnight and *things* hunted the unwary … She didn't like it. And if Zahid was there then at least there were two of them, for whatever good that might do. And maybe Harry, but she didn't even feel guilty for not considering him.

"I *was* going home," he said. "But you got in my head, so now I've missed taco night, missed back and biceps at the gym, and will probably have to sleep on the sofa when I do finally get home, because it stinks like bloody burning tyres down here, for some reason."

"Does it?" Adams asked, frowning. "That's weird."

"Tell me about it. I'm never getting the smell out of my beard."

"Well, I'll be back soon as I can."

"How soon's that?"

"Soon."

Zahid sighed so heavily there was a moment of static on the line, a crackle that set the hairs on her arms shivering away from the skin.

"Zahid?"

"Yes, yes. Look, it's freezing down here as well as reeking. Is there really any point us hanging around the damn bridge? I know it's the one common thread, and you've got your weird cult angle going on, but do you really think they're going to waltz down the path in their robes in the middle of the night and try to grab someone? There's no kids here anyway."

"No. No, you're right," she said, fairly truthfully. "Seriously, you go home. You didn't need to stay."

"I know."

She snorted. "I thought Harry was running you back."

"Have you seen his car? It's a moving health code violation."

"So get an Uber."

"You'd think I was on a DCI salary."

"If you bought less protein shakes you could probably manage it."

"Says the woman single-handedly supporting London's coffee industry."

Adams indicated to swing into the parking garage. "Night, Zahid."

"Yeah." He didn't hang up, though, and before she could disconnect he said, "You sure you're alright, Adams?"

"Knee's a bit sore, but otherwise, yeah."

"Not what I meant." His voice was lower, and she had the sense of him moving away from whoever he was standing with. "I know you really want to break this, but go easy. That Fox Mulder thing's going to stick, you know?"

"I know," she said, pulling up at the barrier. "But if I find them, it won't matter."

"*If*," he said.

She hung up, and pressed the palms of her hands into her eyes for a moment, leaving swirling lights behind when she took them away. They reminded her of the migraine spots at the bridge. If they had been migraine spots, of course. It sounded preferable to the alternative, which was worrying.

THE DESKS WERE MOSTLY EMPTY, monitors turned off, and there was only one detective sitting amid a pile of printouts when she walked in, sifting through them with frustrated little mutters and taking spoonfuls of ice cream straight from a large tub balanced precariously on his knee. He nodded at Adams as she went past, and she nodded back, heading for the locker rooms. Her gym bag was stuffed unceremoniously into the bottom of her locker, under a single spare white shirt on a hanger. She dug out leggings, trainers, and a hoody, but no top, so her current shirt was going to have to do. Hardly her best look, but with the big yellow police jacket from the back of her car she'd be prepared for … well, whatever she needed to be prepared for.

She changed quickly, taking time to smear a little antiseptic cream on her knee and slap a plaster over the worst bit, more so it didn't stick to her leggings than because she was worried about it. Although who knew what she'd been rolling around in. She made a face and shoved her street clothes into the locker, then turned and hurried back to the main room, almost barging into the DCI as she pushed through the door.

"Oh! Sorry, boss."

"Adams. I was looking for you."

"Right." Adams wasn't sure how to respond to that, so she just tried for an expectant smile. The DCI looked even more tired than earlier, mascara seeping into the lines around her eyes and lending them dark shadows.

"Any luck?" the DCI asked.

"No. But I'm heading back to the bridge now. Keep an eye on things, like."

The DCI examined her, her gaze resting on Adams' scuffed knuckles. "Any trouble?"

"Not exactly." The DCI raised her eyebrows, and Adams tucked her hands behind her back. "I mean, I got jumped, but no harm done."

"By who?"

"I didn't see them."

"You didn't see any*thing?*"

Adams wasn't sure if she were imagining the emphasis on *thing,* creating something out of nothing. The DCI's gaze had shifted to her face, and the younger woman struggled not to look away or fidget. Her feet seemed to want to do a weird little lying shuffle, and she wondered if the DCI had kids. That look would give her mum's one a run for its money.

"It was really foggy," she said.

The DCI grunted, and finally stepped back, looking at Adams' legs. "Going for a run?"

"My trousers have a hole in them."

"Unfortunate." The DCI waved Adams into the room, and she crossed to her desk almost cautiously, the older woman following. "Anything from records?"

"Not as I know. I'll check now, but probably nothing till tomorrow." She sat down at her desk, pulling open the bottom drawer to fish out her spare takeaway cup. The Yorkie bars stared up at her accusingly, and the DCI clicked her tongue.

"Not much good in there, are they?"

"Um … no?"

"Keep them handy, I said." The DCI turned away as Adams stared at her. "And make sure your bloody torch is good to go." She strode off, heading for her own office, snapping at the other detective as she went, "For God's sake, Gary, you're dripping ice cream on the crime scene reports. Use a damn napkin, can't you?"

"Sorry," Gary mumbled, using his sleeve to wipe ineffectually at the spill.

Adams watched the DCI vanish through her office door, closing it surprisingly softly behind her. The blinds were drawn, and she wondered what the older woman was doing behind them. Reviewing case notes, or drafting press statements, or stockpiling chocolate bars in case of a worldwide shortage? She pinched the skin of her forehead with one hand then grabbed her spare mug and the Yorkie bars out of the drawer, the dark blue packaging crinkling under her fingers. *Keep them handy.* She suddenly thought of the shiny foil wrapper of the Freddo drifting down out of the night, like the shed skin of an insect.

She shook her head and frowned at the pile on the desk, then went back to the locker room. She came back a moment later with the empty gym bag in one hand. Well, almost empty. The metal duck rolled softly in the bottom as she threw the Yorkie bars, the last creme egg, her phone, a handheld radio and mic, and her mug in on top of it, trying not to think too much about things. Sometimes thinking just got in the way. Sometimes you had to simply act.

THE STREETS still rumbled with life, people finishing late shifts or starting even later ones, taxis and Ubers and delivery drivers, groups and couples still drifting to bars and pubs and homes. DS Adams found her gaze drifting over them as she waited at the lights, not in the usual, automatic, looking-for-trouble type way, but searching for something *different.* Looking for some sign that they were *other.* Were her legs just a little too long (probably not, she was probably a model)? Was his back angled in a way that just didn't sit right? Were those horns? Wings? And if anyone had a tail, how the hell would she know, given all the long coats on a December night? Although she supposed she could rule out tails on anyone wearing skinny jeans.

A horn parped impatiently behind her, and she raised an apologetic hand to the rear-view mirror as she pulled away from the lights. This wasn't what she should be thinking about, even if *this* was actually a thing and not just some dislocated soul's way of understanding a world that he was out of step with. The more she thought about it, the more she liked the idea of robotics. Traffickers got smarter all the time. It could be a way to snatch kids without risking exposure, and maybe the adults had just been wrong place, wrong time. Although that didn't explain the historic pattern of the missing around the bridges. But maybe there was no pattern. Maybe she was making it up. The human mind always tries to make sense of what's around it, to impose order on chaos, but that doesn't mean that what it creates is true.

She pulled into the parking area by the market, her stomach suddenly tight. The lights of the riverside path were warm but watery, as if seen through a rainy window, and the bridge loomed beyond them, plucking at her attention. She parked behind Harry's car and got out slowly, examining the market. No Zahid that she could see, and no one else, either. The absence of uniformed officers still seemed strange, to appease the public and media if nothing else, and she wished that she'd thought to ask the DCI about it. But she'd been too busy being told off for not carrying chocolate at all times. She shook her head and went to open the boot.

She clipped the radio to her leggings, running the line for the mic across her back and attaching it to her opposite shoulder, considered it for a moment, then pulled the drawstring of her leggings through a bit and tied it onto the radio's lanyard. Losing a police radio while having an unauthorised and unaccompanied clamber around a bridge in the middle of the night wouldn't go down well. She swapped her hoody for her heavy, bright yellow police coat and zipped it up, then loaded the cavernous pockets from the gym bag. Yorkie bars, two packs in one chest pocket, one in the other. ID and phone in an inside pocket, along with her keyring and its little but sometimes useful multitool. Head torch in the left lower pocket, cuffs in the right. Baton in with the cuffs.

She considered the big Maglite that lived in her boot for a moment. It'd be too awkward to hold onto while clambering about, but it might be handy. She wedged it into a pocket, the weight of it reassuring. And then the only thing left was the little metal duck, the streetlights giving its body a burnished glow and lighting sparks in its LED eyes. She picked it up, rubbing her thumb over its smooth head, then tucked it in with the Yorkie bars on her right, shut the boot, then opened it again and slung the empty bag across her body, cinching the strap tight. Then she walked into the market with the slow, let's-be-having-no-nonsense tread she'd used a thousand times.

The market was empty and shadowed, the shutters closed tightly on the stalls and the signs above them dull and bland without the festive lighting. The faintly metallic scent of the river snaked up to greet her, and somewhere over it she caught a whiff of cooked onions. The tree loomed above her, rendered dark and unfamiliar in the night, and she had a sudden sense of sorrow for it, torn from its roots in some faraway, rich-earthed forest to die here among the concrete and the stone.

But she wasn't here to worry about the feelings of trees. She skirted it, her eyes already on the bridge, and almost walked straight into Mirabelle. The other woman jumped back, a fleeting look of fright on her face, then managed a smile.

"DS Adams. I thought you'd be around somewhere." She had an insulated bag slung across her body, and Adams smelled cooked onions again.

"What're you doing here?"

"Delivery," Mirabelle said, and tipped her head behind her. Harry waved at Adams with one hand, clutching a paper bag in the other.

"Just can't stay away, can you, Adams?"

"Seems not."

"Have a sandwich." He nodded at Mirabelle. "Go on, give her a sandwich."

Mirabelle looked at Adams, that same evaluating look, and shook her head. "She doesn't want a sandwich."

"No, I don't," Adams agreed, although they smelled a lot better than her half-eaten veggie burger had tasted.

"Go on," Harry said. "It's good for you."

"I—"

"It's too late," Mirabelle said, talking over her. "The time for sandwiches is gone."

Adams looked from her to Harry, who was scowling. "What?"

"Give. Her. A sandwich," Harry said, his voice a growl.

Mirabelle's lip curled. "Watch your tone, McMartin. This isn't on me." She looked at Adams. "Mind him. The small dogs always bite the hardest." She turned to walk away, then stopped and swung back to Harry again. "I gave you the wrong one. Swap." She dug in the bag, grabbing out an identical-looking paper bag and exchanging it, then walked off in the direction of the street without looking back.

Adams looked at Harry again. "What was that about?" she demanded.

"Nothing," Harry said, his tone still hard-edged. "You should've had a sandwich, is all."

She thought of Theo snatching the sandwich off her, and Jack saying, *I don't eat those,* and said, "Why?"

"Well, they taste bloody good," Harry said. He sounded very much like his normal self now, but he was looking everywhere except at her.

"Right." The toasties would have to wait. She had bigger things to worry about. "Where's Zahid?"

"Home, I'd've thought."

She examined him for a moment, but he just looked like Harry, a little hunched and confused by life, and trying to get through it all by the easiest road possible. "And Alex?"

"He's patrolling. What're *you* doing?"

"Bit of my own patrolling."

He rubbed his mouth, looked at his sandwich, then said, "The bridge isn't our business."

The world shivered around her. *He knew.* "The kids are."

"Some things have to happen—"

"Like floods and forest fires?" He spread his hands, not replying, and she said again, "Where's Zahid? He hasn't gone home, has he?"

"He'll be fine."

She stared at him, wanting to grab the front of his jacket, to force him to tell her, but she had to think of the kids first. *Had* to. "What about Jack?"

Harry took a bite of sandwich. "You should've had one of these. They really take the edge off."

Adams pressed one hand against the nape of her neck, feeling the scabs under her fingers. "What's happened to Jack?"

"No idea. You were the one running around with him. Bad company to keep, you know."

She watched him chewing placidly on his sandwich like a cow on its cud, and wondered if it was still considered assaulting a police officer if it was also a police officer *doing* the assaulting.

"What do you know, Harry? About the bridge?"

"That it's not our business." He'd kept his back to it the entire time, and he didn't look around now. "Some things just have to be left alone."

"Kids, Harry. *Kids.*"

He nodded. "Unfortunate. My dad was on the job last time it happened. Easier to deal with back then."

"*Deal with?* You mean cover up, don't you?"

He spread his free hand, the other still clutching the toastie. "Words are just words." He took another bite and wrinkled his nose. "I think she burned the onions."

Adams shook her head and started for the bridge, hissing as she did so, "If you knew and you did nothing, Harry – I'll have you."

He grabbed her arm as she went past him, pulling her to a stop. "But we have to do nothing," he said, sounding almost apologetic. "You have to be careful even about seeing. And if you do see, you don't interfere. There are other things than bridges."

"Get off me."

"I can't let you go. What if something worse happens because you interfere?"

"Worse than lost kids?" She tried to pull away and he tightened his grip, fingers grinding painfully into her arm.

"Maybe. We don't know. There has to be balance. Certain things must be maintained, even if a few have to suffer for it." Then he hiccoughed. "Ugh. There's definitely—*hic*—something wrong with those onions."

Adams twisted out of his grip, his fingers slipping on the slick surface of her jacket, and when he grabbed for her a second time she jumped back. "Don't try this, Harry."

"*You* don't try it," he snapped irritably. "Just stop being such a bloody star for once, can't you? All you have to do is not go up there, and stop running about with crazy people. Let things be. Some things protect themselves."

"So what're you doing, then?"

"Stopping you messing everything up," he started, then pressed a hand to his belly and coughed slightly. "You can't go up there." He took a step toward her, and she took the baton from her pocket, shaking it out. "Oh, come on," he started, then abruptly turned and lurched away, one hand over his mouth.

Adams watched him go, her heart going too fast, then looked at the abandoned sandwich splattered on the ground in front of her.

"Thanks," she said, even though Mirabelle wasn't there to hear her. Because forest fires could be fought, and floodwaters could be escaped. One just had to be ready for them.

And have a little help.

Adams turned to the bridge, and the Thames running

opaque as the Lethe beneath it. The Christmas village was dark behind her, and she was alone on the river path, the city distant and disinterested, leaving her to the monsters. She touched her pockets. Baton. Head torch. Yorkie bars. Duck.

"Sorted," she whispered, and marched into the dark.

16

INTO THE LAIR OF THE BEASTS

STANDING AT THE BASE OF THE BRIDGE ITSELF, STARING UP, SHE thought she probably should have packed a lifejacket instead of a duck. And a climbing harness would've been nice, too. It all looked disturbingly *high* up there, and though she wasn't afraid of heights, she didn't much fancy the idea of falling straight into the Thames if she missed her footing. Or something missed it for her. She looked down at the water, her eyes watering in the cold air. The fall wasn't so bad, but the river had the sort of currents that were both unpredictable and ravenous, and it'd be cold enough to stop her breath when she hit. *If* she hit, obviously, as she had no intention of doing so.

And a climbing harness would've helped with that, but she was here now. She could feel the tug of weariness in the weight of her limbs and the itchiness of her eyes, the tightness of fright in her neck and shoulders, but she knew that if she called it off, if she went home or tried to find backup, she wouldn't come back. Or she'd come back in the sensible, Zahid-approved way, with not only a harness but backup and floodlights and whatever weapons might be handy against sentient bridge monsters and-slash-or scary robots. And they wouldn't find anything. Just as she knew, if she waited for daylight, there'd be nothing here either. Or there would be, but it'd be *deeper.* More hidden. Harry was right on that, at least – some things did protect themselves. Now, right this minute, exhausted and hungry and with her nerves rubbed raw by caffeine and cold – now she could see. Swirls in the Thames of more than turbulence. Lights in the streets that moved too erratically for even cyclists. And a dog standing in the middle of the riverside path, beyond the bridge, watching her with its shaggy fur rendering its outline indistinct.

She nodded at it, and it tipped its head. It looked big now, even larger than a Labrador, and she wondered how she'd thought it was small when she'd first seen it. She glanced back the way she'd come. There was no sign of Harry. Whatever the toasties were meant to do (cheese-based soporific, maybe, countering views of the deeply real? Or hallucinogenic? She was willing to consider either), Mirabelle had evidently done some doctoring. There was no sign of any other officers, either, and she had an idea why. The creatures had to be allowed to hunt, after all, didn't they?

She took her phone out and tried Zahid, almost dropping it when it rang. She'd half expected him to be at the bottom of the river.

He picked up on the second ring, his voice low. "What?"

"Are you okay?"

"Sure. Why?"

"Did you have a toastie?"

"A *what?*"

"A toastie. From the van."

"No, I didn't have a bloody toastie, Adams. Harry insisted on buying me one, and that bloody Alex was all on about the cheese being good protein, but come on. Carbs, you know? I snuck it in the bin when they weren't watching."

Adams breathed out slowly. "Okay, good. Listen, you need to go back to where we found Jack. I think he's in danger."

She was aware of movement at his end of the phone, him getting up from wherever he'd been sitting. "Adams—"

"No, listen. Harry is ... I don't know, exactly. But he knows more than he's saying. And I'm worried he's done something to Jack. I mean, he likely won't know where Jack *is*, but he might have a way to find him, and I think we need to get him into some protective custody." She expected Zahid to start shouting at her for having a Jack fixation, but there was no immediate answer. "Zahid?"

"Alex and I did a turn down the river together. He asked where we'd found Jack."

"You told him."

"I didn't see any reason not to."

Adams swore, then said, "Right. Well, can you get there?"

There was a pause, then he said, "What are you doing?"

"Following a lead on the kids. But Harry's talking cover-ups, and there's no other officers here. *None,* Zahid. Where is everyone?"

Zahid was quiet for a moment longer, then he said, "Tell me you're not going into something on your own."

Adams glanced down the riverbank. The dog was still watching her. "Sort of?"

"So yes, then."

"Find Jack. And there's others there too. Make sure they're safe, Zahid. They're still people."

"I know that," he said, a touch of irritation in his voice, then he sighed. "I do know. I'm on it. Where are you going to be?"

"The bridge. I've got it covered." She hung up before he

could object, hoping she was wrong. Hoping Harry – and Alex, if he were part of this too – were nothing more than interferers, casters of misdirection, making sure *different* theories stayed as jokes.

But she couldn't be sure.

ADAMS TUCKED her shirt into her leggings, checked the laces on her trainers, and made sure the Velcro pockets of her jacket were firmly sealed down. There was enough light from the river walk and the general city loom of illumination that she didn't need her torch – or the duck – just yet, and there was no need to announce her arrival. She padded over to where the heavy girders of the base pressed down into the earth, took a deep breath, and swore at the city, hidden monsters, Yorkie bar–wielding DCIs, and life in general. Then she started to climb.

The metal access ladder was set back into the superstructure of the bridge, the rungs skinny and slick, and cold enough that she added gloves to her list of things she should have thought of. It only took her up a few metres before she met a sturdy padlocked gate surrounded by spikes and wings of sharp metal intended to discourage nighttime climbers such as herself. She added bolt cutters to her list and manoeuvred around the barrier precariously, tearing a jacket pocket and swallowing yelps as the metal gouged her through her leggings.

But then she was safe on the other side, standing on a skinny metal walkway with another ladder leading up into the gloom. She made sure nothing was going to fall out of her torn pocket, blew on her hands to warm them up, and carefully ignored the way the city lights had dimmed as her perspective widened, and sounds had grown muted, like someone had closed a door firmly behind her. None of that mattered right now. All her attention was on the deep shadows gathering in the underbelly of the bridge, shadows that could hide anything – and quite possibly did. She started up the next ladder, listening for scraping steps and soft chitters in the dark.

She was in the lair of the beasts.

And she was also very cold. She was glad it wasn't windy. It was precarious enough as it was, and the cold metal of the ladder stung her fingers, rendering them stiff and weaker than they should be. Tension strummed across her shoulders, and her every sense strained as she peered about, the scabs on the back of her neck stinging and her injured hand throbbing. She didn't pause, though, just kept moving steadily, up and up into the tangled girders of the bridge, trying not to think about the fact that she'd been climbing for far longer than she should have been, given the fairly low profile of the bridge itself.

But finally she reached the narrow maintenance walkways that spanned it, and eased off the ladder onto the first of them, giving herself a moment to catch her breath and look for ambush. Nothing revealed itself. The corners and angles remained resolutely obscured by shadow and lingering pockets of mist, and all that moved were distant headlights on the periphery of her vision, and the occasional angry protests of pigeons as she disturbed them from their roosts.

She edged forward. The further she moved from the bank, the quieter the city became, until she was aware of the hungry mumbling of the Thames at the bridges' supports, and the creak and groan of settling metal. She'd expected the cars would be louder here, even given the strange acoustics of the bridge (of the bridge *monsters*, really, but she still wasn't quite ready to consider that yet), but they seemed more remote than ever, nothing but a hum on the edge of hearing, irritating as a fly stuck in a closed room. The whole structure trembled just faintly with the assault of the vehicles, giving her the disorienting sense that she was standing atop some giant, slumbering beast, listening to its snores. Although she supposed she'd actually be in its belly, which was a thought she pushed away as quickly as she could manage.

She turned carefully on the narrow walkway, the railings waist-high but with wide gaps beneath them, and peered back toward the riverbank. It was distant and dim, almost out of focus, and she had a sudden, swooping sense of vertigo that made her drop into a crouch, breathing hard and squeezing her eyes shut. For one moment she felt utterly dislocated, everything rendered directionless and confusing, and she was so much flotsam in a vast, breathing, indifferent city, as likely to be falling as rising. She slipped a hand into her pocket and squeezed the duck, hard enough that the edges of its wings bit into her hands, savouring the discomfort and willing clarity and noise to return to the world, to remind her of where she stood.

It didn't, but when she opened her eyes the vertigo had passed. She stood, feeling small against the vast bulk of the unknown around her, and thought, *see*.

The bridge swelled, bigger than its physical dimensions, painted in stark metal against the night. Somewhere in her peripheral vision she was aware of lights and roads and all the human debris of existence, but it was nothing more than a backdrop. She pushed it away, just as she pushed away the arguing and banter of colleagues and the general chaos of the station when she was working. It was nothing but background noise. All that mattered was what was in front of her. And what was in front of her was … she squeezed the duck in her hand again, her heart a little too fast for the climb to justify, sweat prickling her back. What she was seeing was impossible. But being impossible never stopped anything being real. She resisted the urge to look away, and *saw.*

Adams remembered, very distinctly, being a small girl – smaller than one brother but bigger than the other – and finding a plant in the local park with three leaves at the end of one small branch, all bound together with a thick, white, gossamer coating, opaque and almost pearlescent. Morning dew had beaded it softly, and she'd thought it was quite beautiful. Until her younger brother had rushed up, demanding to know what she was looking at, and promptly poked it with a stick. The soft shell of webbing had torn, and tiny spiders had erupted from it, rushing everywhere in panic as their home was destroyed. Adams had been less horrified than fascinated, that all these little creatures had been living in such a wonderfully crafted and secretive home, and also furious that her brother had destroyed it. She'd immediately retaliated on behalf of the spider by tackling him and trying to rub his nose in some old white dog poo, but her mum had spotted her and refused to believe that destroying a spider's nest was a gross enough transgression to merit rubbing one's sibling's nose in excrement of any form. Adams still felt she'd been in the right, and had taken every opportunity for far longer than was probably reasonable to launch spiders at her brother at unexpected moments.

Now she blinked at the night, which for a moment had felt far more distant than the spring chill of that half-forgotten morning. There were no plants here, no annoying brothers or dog poo, but that little cocoon of baby spiders reminded her very much of the patches she could see tucked into the superstructure of the bridge. Admittedly, the spider's cocoon had been white, and these were more shadowy greens and greys, and if these ones *did* hold spiders she didn't like to think what size they might be. That cocoon she'd been able to cradle comfortably in her child's hand. These ones looked like they could cradle the child. She swallowed hard, peering into the dark. Three close to her. A glimpse of another further on, and a suggestion of a fourth, and then there wasn't enough light for her to be able to see into the distant reaches toward the other side of the river, but she'd bet her favourite takeaway cup that there were six. Six child-size cocoons, looking like nothing so much as slightly deeper pockets of shadow, or simply grime collected from the exhausts of cars and boats and lives.

"Okay," she said, her voice quiet in the night. "Okay, sure." Because if she was thinking about mind-altering toasties that were possibly counteracted by exceptional brownies, and carnivorous bins, and dogs of unfixed size, then why not? She let go of the duck and gripped the railing instead, leaning over precariously as she scanned the underside of the bridge. There weren't any other proper walkways that she could see, but there were handholds and grips, she supposed for if workers had to clamber out and do repairs or something of the sort. "With harnesses," she muttered to herself, slinging a leg over the railing. "And lifejackets. Probably immersion suits as well." Although she supposed that'd make the climbing a bit tricky, even if she really fancied the idea of an immersion suit if she fell. And a hardhat.

Trainers and cold, stiff hands didn't make for the best climbing gear, but she took a final look around, half-expecting something to come rushing out of the dark, all long limbs and wrong angles, but the bridge was still. The things were sleeping, or off hunting, or something. Maybe they didn't even live here, just stashed their catch. Either way, she didn't see them. They probably didn't expect her, not after the encounter earlier. "That's because sensible people don't come back," she muttered, grabbing a handhold and swinging herself away from the dubious safety of the walkway. "Sensible people get hoisted into the air by a monster and they don't come back, ever. Of course, *really* sensible people don't even see monsters, so there's that. It's a bad sign."

So was talking to herself, probably, but it stopped her thinking too much about what she was doing. Which seemed wise, considering that she was up on a bloody bridge over the Thames in the middle of the night, with no safety gear, alone, and with no evidence other than the sort of things that likely got you sectioned, even in these slightly more tolerant days. She was momentarily distracted wondering how many people had ended up institutionalised because of what they'd seen. More than was comfortable to think about, probably. But even if she didn't end up sectioned, she hoped she never had to write a report on this. More than that, she hoped she was wrong. That she'd had a momentary lapse of judgement, too much caffeine and too little sleep, and was following a completely ridiculous wild beast chase. Because, if she wasn't, then bridge monsters that stole children and bins that ate people actually existed, and that meant she didn't know this world at all.

She slipped once, her foot sliding off a skinny metal handgrip, and her arms jerked in her sockets as she caught herself, thudding into the girder in front of her and feeling one hand start to loosen. She kicked her feet frantically into the frames, finding footholds in corners and angles, and hauled herself back up, resolutely not looking at the river funnelling hungrily beneath her, far more distant than the height of the bridge gave it any right to be.

She seemed to have been climbing for hours, the bridge curving still higher in the middle, and her muscles were starting to shake from cold and effort. She had to keep stopping to shake life back into her hands. But she was gaining. The cocoon was coming closer, still and silent, revealing itself as less of a cocoon and more of a thick, opaque wedge pressed into the corners of the structure, well-fastened and solid. The traffic noise faded even further as she climbed on, an alien sound that belonged to a distant overworld. Here was only sneaking wind and sibilant water and the crash of her own heart.

Round one final support, and up into the far reaches of the bridge, where the cars should have been thundering right above her head, but the only evidence of them now was that faint thrum coming through the bridge itself. No wonder no one ever heard the kids. She braced herself as well as she could, one arm hooked through a handhold, and stared at the webbing. It was squished into a corner between the underside of the bridge above her and a girder, milky and opaque, just as she remembered from the spider cocoon. She reached out a hand hesitantly, and her fingers slid over it, the surface slick and cool. She tried pinching a bit between her fingers, but she couldn't get any grip on it. Scratching just sent an unpleasant sensation shuddering down her spine, like nails on a chalkboard, and she flinched, then poked it as hard as she dared. There was no give to it whatsoever.

"Dammit," she muttered, and peered around. The bridge still looked empty, but it felt like she'd been up here for ages. The beasts would have to come back sometime. She fumbled in her pockets to find her keyring and the multitool attached to it, unfolding the serrated blade. The ads all reckoned it could saw through wood, but given the size of it she imagined that meant a stick for the dog, not logs for your cabin. She tried an experimental swipe at the web, and it parted under the blade grudgingly, curling slowly away in layers under its own tension. She cut again, more deliberately this time, keeping close to the edges. There was no telling who – or what – was inside, and she didn't want to inadvertently give someone a haircut (plus, that long-ago memory of the spiders boiling out of the cocoon was still very much with her).

The fabric (*web,* her mind insisted) parted easily enough, but it was thick and sticky and slow to peel away from what was underneath. Adams kept going, slicing a little then pulling the loose material back, glancing around occasionally, aware she was taking too long and not able to do anything about it but keep going. Warmer air seeped over her fingers, the inside of the cocoon unpleasantly clammy. She still didn't – *couldn't* quite accept what she was doing, couldn't believe that this was part of her city, but she kept on grimly, sawing doggedly away and digging for the centre of the web. And maybe there was still an explanation for this, some natural phenomenon a biologist would be happy to explain to her somewhere nice and clean and warm and clinical, something to do with rare migratory birds or some invasive species of insect, and there'd be no children in here, because it just *didn't make sense.*

Then she tore a final, sticky layer back to revel one small, shoeless foot, the sock decorated with pugs wearing glasses. Adams flinched back, almost dropping the multitool and momentarily forgetting she was clinging precariously to a girder and one handhold, and wouldn't *that* have been a fantastic turn of events. She lurched forward again, resettling herself in her perch, and grabbed the foot, feeling the warmth of it. She pinched a toe, and for one panicked moment there was nothing but stillness, then she felt a lazy twitch against her hand.

She closed her eyes, swearing softly and gratefully under her breath, then reached for the mic on her shoulder. She stopped before she keyed it, though. Harry might be down there still, and the last thing she wanted was him to know she'd been successful. Who knew what he might do to keep his mysterious balance. She grabbed her phone out of her pocket instead and opened it to her last calls. Her thumb hovered over the dial button next to Zahid's name, then she looked along the shadowy labyrinth of metal girders and opened a text message instead.

Ambulances & backup to bridge. NOW.

She hit send, swapped the phone for the multitool, and went back to sawing through the webbing, her breath harsh in her throat.

There were still five more cocoons.

17

A PAINFULLY SLOW RESCUE

GETTING THE KID DOWN WAS TRICKY. TO REACH THE LAST OF the webbing holding them against the steel, Adams had to clamber into an even more precarious position, working with both feet on a slippery girder and her knees braced against another, one hand holding the kid in place and the other still wielding the multitool. She was trembling by the time she cut the last swathe of webbing free, half convinced she was going to lose her grip and send one or both of them straight into the waiting maw of the Thames. Or lose the multitool, which would be almost as disastrous. And in between it all she kept checking the riverbank for lights. Where the hell was Zahid?

Finally the kid – a girl of about eight or so, her hair mostly secured in two dark braids and her puffy pink ski jacket half unzipped, exposing a bright blue jumper with a Christmas penguin on it – was all but free, only secured by one stretch of webbing across her skinny chest. Adams settled herself in place as securely as she could, trying not to think about all the ways this could go wrong, and swung her gym bag around to her front, checking the straps. Her big brother had given it to her for Christmas a couple of years ago, so it was some fancy brand, technical this, stress-tested that thing. She didn't really care about the details, but what she did care about right now was that it was cavernous when it was zipped out to its full size, and that the webbing straps were stitched firmly right around the body of the bag, and that the clips and fastenings were all hefty stainless steel, no plastic.

She frowned at it, zipped it open, then wedged her shoulder into the girl's belly and sliced the last of the bindings free. The girl flopped onto Adams' shoulder in a fireman's carry, just as she'd practised in some half-forgotten training day, and she had one small moment of triumph before her feet started slipping off the girder, and the girl started sliding off her shoulder. She trapped the girl in place, shoved her multitool into the phone pocket of her leggings, and managed to fling her arm around an upright in time to scuffle for better footing. She waited, heart going too fast, then slowly manoeuvred the girl's body into the bag. It wasn't exactly secure, but it worked, after a fashion, the girl's limbs flopping out and looking like they'd catch on every girder they went past. The bag seemed fine with the weight, at least, and Adams carefully shifted it around to her back again, the strap pinching the skin at her neck and across her chest.

"This is going to be fun," she muttered, and eased herself toward a new handhold. The girl's weight shifted, and Adams wobbled on the girder. She took a stumbling step forward and her knee crashed into an upright, but she managed to wedge herself into a corner and take a couple of shaky breaths. She patted the bag on her back, checking the girl was secure, but she hadn't moved. Now just to make sure she didn't slip, lose her balance, or walk into a beam and give the kid concussion. She risked another look at the riverbank, but the market was dark. No bobbing torches, no floodlights, no flashing lights. But there was precisely nothing she could do about that, so she started moving again, concentrating on the next handhold, the next step, the next careful swing across empty space. It was all she could do for now.

The worst bit was trying to get back over the walkway railing. It was high, and the walkway itself was narrow, and Adams was shaking from the cold and her trek across the underside of the bridge. There was one horrible moment, when she had one leg on either side of the railing, where the girl's weight shifted and almost pulled her backward. She flung herself forward so wildly that she thought she was going to somersault straight across the walkway and out the other side, but she dropped hard onto her knees instead. There was a crash as she hit the metal grating, and she winced at both the echo of the sound and the sting of the impact, but she was safe. Relatively speaking, anyway.

She sat down carefully, letting the bag ease onto the walkway behind her, then ducked out of the strap and turned around. "Hey," she whispered, clicking her fingers in front of the girl's face. "Wake up. Come on." There wasn't so much as a twitch in response, and she peered back at the riverbank again. Still nothing, not even a little flurry of activity from the officers already on the scene – unless Harry had quashed it, of course. It was possible, but not for long. Zahid should be there shortly. She took her phone from her pocket. If Zahid hadn't seen the text then she could have a problem—her text sat unsent on the screen, and she poked it irritably. Her phone helpfully asked if she'd like to try sending it again, so she did. It sat there for a moment, then said sorrowfully that it hadn't sent.

She checked the underside of the bridge. Still no movement that she could see, but time seemed to be running faster than the river beneath them. She *needed* help. She hit call, and her phone considered it for a moment, then bleeped a disconnect at her. She checked the display. No signal. Here, in the middle of London, no signal. Just like the alley, but at least there she'd been able to blame the high walls. She tipped her head back, running a hand over her face, then tried 999. Emergency calls always went through, no matter what.

Except when you're in the realm of the bridge monsters, apparently. She cursed, gave the girl a guilty look, then shoved the phone back in her pocket and looked around. She needed to get to the next cocoon as quickly as she could, since it seemed there was no help coming. But she couldn't just leave the girl here. If she woke up and rolled over she could go straight through the railings and into the water. Adams toyed momentarily with the idea of handcuffing the girl to the bridge for her own good, then dismissed it. She'd have enough to explain after all this without throwing small children with dislocated shoulders and broken wrists into the mix. Or, worse, small children that have fallen off bridges because handcuffs aren't really designed with eight-year-olds in mind.

She leaned forward and pinched the girl's earlobe. She flinched slightly, but it was a sleepy, unfocused movement, and her eyes didn't flicker. Adams took off her jacket and laid it over the girl, then stood up and stretched out her aching back. She could try shouting, but she was almost certain that while a phone call *might* draw attention to her, a shout was certain to. And the odds of anyone hearing it seemed slim. Not only was the shore distant, but that heavy thickness still hung around them, swallowing sound, offering cover to whatever it was that enjoyed shoving kids in webs. Adams was done trying to figure out what such things might be. It didn't matter. All that mattered was getting the kids out. She supposed she could carry the girl all the way along the walkway and down the ladder, then come back for the others, but she had a feeling it wouldn't work. That she'd struggle to find her way back again, as if she'd been offered this one chance while everyone's back was turned, sneaking into a part of the world that was never meant for her.

She sighed, and tried shaking the girl gently. "You in there?"

The girl made a sleeping noise. It wasn't much, but it was better than the utter lack of responsiveness so far.

Adams fished in her jacket pockets until she found a Yorkie bar. She opened it, waving it under the girl's nose. "Snack?"

The girl twitched like a sleeping cat.

"Here we go. Chocolate, look. Yum!" Adams broke the end off the bar and popped it in her own mouth, almost wincing at the heavy sweetness of it. At least it might fend off the cold a bit.

She was adding water to her mental list of things she should have brought with her when the girl opened her eyes and stared at her in a horrified, unfocused way.

"Hey!" Adams managed, almost choking on a piece of chocolate. "Hi. Um … Detective Sergeant Adams, Met Police. What's your name?"

The girl just stared at her, eyes wide.

Adams offered her the rest of the chocolate bar. "Yorkie?"

The girl looked at the bar, then at Adams, then at the echoing confines of the bridge. "Where are they?" she whispered.

Adams swallowed, her throat sticky. Maybe an eight-year-old wasn't any more reliable a witness than Jack, but it made it more real somehow. She waved the Yorkie bar at the girl. "Have something to eat. You need it."

The girl took the bar, but didn't bite into it. "They'll be back. They *always* come back."

"We'll be gone before they do. Eat up. You need some sugar."

The girl did, the sharp-edged wind toying with the hair around her face. Once she was done, Adams said, "What's your name?"

"Safa."

"Hi, Safa," Adams said, trying to sound perky and upbeat. "Can you sit here safely and not go anywhere? We don't want you falling."

Safa gave her a narrow-eyed look. "I'm not a *kid.*"

"Right." Adams gave up on sounding perky. "You do that, then, and stay quiet, okay?"

Safa rolled her eyes. "*Obviously.*"

"And give me the bag."

Safa shuffled off it, and Adams slung it back across her body. Safa tried to hand the jacket back too, but Adams shook her head and tucked it closer around the girl, then wrangled the Maglite out of a pocket and offered it to her. "Keep it off. But you can flash it at me. You know, as a signal. If … just as a signal."

Safa took the torch without speaking, her face unreadable. It looked outsized in her small hands.

"Right," Adams said. "Good." She checked she had the multitool in her leggings pocket still, and eyed the next cocoon. It wasn't too far away. Now that she knew how to do it, she could be quicker, too. Maybe this might be okay. Maybe. She slung a leg over the railing, and Safa said, "Wait."

"What?" Adams said, barely biting down on her impatience.

"Be careful. They're really fast. You don't see them coming."

"Awesome," Adams said, and picked her way into the tangle of girders and struts and uprights, trying not to look at the river, or to spend too long searching the shadows for movement. Was she doing the right thing? Maybe she *should* have got the girl down first, out of harm's way, then come back later with a proper rescue team with harnesses and nets and survival blankets, not just her with her fancy gym bag and a pocketful of Yorkie bars. But she still had the sense that time was running out, and that if she left she'd never make it back again. The beasts would move, and this pocket in the world would close, and the kids would be gone forever. This was a one-time only deal. She felt it in the same way she felt the connections of cases twisting together, that sparkling frisson in the tips of her fingers and her heart. And sometimes that was the sort of thing that solved cases, not logic and facts.

So she swung herself through a gap between two girders to the next cocoon, wedged herself into place, and started cutting.

THE SECOND CHILD WAS A BOY, smaller than Safa, and Adams was so certain he was just going to flop straight out of her bag that she considered trying to zip him into it entirely. But trying to tuck his legs and arms in was too difficult while she was clinging to precarious footholds, so she just settled him against her back as well as she could. Despite her doubts she got him back to the walkway more quickly and easily than she had Safa, laying him next to the girl and telling her to both get him awake as fast as possible and also, since Safa was now in charge of the Yorkies, for no one to eat so much chocolate that they were likely to be sick on her. Safa gave her another eye roll as she covered the boy with Adams' jacket, but Adams felt that was probably a good sign.

She set off again, sweat chilling on her forehead and soaking her shirt from the effort of the climb and lugging small children about the place. Her shoulders ached, and her legs shook, but she kept on doggedly, her movement across the girders becoming more surefooted and swift as she worked.

She found two more boys, then a second girl, and by the time she got back with her Safa was already feeding the third boy a Yorkie bar.

"How we doing?" Adams asked, laying the girl down on the walkway and trying not to bleed on her. She'd torn her hand on something, and the blood was collecting in the creases on her palms.

"Everyone's mostly awake," Safa said.

"Good." Adams wiped sweat off her forehead with one arm. Five down, one to go. "Safa, are you a good climber?"

"I do gymnastics," she said, matter-of-factly.

As far as Adams knew, that involved more controlled falling than climbing, but it was something. "Cool," she said, and nodded at the boys. "How're you all doing? Think you can climb down?"

"This isn't organic," the biggest boy said, staring at the Yorkie bar in his hand. "I think I'm allergic to it."

"To chocolate?" Adams asked.

"To non-organic food. Mum said."

Safa snorted loudly, and Adams bit the inside of her cheek to stop herself from laughing. "We'll get you something else when we get down." She pointed at the smallest boy. "How about you?"

"I like it," he declared around a large mouthful of chocolate.

"But I need something *now,*" the bigger boy said. "It's not fair that you have something and I don't!"

"Then eat the Yorkie," Safa snapped.

"It's not *organic!*"

"I'll have it," the third boy said, snatching the bar off the bigger one. He tried to grab it back.

"But I want something to eat!"

"Jesus," Adams said, pinching the bridge of her nose. "You'll all get something to eat, okay? Now can you climb down or not?"

"It's high," the third boy said, looking at her dubiously. "Shouldn't we have parachutes or something?"

"It's not right, not having organic options."

Adams had the passing thought that she might prefer dealing with the Friday night post-pub crowd to this, and said, "You'll all get something, but if you want to get home, you have to climb. Or the monsters'll be back."

Four small faces stared at her, then the smallest boy burst into tears.

"Dammit," Adams said.

"Well done," Safa said, hugging the little boy. "Look, it's an adventure," she added over his head to the others. "All you have to do is climb down, right?" She nodded at the biggest boy. "Briar, you can go first. Noah can go last, and Alfie can be in the middle. Right, Alfie?" she added to the little boy, who was still snuffling. He gave her an uncertain look, then took another bite of chocolate bar.

"You're going too," Adams said to Safa, and the girl gave her a cool look.

"I'll stay and help. You're really bad with kids, you know."

Adams opened her mouth to argue, then shut it again. "True."

"Didn't you ever have brothers or sisters?" Safa asked, cleaning Alfie's face with her sleeve.

"Two."

Safa did the eye roll again. Adams hated to think what she'd be like in about six years or so. "I bet you were the boring one who always did what she was told."

"Well, I *am* a police officer," Adams protested, then shook her head. "Look, this isn't a discussion. It's dangerous up here, and you need to *all* head toward the ladder, now."

Safa pointed at the new girl, still unconscious on the walkway. "And what about when she wakes alone and freaks out, and falls off into the river?"

Adams scowled at Safa, uncomfortably sure she was being out-argued by an eight-year-old. Then she looked at the other girl, sighed, and said, "Bollocks. You're right."

"You said bollocks," Noah said, and giggled.

Adams thought that was hardly the worst thing they'd been through over the past couple of weeks, but she made a contrite face and took her phone from her jacket, swiping through the screens to get to Zahid's number. It still showed no signal. "Here," she said, giving it to Briar. "It's unlocked. When you get down, you hit dial. There's a police officer going to answer"—*hopefully*—"and you tell him you're at the bridge, alright?"

"Alright," he said, tucking the phone carefully into the inside pocket of his own coat. It looked like it cost more than the phone did.

"And you *run,*" she added. "You run straight to the Christmas village, and you don't stop until you meet a detective called Zahid, okay? You don't stop for anyone else, even if they say they're police."

"Can we have a Taser?" Noah asked.

"What? No."

"Why not? That'd show them!"

"Because I don't *have* a Taser," Adams said.

"That's rubbish," Briar declared.

"No it's not," Safa said. "What if you electrified the whole bridge?"

Everyone stared at her, and Adams said, "What she said," then gestured to them to get up. "Come on! You need to move."

The three boys and Safa got up, clinging to the railing. Briar peered over the edge. "It's really high."

"Not really," Safa said. "Kilimanjaro is high. Or the London Eye. That's *really* high."

It seemed the boys couldn't argue with that logic, and they started to shuffle down the walkway, clinging to the railing on both sides. They looked desperately small, even Briar, and Adams wondered again if she was doing the right thing. But at least if *some* of them got away—

Noah looked back at Adams, his eyes wide and his nose pinched and pink with cold. "It *is* high," he whispered. "Are you sure we shouldn't have parachutes?"

"Just look where you're putting your feet and hands," Adams said. "Hang on tight, and don't look past the walkway."

Noah didn't answer, but he turned back and trailed dutifully after the other two boys, tiny and fragile against the night. Adams clutched the back of her neck as she watched them go, trying to look confident and in control. Grown up. Judging by the look Safa was giving her, she wasn't doing any better at that than at being perky.

"Go on, then," the girl said. "There's still one to get."

"You should have gone with them," Adams said. "They need you."

"You need me more. You're *awful* at this."

Adams accepted the criticism with a sigh, deciding to assume it was directed at her child-wrangling skills rather than her policing skills, then swung back over the railing. One more. One more to claim back from the shifting, treacherous shadows. One more to free before the monsters returned.

She hoped she still had time.

18

DUCK IT

ADAMS PEERED BACK INTO THE SHADOWS OF THE BRIDGE'S underbelly as she worked on the last cocoon. It was almost directly over the walkway, nearly at the halfway point of the span across the river, and she wondered why the pouches were all clustered on this side. Was the other side of the bridge no good for nests? Was the light wrong? Or the angles? Did it have some sort of monster-repellent paint on it? If so, she wanted some, preferably in aerosol format.

She couldn't see the kids from here, couldn't tell if they were still milling about or had followed instructions and were trekking back along the walkway to the ladder and the—

"Oh, f—" She stopped, glancing at the cocoon, which seemed reproachful. "Fox," she mumbled, and attacked the webbing more enthusiastically. *The gate.* She'd forgotten about the damn gate. She'd barely managed to get around it – how the hell were a bunch of tiny humans meant to do it? Tiny, exhausted, and non-organic-intolerant humans. She didn't even know how *she* was going to get them around it, but given the choice of facing bridge monsters or risking a few bruises, she'd throw them over the bloody thing if she had to.

She looked either way along the bridge, then sighed and checked the radio was on. She was just going to have to risk it. Zahid had to have alerted someone else by now. She keyed the radio on her shoulder. "All stations, all stations, Detective Sergeant Adams. Urgent assistance required, repeat, urgent assistance required."

There was no response, not even a scraping of static, and she checked the volume, twisting the squelch button until it gave a little crackle. Even so, there was still no response when she tried a second time. Of course there wasn't, any more than her phone had been able to get reception. It wasn't atmospherics, or interference, or anything else. She'd crawled through a crack in the world, following beasts and children, and there was no reaching the world she knew without climbing back out.

Which was what she was going to do. She shifted her position, arms and shoulders aching, legs shaky, and peeled back a swathe of webbing, exposing an outflung arm and a small pale hand. She cut again, careful to avoid the vague outline of the kid's body, aware of a timer ticking at the back of her mind. She'd been up here half the night by the feel of things, but she couldn't have been. Zahid would've been here by now. Unless something had gone wrong. Of course, it was also possible that time just *stopped* in the strange, dark quiet of the underbridge world. She wasn't ruling anything out.

She tore another strip of webbing away, the kid emerging as a boy with his head resting on his chest, looking like he'd just fallen asleep in front of the TV, waiting to be carried to bed. The river gave a sudden chuckle beneath her, as if amused at her efforts, and somewhere she dimly heard a horn. She had the horrified thought that things were *ebbing,* that whatever had been holding them in its grip was starting to release. Which should have been a good thing, if the world she knew was getting closer, but it didn't feel that way. No, it felt *noticeable.*

The webbing was gunky, clogging up the tiny teeth of the multitool, and she wasted precious seconds trying to clean it off. Her hands were trembling, and she wanted to believe it was a mix of cold and prolonged stress, but the world was taking on strange migraine edges, and she thought of the dog with his humorous grin for some reason. Her grip on the girder slipped a little, and she winced as metal bit into her torn palms, then readjusted her position with her breath harsh in her throat and her heart running far faster than seemed reasonable. Focus. The last thing she needed was to slip and end up with a kid in need of stitches. That wouldn't read well with the press.

She was down to one final stretch of webbing when her radio belched static, making her yelp and drop the knife. She lunged forward, managing to trap it between her hand and a girder, using the sort of language that she really hoped the kid couldn't hear. She keyed the radio.

"All stations, DS Adams."

Another blast of static, nothing discernible in it as words.

"All stations, DS Adams."

A pause, then the radio blatted again, a ragged chorus of electronic noise that bounced around the bridge, and buried within it one word, the voice garbled beyond recognition. It was the word that mattered, though.

Coming.

Adams lunged for the cocoon.

They're coming.

"Safa!" she yelled, not looking around to see if she could spot the girl. There was no time for that, and no time for secrecy. She couldn't have said why she was so sure that the word had been meant for her, but she knew it the way she knew certain alleys weren't to be walked down, even by police. "*Safa!* Move! Start down *now!*"

There was a small shout in the distance, nothing that Adams could interpret, so she just yelled again, "Get out of there *now!*"

She wrestled the blade shut on the multitool and tried to shove it into the pocket of her leggings. She missed and it clattered away, but she didn't bother to look for it. There was no time. She half fell forward onto the cocoon and tore away the last of the binding strands in great handfuls. How long would it take for the beasts to get here? And how did they move, anyway? They seemed to have an unreasonable amount of legs, but that might not be so helpful with all the girders on the bridge. Maybe gravity wasn't really a thing for them. She was momentarily distracted by the horrifying thought that they might have wings secreted somewhere on their bony carapaces, and pushed it away as the boy slipped, almost sliding out of the cocoon entirely.

"Focus," she muttered to herself. "You can work on the fairy tales later." And they had to be fairy tales, right? Like her mum's ones, though, all fierce and monstrous and blood-soaked, rather than her dad's rather more sanitised versions. She'd always preferred her mum's, but they all had one thing in common. If you faced the monster, you could beat it. If you were canny and careful, if you were sneaky and brave all at once, you could win.

She scooped the boy into her bag, wobbling as his weight pulled her momentarily off balance. And fast, she added to herself, as she began to edge down to the walkway. Canny and careful and *fast.*

IT SEEMED to take far longer to get down out of the tangle of girders and onto the waiting walkway than it should have. The uprights were too far apart, her footholds too slippery, the boy impossibly heavy and awkward for such a small burden. She lost her footing twice, barely saving herself with back-twisting lunges for new handholds, and missed her grip a couple more times, and just as she was making a final jump onto the walkway the kid slid out of the bag with all the grace of a sack of spuds. She grabbed him with one hand, trapping him against her hip, and took a giant, ungainly step down, as if she thought she were doing a moon landing. She dropped clumsily to the metal lattice flooring before she could moon stride straight off the other side, managing to whack one hip and one elbow on the way down, before crashing to her knees hard enough that she felt the entire walkway shake. The kid seemed to be unscathed, though, which was something.

She hunkered there for a moment, breathing hard, then untangled the kid from the bag, abandoning it where it lay. She scrambled to her feet and hoisted him onto her shoulder in a fireman's carry, turning to peer down the walkway as it vanished into the dimness toward the bank.

"Safa!" she shouted. "Safa, you better be bloody well climbing!"

There was no answer, and no knowing if the kid had listened, and she set off down the walkway as fast as she dared, head down to avoid banging it on low-hanging girders. Her trainers clanged too loudly on the metal and her breathing was ragged and painful, her knees and shoulders and hip and elbow and *everything* screaming protests at her. But none of that was as awful as the sense of *things* circling in the dark, the intensity of it so tight that she was surprised she was breathing at all. How long? How long before the creatures came slipping out of the night? How long to get them all clear?

The river moved heavy and silent below, and the city cast the loom of its lights everywhere but into the vast steel frame of the bridge. The moment of lightness, when she'd heard the water and the distant sounds of traffic, was gone, and the radio, when she tried it, was dead again. Everything had faded, horns and engines and sirens heard as though on a TV through a neighbour's wall. Here was only the rasp and rush of her own breath, the clatter of metal under her heels, and the whisper of wind past her ears, playing across the sweaty nape of her neck and chilling the scabs there. She pushed harder, jogging precariously, the kid bouncing on her shoulder.

"*Safa!*" she tried again, still hoping the girl *had* followed the others down, helping the second girl as she did, but Jesus, they were so small. So small, and so tired, and it was such a long way down, and then there was the *gate*– What the hell had she been thinking, sending them off alone? "*Safa!*"

"Be quiet!" The whisper-shout came back to her, voice strained and small and barely audible over the clamour of her own movement. "Be quiet, you'll bring them here!"

Adams saw the girl now, indistinct in the darkness, huddled at the top of the ladder. Not far to go. She shifted her grip on the boy, trying to ignore a sudden hope unfurling in her chest. Get them all to the gate, and she'd have to just lift them over, or bloody well throw them if she had to, just get them off the damn bridge and onto clear ground, and then they'd run straight for the lights and safety and sanity. She'd come last, make sure no one fell behind, because the things would come from above, wouldn't they? She could almost see them, clattering along with their angular joints projecting high above their skeletal bodies, fast and hungry and raging. But what if they came from the river itself? What then?

She pushed the thought away. No more than ten metres to go now, Safa just visible as a huddled form, the other girl clinging to her with her face pressed into Safa's shoulder.

"Safa? Are you alright?"

"Quiet!" The answer was a hiss, but the fright in it was clear and sharp enough to stop Adams mid-stride. She peered around, shuffling the boy into a more secure position, trying to see the end of the walkway and the ladder down, looking for lights and movement below the final arch of the bridge, where it reached for the ground in a brutal curve. No light, no glow from the phone screen. No movement, no anxious chatter. Just silence, and, now that she'd stopped and was looking properly, mist gathering in the joints and angles of the superstructure.

The night had changed. She couldn't have said how, exactly. Couldn't have said what she was seeing that she hadn't before, other than that coagulating mist. But the underbridge world had gone from feeling hostile yet empty, a lair without a dragon, to being *hungry*, like one of those antlion nests, all treacherous, sliding sand drawing small things to the bottom where the jaws wait. She started forward again, gaze flitting from blank sky to stark girders to the muted colours of the city.

"Safa?" She kept her voice low this time.

"We have to be quiet. They're coming."

She almost flinched, hearing the blare of radio static in her memory. *Coming.* "Can you see them?"

"Not yet. But I can ... when I was in the web, I could *feel* them. I still can. They're almost here."

Adams managed not to shiver at that thought, of the girl tangled in the beasts' nets, feeling their approach like a shadow on the sun. She'd felt the world change when they were around, and she'd barely even been near the things. Safa had been here … how long? She'd been missing two weeks, if Adams remembered right, and she almost always did. The girl must be so tuned into their presence she was basically a human beast detector.

Adams hurried along the last stretch of walkway, trying to step as softly as possible, and spotted the three boys clustered around the top of the ladder, all peering at her anxiously. What were they *doing?* She half-ran the final few strides and dropped to her knees in front of Safa, sliding the boy off her shoulder. "Why haven't you gone down?"

"I did," Briar said. "But it's locked."

Adams managed not to point out that now they *all* had to go down *and* get it unlocked, which would take longer than just her meeting them down there, and simply nodded. "Are they here yet?" She directed the question to Safa, but it was Alfie who answered.

"Yes." He pointed with his hand held close to his chest, the way you do when you don't want anyone to see. "*There.*"

Adams jerked around to stare back down the walkway, her neck twinging painfully with the movement. The bridge was empty, all plain angles and predictable corners, but the mist was thickening and spreading. "I don't see them."

"They're there," Alfie said, and snuffled tears back. "They *are.*"

Adams lifted a hand toward him, hesitated, then patted his shoulder. "Okay."

Safa gave Adams a very adult look of disapproval and reached past the other little girl to pull Alfie into a hug. "It'll be okay," she said. "The detective's here. She's going to save us." Her look became even more pointed, and Adams nodded.

"Yep," she said. "Yes, absolutely." She took another look under the bridge, then got up. "Come on. We're going."

"How?" Noah asked. "It's locked. We need parachutes so we can jump."

"I'd like a parachute," the smaller girl said.

"We don't need them," Adams said, pulling her jacket on. "We're going to climb."

"But we need hardhats," Noah insisted. "And jackets. You're the only one with a jacket."

Adams found herself fixed by five pairs of hopeful eyes, and she picked up the Maglite from where it lay on the walkway. She handed it to Safa. "That's all you need."

Safa examined it dubiously, then switched it on, sending a raw beam of brightness into the night. "It's just a torch."

"Yes. It's a magical one." Safa gave her a sceptical look, and Adams shrugged. "Fine, it's just a torch. But the monsters don't like the light, I promise you. So you head down first with it. You—" She gestured at the other girl.

"Dotty," she said. "What about bungy cords? Or a giant trampoline."

"That'd be *so cool,*" Noah said, looking at her admiringly.

"They're *here,*" Alfie whispered from under Safa's arm. "They're here *now.*"

"Ladder," Adams said, pointing. "*Go.*"

Safa got up, Alfie and Dotty still clinging to her, and gave DS Adams a worried look. "What about him?" she asked, nodding at the newest boy.

"I'll deal with him," Adams said, and turned to Briar. Safa wasn't getting untangled from the other two any time soon. "Actually, Briar, you'll have to go first."

He gave her a wide-eyed look, but got up and hurried to the ladder as she waved him over.

"You went down before, didn't you?"

"Yes," he said, glancing around at the mist. It was creeping toward them, and the unspoken part of his answer was clear. *Not with them here, though.*

Adams ignored it. "Good." She grabbed his shoulder as he tried to peer past her, presumably checking the ladder for lurking monsters. "Turn around. Feet first. Do *not* look down." He turned obediently, and she looked past him. No beasts waiting to snatch him up that she could see, so she let go and patted his back lightly. "Go."

Briar nodded jerkily, and grabbed the railings, fumbling his steps as he tried to clamber into the ladder. Adams could see his hands shaking, and she caught his shoulder again, more gently this time.

"Steady. Wait a moment." The skin on her shoulders was prickling, and she almost thought she could *smell* them coming, smell something both metallic and feral. But there was no point rushing if it meant none of the kids even made it down. She crouched down, whispering to him. "I need your help. Safa's doing really well, but I need someone at the bottom to help everyone down. Can you do that? Can you help them?"

He looked at her uncertainly. "I think so."

"I know you can. Have you still got my phone?"

He nodded. "There's no signal, though."

"There will be when you get down." *I hope.* "And there's a torch on it, so use it. Now lead the way. I really need your help with this."

"Okay." He gave her a grin that was half defiant, half terrified, then grabbed the railings rather more steadily. "Alfie, you come after me, okay? You're my backup."

Alfie gave him a dubious look. "Is it safe?"

"Can you climb?" Briar asked.

"I have bunkbeds at home."

"Exactly the same," Adams said. "Now let's go."

"Yeah," Noah said, getting up. "Then we can call the *army* on those spiders!"

That roused everyone, Dotty scrambling to her feet as

Alfie picked his way so carefully toward the ladder that Adams barely managed to hold back a scream of frustration. The mist was definitely fog now, the city vanishing behind it, and she had the sense of movement in its depths.

Alfie grabbed her hand, startling her. "You have to come too," he said.

"I will," she promised. He still had chocolate smeared around his mouth. "Just go, okay?" She shook her hand free and turned him around, holding his shoulders as he clambered into the ladder. She looked past him at Briar. "Make sure he doesn't fall."

"I will," Briar said, and started to take a hand off the ladder to reach out to Alfie.

Adams clicked her tongue. "*No.* Both hands on the ladder."

"Okay." Briar settled for an encouraging grin at Alfie, and started down. Adams kept hold of the small boy until he was heading steadily and surprisingly nimbly down, then waved Dotty and Noah over. They barely needed any help at all getting started, and, thankfully quickly, there was only Safa and the still-unconscious boy left on the walkway. Safa was leaning over him, waving a Yorkie bar under his nose, the Maglite abandoned next to her.

"Safa. Come on."

"He's almost awake."

"Safa, *hurry.*" The fog was a wall rolling down the walkway toward them, no longer led by fingers of mist.

Safa just about crammed the Yorkie bar into the boy's nostrils. "But what about him?"

"I'll carry him. Come *on.*" Adams checked on the climbers below. They were moving slowly but steadily, and she had the fleeting thought that she hoped the gate was there, that the *world* was there. She couldn't see anything but the thick, curling mist, already threatening to fill the space between them. She crossed to Safa, grabbing her arm to pull her to her feet, and the girl shook her off.

"You can't carry him! What if you drop him?"

"He'll be fine. You have to go." Adams snatched the torch up and shoved it at the girl, then half-dragged her to the ladder.

"You *can't,*" Safa repeated, her eyes wide. Her gaze kept darting to the fog. "Please, you have to get us *all* down, you can't leave him, you have to stop them—"

Her voice was rising, and Adams caught the girl's arms, crouching before her and swallowing her own rising panic. "*Safa.* You've done amazingly, but you have to let me do the rest, okay? This is my job." *Beast-wrangler extraordinaire, that's me,* she thought, and swallowed a ragged laugh.

Safa opened her mouth, and for a moment Adams thought she was going to keep arguing, but she just hurled the Yorkie bar she'd been trying to wake the boy with. Adams ducked instinctively, and it whirled past her ear and struck something in the camouflage of the fog as she pivoted on her heels to follow its path. There was a crackle of the wrapping, then something uncomfortably slobbery. Adams wanted it to sound like a Labrador, but it didn't. It sounded sharper and more ravenous.

She swallowed some very inappropriate language and snatched the torch off Safa, tucking it into the girl's jacket then pushing her at the ladder. "Safa, *go.*"

The girl lunged for the ladder and started scrambling down as Adams turned back and grabbed the boy, trying to heft him onto her shoulder. He shifted in her grip, making some small, half-awake sounds. Bollocks. That was all she needed, him waking up properly halfway down and wriggling free.

Something loomed in the girders, seen-not-seen in the encroaching fog. Adams glanced down. Safa was moving fearlessly, and the others were just visible below her. They seemed horribly slow, but given the fact that they were all under ten and had just been pulled out of some sort of suspended animation in alien cocoons, she supposed they were doing pretty well.

Movement again, angular and rapid, stuttering up the bridge uprights below the children, and her stomach gave an awful, sick twist. No, no, *no.* That couldn't happen. She all but dropped the kid off her shoulder, setting him next to the ladder, and he blinked at her in astonishment.

"Hey," he started, and she waved at him impatiently, leaning over the edge and fishing in her pockets for something, *anything* – her hand closed on her cuffs and she shifted position, not hesitating, twisting into a throw honed by summer after summer of reluctant yet heated family cricket games. The handcuffs whipped into the mist, and she was rewarded with an offended snarl, guttural and sounding as much of crashing metal as wounded animal. It was the sort of sound an engine under strain makes just before it breaks. Movement appeared as currents in the mist, but it was moving up now, away from the kids. Toward her. But that was fine. That was what she wanted.

She looked at the boy. "Can you climb?"

"Um," he said, and she took it as a yes.

"Go," she said, grabbing his hands and hauling him to his feet. She swung him bodily onto the ladder. "Climb! *Hurry!*"

The boy yelped and started down, fast. Adams risked a look down, and saw Safa staring up at her. She tried to wave her on, but the girl pointed past her. Adams spun, but saw only the fog-crowded walkway.

The walkway, and the last of the chocolate bars sitting neatly in the middle of it. Adams pocketed them and zipped up her jacket, the neon brightness of it feeling like armour against the creeping, dim mist. She took a Yorkie bar in one hand and plucked the duck out of her pocket with the other, and walked into the fog. Away from the ladder. Away from the kids.

"Come on, then," she said, as the visibility closed in around her, and the skin on her neck crawled with cold and fright. "Let's be bloody well having you."

19

COME AND HAVE A GO

THERE WAS NOTHING, NO MOVEMENT, NO THINNING OF THE clammy, opaque wall of fog, and Detective Sergeant Adams of the London Metropolitan Police walked forward into it with her duck and her chocolate, her tread measured but not as heavy as she'd have liked in her trainers instead of boots. She put a bit of a stomp into things, both gratified and horrified by the way the metal rang under her feet. The mist damped the sound down, stopping it travelling, but she could feel the faintest shake that the impact set up. She didn't know if it was louder or more attractive than the sound of six kids scrambling down a ladder, but she had to hope it was. She jumped from foot to foot as she kept moving forward, landing with exaggerated impact as she hopped away from the ladder, away from the way down and out of the murk, feeling like she was playing some poorly laid out hopscotch with potentially dire consequences.

"Come on, come on," she muttered, then raised her voice, shouting into the fog, her voice sounding dull and flat to her own ears. "Come *on,* come and have a go if you think you're hard enough … something, something, Derby ambulance."

She couldn't remember the words to the chant. She *should* have been able to, the amount of times she'd heard it yelled outside clubs and boozers at closing time, but maybe some things were wilfully blocked. "I've got chocolate," she offered instead. "Come and get your treats, you spindly bloody mechanical poodles."

Which, she had a moment to think, was hardly the most devastating or provocative of insults, but it was better than a half-remembered football chant.

And was also apparently effective. Movement swelled in the mist, the fog peeling back in a manner that made Adams think of the webbing peeling back from the kids, curling in on itself like it was being pushed apart by unseen hands, and there was a *thing* stuttering toward her from the river side of the bridge. It was running along the outside frame with unnerving grace and speed, and she was completely, entirely certain that it *wanted* her to see, that it had pulled the mist away just so she could gawk with open-mouthed terror. As the thought occurred to her she dropped into a crouch and spun precariously along the walkway, raising the Yorkie bar and the duck above her head and squeezing them both in some terrified instinct. She felt the wind of movement through the space she'd just been in, and caught a whiff of the metal-feral scent again, and something screamed right on the edge of her hearing, shrill enough to set her teeth on edge. She squinted against the glare of light coming off the duck and rebounding on the mist, then released her death grip. The light winked out, leaving her vision printed with afterimages of the girders, and she blinked urgently, trying to spot the creatures again. They'd retreated, wrapping their paths in fog, and she scrambled to her feet, stomping on the walkway again and shoving the duck back in her pocket.

"Hey! *Hey!* I'm not bloody well done with you!"

There was no response, and she was seized with the

sudden, panicked conviction that they were after the kids again, that they'd decided she was too well armed and, while she waved her arms about uselessly up here, they were snatching the children off the ladder like candy canes from a Christmas tree. She spun and sprinted back down the walkway, half-crouched in the hope that she wasn't going to brain herself on a girder along the way. The ladder loomed at her, and she barely stopped before she hit the railing.

"Hey!" she shouted into the dark. "Safa!"

She was rewarded by a small shout, and she dropped through the gap, scrambling down the ladder so fast that she almost stepped on the last boy before she saw him. The kids were clustered around the gate, staring at her with wide eyes, and she shoved the duck at Safa. She grabbed it, handing the Maglite off to Dotty. The torch's light seemed dim against the raw illumination of the duck, and Adams hoped the batteries weren't dying.

"Keep it on," she said to Safa, pointing at the duck. "And the torch. Keep them *both* on." She threw herself back up the ladder.

"Wait!" Briar shouted. "We can't get through!"

"Shout!" DS Adams yelled back, taking the rungs as fast as she dared. "Just start shouting!"

Light flooded around her as she scrambled up toward the walkway, and something screamed, followed by a much more human scream from one of the kids.

"Safa!" she shouted, coming to a halt, hanging from the ladder.

"We're okay!" Adams could hear something like panic in the girl's voice, and sympathised. "They're after you!"

"Good! Keep the lights on!" Adams lunged up again, her wounded palm tearing open on the metal, wondering once again how the hell such a low bridge could have such a long ladder, and then she was throwing herself onto the dim, murky walkway, grabbing a Yorkie bar from her pocket and ripping it open. She found her feet, waving the chocolate over her head as she turned once again toward the river, moving fast, shouting a shaky mix of taunts and fright and fury, hoping that the Yorkie bar was tempting enough – and the duck dissuasion enough – for the beasts to come for her instead of the kids.

There was no time for her to wonder what she'd do if the things *didn't* come after her, how she was going to fight on the ladder or through the girders, before the mist split and the creature rushed her. She had the jumbled images of a grasshopper launching into a jump and a spider's scuttling limbs, and she dived to the walkway, sliding under the thing and hearing an old-engine snarl as it passed over her. She came to her feet to see the second beast coming at her from the side, and she flung the Yorkie bar at it, aiming for roughly where its nose should have been, although she couldn't see anything that looked like a snout. Or eyes, or a mouth, for that matter. She was kind of grateful for the lack of mouth, if she was honest.

The beast snatched up the Yorkie bar before it could connect, and Adams grabbed her extendible baton out of her jacket, snapping it to full length and swinging it as she spun back to face the first beast. It was scuttling toward her, and she caught it a solid thwack on one leg, sending a jolt up her arm from the force of the blow. The creature recoiled with a snarl, giving her a moment of alarming pleasure.

"Come on, then," she said, trying to watch both of them at once. The second one was snuffling with its non-existent snout at the empty Yorkie bar wrapper, and she wished briefly that she hadn't fed so many to the kids. The first stalked after her, shaking out the leg she'd hit like it had pins and needles. She edged along the walkway, further from the ladder, and said, "You want more chocolate? Come on, then. Come on. Follow me. I've got loads. Nice chocolate."

She wasn't sure when she'd changed from insults to wheedling puppy talk, but it didn't really matter. What did matter was that the fog was pressing so tight around her that she could barely breathe, but that had to mean all their attention was on her. So maybe, *maybe,* someone would hear the kids.

She took another bar from her pocket. She only had two left, but it was better than nothing. She waved it at the beasts, wondering how she could be so sure that the second one was drooling chocolatey drool when she still couldn't see a mouth. "Yum," she said again, then yelped as Drooly grabbed at her with one long, glossy leg. She could see bristles on it like metal shavings, and a faint patina of rust, and she slammed the baton down on it, hard. Drooly squalled an objection, and she swung back to face the first beast just in time to duck a claw that would've gone through her skull.

"Bad," she said, breathlessly. "Bad bridge monsters." She scooted further down the walkway, trying to find something to put her back to, and the creatures stalked after her. She could feel their regard, heavy and grave and hungry, and at some level she caught the communication that passed between them, as sure as seeing a couple of likely lads exchanging glances on the street. She hurled the Yorkie bar at them just as they lunged forward, and both beasts turned their charge into a lurch after the chocolate, crashing into each other with a clatter of metallic limbs. Adams turned and sprinted into the fog.

She was fairly sure she didn't even get seconds before the scratch and rush of pursuit swelled after her. It certainly wasn't *many* seconds. She whirled to face them, planting her feet wide and slapping her head torch on, its beam weak and unimpressive compared to the raging floodlight of the duck and the Maglite. But it still collected on the mist and bounced back, and slid off the glossy edges of the creatures' carapaces, and illuminated such lovely detail as the fact that Drooly was *definitely* drooling, and that there were gaps and shadows in the other one's body that were both pointed at her and unpleasantly reminiscent of teeth. Big ones.

Drooly and Toothy loomed over her, brought to a sudden halt by the light, front limbs pawing at the air as they screamed, trying to protect themselves from the onslaught of the cheap Sports Direct headlamp. Adams found herself frozen in place, staring at them as they dropped back to all (six? Eight? Ten? It was oddly hard to tell) of their limbs and lurched back down the walkway into the protection of the mist, hard and angular as crabs. Then she realised that they were going *back*, back toward the kids, and she screamed as well, half-formed threats that made no sense. She lunged after them, swinging the baton with both hands, slamming it ineffectually into a leg hard as the girders here, clattering against the smooth, round edges of a body there, the creatures skittering and roaring as they fled the light.

They should have been running into the dark, off to the sides of the bridge, but the light was confusing them, she supposed, hurting their sensors or receptors or whatever the hell they had. Not that it mattered *what* they had. All that mattered was that they were disorientated, and she needed to keep them on the run, she needed to give the kids time to escape. And if, *if* she could somehow make sure the damn things never left here – well, then there couldn't be any more missing children cases. Not of this sort, anyway. And whatever the exact details – the webs, the fog, the damn *claws* – none of that mattered. All that mattered was that she stopped them.

She was abruptly at the end of the walkway, the creatures shying from a wash of light below that meant the duck was still there – and so were the kids. One of the beasts ventured a little lower, spitting and growling as the light stung it, but it seemed less intimidated than it had before. Either the torches were failing, or they were getting used to them. Adams slammed her baton into the nearest limb she could find.

"*Hey!* Eyes this way, you animated bloody train sets!"

The creature squalled, and edged further into the girders.

"*No!*" Adams shouted, as if it'd just made a mess on the carpet. "No! Get back here *right now!*"

The thing turned its back to her, and she waved the baton at the other one.

"You, then! Get here!"

It swung below the walkway, trying to skirt the wash of duck light, and Adams grabbed at the back of her neck as if she could shake an idea into herself, make herself *think,* because there had to be a way to turn the things' attention back to her, *had to*— Her hand knocked her head torch.

"Oh, you git," she muttered, and switched it off, the underbridge suddenly vividly, painfully dark, the beasts lit from below by the duck, its light deeper and more intense without the torch competing with it. Adams snatched the last Yorkie bar from her pocket and ripped the wrapper open. "Oi! Eyes on me, Meccano-face!"

She felt their attention swing back, drawn by the dark and the sugar, and she backed up a step. That sense of communication again, and she could feel them hesitating. She reached up and pulled the head torch off, switching it on. They flinched, and she flung it straight down the ladder, shouting "Heads up!" as she did so, and hoping she didn't knock anyone out. Light swelled below, as if the duck were feeding off the extra illumination, and the creatures backed into the mist a little further, pulling away from it.

"Come on," Adams said, waving the chocolate bar at them. "This way. Nice chocolate. Nice—!" She turned and bolted, clutching the chocolate bar in one hand and the baton in another, sprinting into the distant reaches of the bridge. The structure rang with the pursuit of many-jointed limbs, faster and surer up here than she was, gaining rapidly, and she dropped to the ground, spinning into a crouch. She looked up to see reaching, clasping limbs, and things that looked far too much like toothy mouths lining them, and jabbed the end of the baton straight into the closest one. Something shattered under the strike and the beast reared back with a scream, and she scrambled to her feet just in time to be knocked straight into the railing by a blow from the side.

The rail caught her in the ribs, jolting a yelp out of her, and she lost her footing, trainers sliding across the mist-damp metal. She hit the side of her head painfully as she went down, lights blossoming in her vision, but twisted as she fell, bringing the baton up to defend herself. Toothy – or it might have been Drooly, she'd lost track – reared over her, and she shoved the baton forward with both hands as hard as she could. It met something that gave with a startling lack of resistance, and the beast screeched in horror. The baton was ripped away, and she looked up to see it jammed crossways in some dent in the thing's carapace, which was frothing with mist and chocolate-tinted dribble. The beast pawed at the baton with two front legs, staggering back, and Adams made it to her knees, snatching the Yorkie bar up from where she'd dropped it and brandishing it at the second beast.

"Wait," she said, trying for the severe tones of a dog trainer, then the chocolate bar was gone, leaving her with the crawling sensation of bristly, wriggling tongues on her hand, like the sticky underside of a starfish. She gagged, and scrabbled in her pockets for something, *anything* that she could use as a weapon, and came up with the last creme egg. It was hardly a weapon, but beggars and choosers and all that. She looked up at Drooly, who was ignoring the still-struggling Toothy and was coming back for more.

"Catch," she said, and hurled the egg straight at the spot on Drooly where Toothy seemed to be having trouble with the baton. Drooly had been rearing up again, chocolate drool dripping from whatever passed as its mouth (or its main mouth, given all the little mouths on the legs), and the egg shot straight past its teeth and into what she hoped was its throat. Drooly stopped dead and gave a horribly human, choking cough, front legs raising to its mouth. It spasmed, scratching for balance, then toppled sideways off the bridge with its legs folding around itself like a dying spider. It bounced off a couple of girders, then vanished into the mist. Adams watched it go, still on her knees, and teetered for a moment on the brink of a precipice made up of screaming questions, mostly chocolate-based, but also involving ducks, lights, and alien anatomy.

Then the scuttle of claws thundering toward her brought her back to her feet, and she staggered as she rose. She cast around for a weapon, but there was nothing, not even a loose bit of metal to tear free, no handy abandoned tool bag of hammers and screwdrivers. Just her, baton-less and duck-less. She shrugged her jacket off as Toothy emerged from the fog, running across the supports of the bridge as effortlessly as if it were flat land, sliding from running upside down to sideways to upright without ever changing pace. The fog parted in front of it, giving her a clear view, and she knew, *knew* that the mist was responding to the beasts, showing her what was coming in order to freeze her in terror, but she was past that now. Way, way past that.

She set her feet wide, brandishing the jacket like a matador, and bellowed, loud enough to tear at the lining of her throat, "*Come and have a go if you think you're hard enough!*"

Toothy screamed, a hurt and furious sound that made

her falter, less in fear than in a sudden horror that she'd sent its mate off the bridge, sent its soul (and sole) companion to the river and left it alone and bereft, then it reared over her, and she forgot everything except the need to *stop it.*

Toothy lashed out and Adams swung the jacket, tangling the thing's limbs in the heavy cloth, and they had a brief tug of war before she reclaimed the coat with the sound of tearing fabric. "Have to try harder than that," she managed, panting, then wished she hadn't as Toothy leaped upward then came plunging down, all its legs aiming at her. She scuttled back, the wind of its landing too close, one of the bristled legs tearing past her body and leaving a burning sensation in her arm that was too sharp and fast for her to really register. It lashed out again, and she flailed with her jacket. Toothy snagged it, and they tussled for a moment before Adams lost her grip. The beast shoved the jacket in its maw eagerly, and Adams turned and sprinted down the walkway, heading for the centre of the river.

She'd barely made it half a dozen strides before the bridge shook with pursuit, and she spun back to face the beast, one leg back and both hands raised in fists, as if she were about to invite the bridge monster for a gentlemanly boxing match. "Come on!" she yelled at it, as if she had any say in the matter. "Come on, *come on!*"

Toothy scuttled forward, legs straddling the railing, and Adams glimpsed pointed, claw-like feet, more like a crab than a spider and she wondered briefly how the hell it stayed on the bridge. Was it the bristles? The *mouths?* She shuddered with the thought of the thing basically licking its way across the girders. Toothy swiped at her, a leg coming far too close to her stomach, and she jumped back, lurching against the railing and getting a dank whiff of the river. The creature made a guttural sound, a hoicking cough that sounded alarmingly like a cat hacking up a hairball, and she had an idea it was laughing. Or screaming.

Her foot caught on something. The bag. She snatched it up just as Toothy swung a limb at her, and she snarled its claw into the cloth as she fended it off, trying to cling to the bag's strap in the vague hope of somehow entangling the damn thing. The creature simply pulled her off her feet, and she let go before she was swept from the dubious safety of the walkway. She landed badly, her foot slipping on something that clattered noisily, and she barely avoided falling through the railings. She risked a glance at what she'd landed on, and saw old red plastic gleaming dully in the dimness.

Her multitool.

She forced her gaze back to Toothy, half-expecting the monster would have noticed her interest. But Toothy ignored it, creeping across the complicated structure of the under bridge, legs twitching and working independently. She could feel the fury of its regard. She took a slow, shaky breath, and dropped to her knees, diving for the multitool and snatching it up in the same motion. She wrenched the blade open as the bridge monster lunged forward, legs spread in triumph, body bearing down on her. She could smell burning metal and melted chocolate and old, damp spaces, lost and forgotten and not made for the likes of humans, and she shoved the blade forward, clutching it in both hands, closing her eyes and looking away, because there was no point aiming. She was as likely to bounce the knife off the thing's carapace as hit a vulnerable spot.

Bristles tore at her arms as they slid against her, and a claw gouged her side, but her hands were sinking into something cold and terrible, and she felt an awful *pop* as the knife pierced alien skin. She opened her eyes to see her arms buried up to the elbows in the thing's maw. It screamed, and she jerked her hands back, leaving the knife where it was and cringing against the railing as Toothy staggered away, spitting mist and screeching over and over, the sound shrill and cutting and full of a grief that was universal.

"I'm sorry," she whispered, raising one shaking hand to her head. "I'm really sorry."

Toothy screamed again, falling to the walkway with a thud that almost shook her to her knees, and her stomach see-sawed with grief. She'd killed it. Killed *them.* Killed some strange and alien beasts, just because they were defending their territory, their *lives,* and wouldn't anyone do the same? Wouldn't anyone strike out at intruders in their midst? Even if— the kids. *The kids.* She turned and bolted down the walkway, back toward the riverbank, and the ladder, the moment of grief forgotten. Surely the mist would clear now, with both beasts gone, and the weird atmospherics would lift, and they'd be able to shout for help, and even if not, she'd get them all over the gate, she'd piggyback them or break the lock or *something,* it'd be *fine—*

She had one moment to realise that the fog was so thick that she couldn't even see her feet in the dim light anymore, then she was hit from behind. Bristles snagged and tore, and she was wrenched off the walkway with no more hope of resistance than a mouse against a hawk. They were over the railing before she could even try to grab for a handhold, her stomach swooping with horror, and all she could think was *the duck, I need the duck,* although what she needed was a parachute, just like the kid had said, or preferably a bloody big pot of that monster repellent, and then she was falling.

Falling into the dark and the mist and the lost places.

20

A SOGGY END

THE MIST WAS GONE, BUT IT FELT AS THOUGH THE CITY WAS AS well. There was nothing but the rush of cold, clammy air against her skin, the scream of movement in her ears (or that might have been her own scream, but she didn't think so – her throat was too tight for screaming), the beast's limbs rasping across her skin, and the startled realisation that *this was it,* because the river was too far below to make sense, and maybe dimensions were different, or time was, or *something,* but even a short fall into the Thames on a nice summer day rarely ended well, and this was neither warm nor nice nor—

The babble of her thoughts was slapped clear as they jerked to a halt. Adams did scream this time, tight throat or not, as the creature's bristles gouged her torso, and for a moment she was still falling and it wasn't. Then she was stopped so violently by a grip on one foot that her leg felt like it was going to come off at the hip. She gulped air, swinging head first over the murky water of the Thames, the surface too sullen to reflect light. Teeth or mandibles or claws or *something* were grinding against the bones of her ankle. Spots swam in her vision, and she squeezed her eyes closed for a moment, then opened them again. Her captor didn't let go, and there was utter silence around them as Adams swung gently, the night painted in greys and blues. The lights of the city had drawn away, as if to turn their backs on what was happening in their midst.

She waited, expecting an explosion of pain as her foot was crushed, or the stomach-churning moment as gravity took hold when the thing let go. But it just held her, her foot throbbing, and finally she craned her neck to look up at it. In the dim light of the underbridge world the sharpness of its bristles rendered its form fuzzy as a sea urchin, their tips tinged with a warm orange bloom of rust that looked almost soft, like the worn skin of an old teddy bear. The beast was clinging to an arch of the bridge with its back legs, and it looked back at her, eyes or not.

Adams licked her lips, and said, "I'm sorry."

The creature cocked its head just slightly, sending a spasm of pain into her leg.

Adams grunted, fighting a surge of nausea. When it had passed, she said, "I'm sorry I killed your mate, or companion, or whatever."

The beast didn't answer, not that she'd expected it to. She wasn't even sure what she was hoping for, hanging here talking at a being that stank of burning metal and hurt. How could it comprehend her, any more than she it? But maybe it was better than hanging here waiting to be dropped.

"I suppose you're just trying to get by, same as anyone," she told it, and let her head drop back toward the river. The strain of looking past her feet was making her neck ache, not that the rest of her wasn't. "You can't just *take* people, though. Not kids, not anyone. It's not right."

Still no reply, just the steadiness of its regard, and she wondered what it was waiting for. Hoping its mate might come back? Listening to what she had to say? Deciding whether to have her as an early breakfast, or stash her in a cocoon somewhere for later? She hadn't seen any adult-sized cocoons about the place, so she thought the snack was more likely.

She craned her neck again, fixing the bridge monster with a firm *now-then* glare, her hands creeping to the waistband of her leggings. The radio was unclipped but still there, hanging from the drawstring of her trousers, and the mic was still clipped to her shoulder. She eased the mic jack out of its socket and cradled the radio in one hand, working on the knots in the drawstring with the other as she said, "Have you tried, I don't know – sheep? Goats? Cattle are very popular."

If Toothy could have blinked at her, it would have. The thing's non-gaze was unsettling. It wasn't like being looked at by a dog, all good-natured confusion and hopeful misunderstanding, or even a cat, which always felt to Adams somewhat suspicious and judgemental, and made her check for stains on her shirt. This was like looking at another person, someone as hurt and afraid as she was. Someone who, just like her, couldn't understand what had just happened. How the Usual Way of Things had been so categorically upended. She saw Drooly falling again, legs folding helplessly around itself, and took a shaky breath to hold back a sudden prickling behind her eyes. The final knot slipped free under her fingertips.

"I mean, you have to move with the times. Human sacrifice is very passé. Perhaps you could try toasties. Toasties are good."

Toothy shifted, and its grip on her ankle slipped just slightly, sending a jolt of pain straight through her leg and up to her belly. She gasped, using the spasm of her movement to shift the radio into her right hand.

"Chocolate," she said, with something like triumph. "Now

that's the way forward, right?" And she threw her whole body into a crunch, drawing her legs up at the same time, rolling toward the beast. Toothy released her foot with a chirrup of alarm, but she was already hurling the radio, throwing it as hard as she could, praying to the dog or the duck or to whatever small gods might be listening. And maybe one of them was, because the radio flew straight past Toothy's raised forelimbs and smashed into its carapace, and the creature bit down on it instinctively with the same mouth it had been using to hold Adams' foot. In the wind of her fall she heard the snap and crackle of electricity as metallic teeth hit the battery and circuits inside. The bridge monster screamed, and then it was falling after her, limbs flailing in panic, and all she could do was hope that it didn't land on top of her. That would seem chronically unfair.

ADAMS CLASPED her hands over her head, trying to straighten her body before she hit the water, and had time to take one heaving, panicked breath. She crashed through the surface on her side, the impact hard enough to send pain radiating out of her poor abused ribs, and then she was sinking into the cold and the dark, while currents clutched at her and tried to spin her in half a dozen directions at once.

The water was desperately cold, placing vices around her head and her chest, and it was all she could do to resist gasping. She didn't fight the plunge, just let herself sink under her own momentum, counting silently in her head. *One, one thousand. Two, one thousand. Three—* She flared her arms and legs, helping to slow herself as the initial shock faded. *Four, one thousand.* Toothy was in here somewhere with her, but that was unimportant. Now was survival. *Five, one thousand.* Her natural buoyancy was reasserting itself, and she was slowing.

Something flashed past her in the water, buffeting her with a sleek, greasy side, and she flinched. *Six, one thousand.* She opened her eyes, ignoring both the sting of grit and salt and the rush of pale flesh next to her, and twisted around, trying to find a reference. *Seven, one thousand.* There. A murky gleam of lighter water, close enough to what felt like it should be *above* that she didn't think it was some luminescent river monster temping her closer. Although, after the last few days, she couldn't be too sure. *Eight, one thousand.* She swept her arms through the water, kicked her trainers off, and swam.

She broke the surface with a heaving gasp, tasting oil and mud and the acridity of adrenaline, and with an old crisp packet plastered to the side of her face. She spluttered, ripping it off, and blinked around at the night. She was already shivering violently, her teeth chattering, tight bands of ice wrapping around her affectionately. How long? How long did she have before her limbs stopped working, before she couldn't swim properly and the water started feeling warm and inviting and like a good place for a nap? She splashed in a circle, looking for the nearest shore, thinking, *float, don't swim.* That was the advice, wasn't it? But she couldn't remember how long you were meant to float for. Enough to get over the shock of the cold, she supposed, and probably until someone threw you a life ring, but unless Toothy was feeling forgiving she didn't see that happening.

She was almost in the middle of the river, and the current was carrying her away from the bridge alarmingly quickly. The lights of the Christmas market were already being swept past, and though she was gratified to see that there were red and blue lights on the road above it, and searchlights washing along the bank and spotlighting the bridge, they weren't helping her much.

"Bollocks," she said, and started a slow, steady breaststroke toward that shore, trying not to splash too much. Partly to conserve energy, and partly because she wasn't quite sure what might be lurking in the river with her. She didn't fancy defeating bridge monsters just to be eaten by a sea serpent. Although she supposed they'd be *river* serpents in here, not that it made the idea any more attractive.

The second time she took a mouthful of water rather than air, Adams stopped swimming, spitting enthusiastically. The Thames was meant to be clean enough for seahorses to live in now, but she still didn't like the idea of drinking it. Not that she supposed it would make a lot of difference, given the fact that she felt like she had more scraped and bruised skin than she had whole at the moment. Any sneaky little bacteria would be having a field day. She rolled onto her back briefly, staring up at the night sky and resting her trembling limbs for a moment. That was better. Nice, even. She could drift downriver like this. She was well past the market anyway, so it wasn't like it mattered where she came ashore. She'd fetch up somewhere.

"Fetch up as a corpse," she muttered to herself, and rolled reluctantly back to her belly, giving up the breaststroke for a feeble doggy-paddle. The shore seemed to be getting further away, which was unfair. She kept going.

She was gulping water on every second stroke, her body sinking even in the light constraints of leggings and shirt, and she was having trouble keeping her chin high enough to get any air at all. Once she sank so low that the water shot up her nose, and she had to stop swimming entirely, fighting to stay afloat as she coughed and spluttered. Things passed her in the water, turning curious eyes to her struggles, circling just out of reach and watching. Waiting. But she kept going, because to not was to give up, and that wasn't an option. She just sent wordless curses to her silent audience, and paddled on. She wasn't going to fail in front of them.

But the shore seemed to retreat, the current keeping her steadfastly distant, too strong to fight, and the night grew darker and the city more distant. She could have been lost in the middle of an ocean here, for all the help that was coming. And then she was swallowing more water than air, fighting just to stay afloat, never mind hoping for any forward momentum, and that was when she realised that she really wasn't going to make it.

She rolled onto her back one final time, concentrating on floating, and looked at the distant sky, stars hidden by the loom of the city. "Bloody monsters," she managed, and closed her eyes, the water warm and supportive, and felt the strange currents circling closer. She supposed it didn't matter much now anyway, but she still wished she had the duck, for some reason.

When thin, pale light washed over her, she assumed it was either one of those deep-sea fish that have luminescent lures over their toothy mouths, or some sort of final hallucination, so she ignored it. Or ignored it until something hard bumped into her violently enough to send her rolling over facedown, and she somehow fought her head clear of the water to hear someone saying, "Be careful!"

"She's bloody half-drowned already, it's a bit late to be careful."

Hands grabbed her shoulders, and she kicked feebly, trying to help them. There was a clatter of movement above her, and the first voice yelped, "You're going to capsize us! Don't you know how to boat?"

"Sorry I lack your extensive yachting knowledge," the other voice snapped. "Help me, can't you?"

More hands grabbed her, then she was hauled over the gunwale of a dinghy, her spine scraping painfully but gratefully on the wood. She blinked up at Zahid, who said, "Tell me you don't need mouth to mouth. *Please*." His grip on her shoulders was painfully tight.

She coughed, and someone else crouched next to her as Zahid helped her up to a seated position. She craned around unsteadily and looked at Jack, who patted her arm, then peeled off his tartan shawl and put it over her shoulders.

It smelled damp and grimy and utterly, utterly wonderful.

"But are you *alright*?" her mum insisted. "The food there will be awful. I'll bring you food."

"I don't need food, Mum," Adams said, shifting in the hospital bed. Her side sang pain at the movement, the skin torn and abraded, and her lacerated ankle throbbed insistently. She was trying not to think about it, or about the grey phlegm she kept hoicking up, opaque as the Thames. She was trying not to think about *anything*, in fact, because the stark white light of the hospital and the brutally efficient bustle of the nurses was making the chaos of the night before seem more and more distant and foggy on the edges. She liked it that way.

"You do need food," her mum said, frowning. Her makeup was carefully applied and her grey-streaked braids neatly looped on top of her head, but her clothes gave her away. She'd come rushing out in a pair of baggy track pants and a T-shirt under the heavy purple wool of her winter coat, and Adams didn't think she'd seen her mum leave the house in anything less than either an eclectically styled dress or figure-hugging jeans and a well-cut top since the time her brother had broken his ankle trying to jump from the top of the stairs to the windowsill in the hall below. Even he hadn't been able to explain why he'd thought that was a good idea.

"I don't," Adams insisted. "They gave me breakfast."

"What? Reconstituted eggs and half a mangey banana?"

"Porridge," Adams said, then added, "I think."

Her mum rolled her eyes. "That does it. I'm getting you something proper to eat." She got up, then hesitated. "Your dad really had to go to work, but he—"

"*Mum.* I don't need food. I don't need company. I just need sleep." They'd kept her up for the whole rest of the night, it seemed, poking and prodding and feeding her antibiotics, muttering about concussion and shock. She had some broken ribs, but the ankle was the worst. Her tendons had survived, but the lacerations ... She'd told the doctors she caught it on a torn cable on the bridge, and no one had questioned it. They'd just added tetanus shots to the seemingly endless parade of jabs they insisted on giving her.

"Well, while you sleep, I'll go home and whip something up," her mum said, leaning over Adams and tugging the blankets up to her chin.

"I'm going home this afternoon. You don't need to bring me anything."

"Your dad and I will pick you up, then." Her mum took her phone from a cavernous patchwork handbag, squinting as she poked at the screen. "I'll tell him to finish early."

"He's a teacher, Mum. I don't think he can skip class. Sets a bad precedent." Adams pushed the covers down again. "I'll get a lift home."

"You're not going to *your* home. You're coming back with us."

"*No.* No," she added, and patted her mum's arm to take the sharpness from the word. She wished her mum would just go. She didn't want anyone talking at her about the terrible band her third cousin had hired for her wedding, and how everyone had been forced to do the Macarena at least four times, or how the shop down the road had gone a bit funny and was selling crystals instead of aspirin, or how the neighbour's son had set up a private medical practice and was single, didn't she know. She just wanted as much silence as the shared ward would give her, to stare at the slice of grey sky just glimpsed through the window and to figure out how to think about things. She felt that something in her might break at any moment from the struggle of holding two realities at once. The edges of her world had torn, leaving ragged, toothy edges, and she needed to stitch them back together before she simply shredded herself on them.

"You can't be home alone." Her mum said it as a declaration of fact, and glanced around for support from the other residents of the ward. A man snored two beds over, and in the bed nearest the door a young woman giggled at something on her phone, headphones clamped to her ears. An older woman in a lavender nightie held a magazine up in front of her face, but Adams could see her peeking over it at them. She doubted she was as interesting as the entangled love lives of three *Big Brother* contestants, though.

"Mum—"

"You have to stay off that foot. The doctor said." Her mum's face was tight with worry, and she put a hand on Adams' arm. "Please, love."

Adams swallowed some very well ingrained guilt and said, "No, Mum. I need to be in my own space. And you've seen my apartment anyway – I can basically reach the fridge from the sofa."

Her mother sighed. "So stubborn. I know where you get it from, you know."

"You," Adams said, grinning, and her mum swatted her arm lightly.

"Horrible child. That's all your father."

"Sure it is."

"I'm making you food, anyway." Her mum got up, gathering her bag and phone and hat and scarf. "*And* we're picking you up this afternoon, because your father will want to see you. And if you still want to go to your place, fine, but at least you'll have something to eat. You're skin and bone, you are."

Adams looked down at herself and considered that her mother's beauty ideals and the world's at large were a rather long way apart, and also that she preferred her mum's. "Alright. I'll take the lift, and I'll take the food. But don't be trying to drag me to yours. That'd be abducting a police officer. I'll have you."

"It doesn't count when it's your parents," her mum said, and leaned in to give her a hug that was scented with familiarly warm, earthy scents that made Adams blink a little harder. She kissed her mum's cheek.

"See you then."

"You will." Her mum lingered, a strong, rounded woman with lines at the corners of her eyes that spoke of a life well-lived. "If you need to talk, Jeanette—"

"It's fine, Mum. *I'm* fine. I'll message you when they give me a release time."

"You'll call me, like a proper human being." She examined Adams for a long moment, and Adams tried to look as strong and resilient as the woman in front of her. Eventually her mum sighed. "The *Thames*. Honestly, Jeanette."

"It wasn't by choice."

"Still." Her mum looked at the window, tapping her fingers against her thigh, then dug suddenly in her bag and fished out a small bundle. "Keep this." She pressed it into Adams' hands, then sailed out the door with her head high and her purple coat swirling around her, making a young doctor on his way through the door leap back in alarm before she could mow him down. Adams opened her hand and looked at what her mum had left her. Dried herbs. A feather. Some leaves, all bound with a tight coil of red wool, and she knew it'd be knotted seven times exactly. Knew it because it was what her mum used to put under their pillows at night when they were small and had nightmares. It was what she put above the door in Adams' apartment when she first moved out, and what she insisted Adams put in her locker at work, and in the glovebox of her car. A charm, a promise, a way of keeping the unnamed dangers of the world at bay.

Adams reached over and set it on the table next to the bed, by the little metal duck. A uniformed officer had brought it in for her that morning, along with her phone, which had miraculously survived the night with nothing worse than some chocolate caked on one corner. The kids had already been bundled off in their own ambulances by the time the police launch had surged up to the wobbly wooden dinghy in answer to Zahid's call. As Adams was hauled into the warmth of the cabin she kept asking and asking if they were okay, if they had been found, was anyone hurt, *where were they?*

It had been the officer who had given her the duck in the first place who had crouched in front of her, chafing Adams' hands in her own, and said, "They're safe. You've done your part. Rest now."

Adams stared at her. "The duck ..."

"Also did its part." And she had wrapped Adams in a second blanket, tugging it firmly around her. Adams could smell the river deep in the woman's pores, and see the strange tawny colour of her eyes, like damp driftwood on wild beaches.

Adams leaned forward until her forehead almost touched the other woman's and whispered, "What were they?"

The officer had smiled and said, "Old, old things." Then she'd moved away, and Adams had turned to watch the riverbank through the open back of the launch. Watching for *them.*

She'd seen them from the dinghy as Jack paddled for the bank as quickly as the load and the currents would allow. They'd been emerging from the water like drowned gantries being revealed at low tide, limbs high and angular above them. Angular and sagging with weariness and pain in places. Mist swathed them, but she'd felt them see her, felt them turn their regard to her. Felt their fear, and she'd hated herself a little for it.

Then she'd seen the lights of the ambulances, and known the kids were safe, and the hate had mostly gone. She wondered if the creatures would come back. Not here, though, she thought. Maybe somewhere else.

She closed her eyes and tried not to think of bridges.

21

DOGS CAN'T POINT

ADAMS HOBBLED INTO THE OFFICE, WALKING AT A LEAN AND very nearly losing precious amounts of coffee over her fingers as she struggled to navigate the door with a crutch in one hand and two mugs in the other.

"Adams!" Zahid bounced up from the desk and strode over to her, relieving her of the mugs and leaving her to deal with the door. "Is one of these mine?"

"The one that smells of sadness and grass clippings."

"Excellent." He slurped from the disposable mug and made a face.

"Do *not* complain," Adams said. "Jack was right. Almond milk's bad for the planet."

"What the hell is this, then?"

"Potato milk. Next big thing, apparently." She managed to untangle herself from the door, which seemed determined to close on her bad leg, and reclaimed her mug from him. "What've we got on?"

"Spate of break-ins. A home invasion. Nessie on the rampage."

"Oh, ha." She hadn't said anything about bridge monsters

to anyone, obviously, but the taint of Jack's reports and Harry labelling her Fox Mulder followed her anyway. Her official report was that she'd followed a hunch regarding how the kids could be hidden, and found them drugged and secured in mountain-climbing tents up in the bridge framework. She'd freed them while their captors weren't around, but had inadvertently ended up in a confrontation upon their return. She could only describe said captors very vaguely owing to the poor lighting, and in the resulting tussle they had all unfortunately ended up in the water. As far as the kids talking about giant, chocolate-loving robot-spiders and cobweb nests, she just supposed that was one for the psychologists.

Zahid had made it to the warehouse just after Alex, and in time to see him hefting a Molotov cocktail straight into the makeshift tent city. He'd seen something else as well, but all he said when Adams pressed him was, "I think the fumes from the gasoline were pretty strong." He'd been much more vocal on how he'd tackled Alex and subdued the younger man, though.

"I was like, *bam,* and he ducked, and threw a punch like *boof,* and then I got him like *yeah—*"

Adams had tuned out somewhere around there.

Jack had been more forthcoming, though, when Adams had found him on the riverside a few days after he'd dragged her from the river. He was sitting on the bench closest to the bridge, and grinned at her when she limped over to sit next to him.

"Hello, detective monster hunter," he said, and she snorted.

"Yeah. How are you, Jack?"

"Good, good. Good," he said, ducking his head in time to some tune only he could hear. "The bridge is safe, the river is quiet. Good."

"Have your friends come back?"

"No. How could they?" He gave her a cool look. "You're telling yourself stories. Making excuses. Thinking it didn't happen."

Adams looked at her hands, the knuckles raw and one palm still bandaged. The doctors kept muttering about various infections she had to watch for, but so far she mostly just felt sleepless and irritable. Even a sheet felt too heavy against her raw skin half the time. She'd grazed one side of her body so badly that it seemed she'd never be comfortable again. "*Something* happened."

He nodded. "But you're thinking, well, not *that* something."

Adams thought of hulking limbs against the night and her mouth twisted. "How did you know how to find me?"

"When the big one who smelled of burnt sugar and broken cameras came, I heard his radio. I knew you were on the bridge, and when the beasts left us – he was going to chase us to them, you know? Until your friend stopped him."

"Zahid has his uses."

"He couldn't see, but he stopped the big one. And the beasts ran when they saw him, because they can only hide so much without the mist." He paused, examining the bridge. "And while your friend and the big one were fighting I grabbed the radio and tried to tell you the monsters were on the way back."

"I heard," she said. "Thank you."

He shrugged. "You tried to help. Not many do."

Adams watched the sun on the river, shattering like spilled glass on the wavelets, and tasted the wet, dank muddiness of it at the back of her throat. "And you saved me."

"You matter," Jack said. "Everyone does, but you *see* that everyone matters, and so it mattered that you were safe."

Adams touched the back of her neck, where the scabs had all but gone. "And the dinghy?"

"It's ours. We didn't steal it or anything, it just washed up. The river gave it to us, you know."

"Of course."

"So I said to your friend it was faster in it than on the roads. He's not good with boats, though. Can he swim?"

"I don't know."

"He should. Everyone should swim. Not swimming is trouble. What if the world sinks?"

"I'll tell him to get some lessons. So you paddled the dinghy down – did you see me fall? How did you find me?"

"Mirabelle."

Adams thought of Harry rushing away, hand clutched over his stomach. "Really? Because she could've helped me get the kids off, and she just left."

"Sometimes it's not safe to help too much," Jack said. "Sometimes helping too much can destroy the helper. Or mean the helper can't help again, you know? And small helps in the right place can remake the universe."

"This is like having a conversation with a fortune cookie," Adams said, thinking of the duck and the Yorkie bars. And brownies.

"Sorry. Some days are like that. It's when the world is clearer."

"What worries me is it makes sense. So Mirabelle saw me?"

"No. No one could've seen you in there without a searchlight. Not in the Thames. It's hungry, and it would have kept you. But the dog watched you, and she watched the dog, and then she pointed me where to go from the bank."

"The dog?"

"Mirabelle. Dogs can't point." He frowned. "Or I suppose they can. Not properly, though."

"I thought I imagined the dog."

"You might've. I didn't see it. Maybe Mirabelle imagined it too." He shrugged.

Adams leaned back in the bench, shifting her leg carefully. The sun was unseasonably lovely, and it was making her tired. Or the conversation was. But she had one more question. She wasn't sure if she wanted the answer or not, but she had to ask.

She twisted on the bench, pulling the scarf away from the nape of her neck. "Is that from them? The bridge?"

"Maybe," Jack said. "It looks sort of bitey."

"I wondered if maybe … I mean, it happened right at the start. I thought perhaps that was what made me start seeing *stuff.*" She waved vaguely on the last word. She still wasn't sure how to talk about it. Detective sergeants who wanted to make superintendent one day did not talk about bridge monsters and hungry rivers.

Jack snorted, and gave her that startling grin. "Even if it was them, you didn't see because you were bitten. You were bitten because you *see.*"

"Oh." Adams resettled her scarf and adjusted her leg again. "Fantastic." They sat in silence for a while, watching a tug labouring upstream with a couple of barges in tow, then she added, "Have the bins been behaving themselves?"

"Not bad." He gave her a sidelong glance. "Are you staying?"

"Staying where?"

He waved without answering, at the Thames and the pale January sunlight and the thin white sky, and she opened her mouth to say *of course* she was, then shut it again. The bridge was too big, pressing too close above her, even though she knew the spans were empty. It was still there, even if the beasts were gone for now, a steel-clad reminder that the city was home to things older and stranger than she knew how to comprehend. She got up abruptly. "Can I buy you lunch?"

"No thanks," he said. "I've got brownies."

"Of course." She hadn't had the brownies, but she hadn't had the toasties, either, even though they both kept turning up on her doorstep, each smelling of their own glorious temptation. One to forget, one to *see,* and she couldn't seem to make herself do either. She was adrift between two worlds.

NOW ZAHID LED the way to their desks, and said, "Herself wants to see you."

Adams sighed. "Already? I've just got in."

"I'd guess that's why. You know, make sure you're not completely traumatised and likely to start shouting about cults down at Hyde Park over the weekend. Give the Met a bad name, that would."

Adams turned and hobbled toward the DCI's office, taking her coffee with her. The room felt hot and over-crowded, even with just half a dozen or so detectives in. She could feel eyes on her, and glanced around as she raised her hand to knock, half-expecting to see officers leaning toward each other, hissing about the detective sergeant who believed junkie tales about monsters in the Thames.

The only one looking at her was Harry, though, and she glared at him, her lips drawing back from her teeth almost involuntarily. He looked away so fast he seemed at risk of whiplash, a flush rising in his cheeks. She hadn't told anyone about him trying to stop her getting to the bridge. She didn't know how. *I'd like to make a complaint against my fellow officer for trying to feed me toasties.* No. That wouldn't work, and neither would saying he'd tried to stop her doing her job. All he had to say was that he'd wanted her to wait for proper backup and equipment, and then she'd look like the reckless, overly ambitious, hungry-for-glory DS so many of them wanted to see her as. It'd all go the wrong way far too quickly.

She turned back to the DCI's office and knocked firmly.

"Yeah," the DCI shouted from inside, and Adams struggled to get the door open and manoeuvre her crutch and coffee around it.

"You wanted to see me, boss?"

"Adams, wonderful. Sit down." The DCI watched her as she pushed the door closed and limped over to one of the uncomfortable chairs, sinking into it gratefully. "How're you doing?"

"Healing up. Might need a bit of physio on the ankle, but that's all."

"Good news." The older woman examined her, and Adams struggled not to look away from the DCI's cool gaze, forcing herself not to fidget or slurp coffee to break the moment. "And the rest?"

"Boss?"

"The rest, Adams. Yorkie bars."

Adams swallowed hard, her throat clicking, and took a sip of coffee after all. "I don't want to talk about Yorkie bars," she said finally.

The DCI tipped her head slightly. "Are you sure? You seem to have a knack for Yorkie bars."

Adams shook her head. "I don't much like Yorkie bars."

"No one's asking you to. Just that you learn how to use them. It's another aspect of policing, is all, and not many have a talent for it."

"I'm not sure that I do, either."

"Oh, you do. I've known people with a lot more experience of Yorkie bars who couldn't have shifted those damn things. I mean, *I've* never even seen them before, and that's saying something." The DCI shook her head and opened the drawer of her desk, taking out a couple of foil-wrapped chocolate Santas. She slid one across the desk to Adams and started to unwrap her own. "You saved the kids *and* nailed the bloody things. That's a proper rare talent."

Adams heard the scream of grief as the monster lost its mate, and felt again their fearful gaze as they crept into the night. She could still feel her own sense of loss and disorientation as an echo of their own, just as it was an echo of Jack's, trying to piece together a reality from scraps of a world that didn't seem to fit anymore. A world that she was part of making more hostile. That didn't feel like talent. It felt like the sort of blind cruelty that crushes beetles underfoot for the sheer joy of hearing them shatter. She wanted her world to fit again, but she wasn't going to shatter anyone else's for it.

"No," she said aloud. "I don't think so."

"We need people who're good with Yorkie bars, Adams. There aren't many of you."

"I'm not who you need."

The DCI took a bite from the Santa, watching her. "You know about them now, though. That changes things."

Adams shook her head. "No. It doesn't have to. I don't *have* to see, and I don't want to. It's ..." She waved a hand vaguely, trying to find the words, and thinking of the dog. She'd only seen it twice since the river. Or, rather, she *thought* she'd seen it. Once it had been jumping on a trampoline in a distant backyard at three in a rainy morning, barely visible with its dark hair flying joyously in the night, and she'd woken the next day with no memory of either getting up to see it or of going back to bed. The other time had been in the wee early hours of the morning in the hospital. The dog had been standing at the foot of her bed, firmly

Labrador-sized, and staring up at her with its hidden eyes. By the time she'd sat up, it was gone, and there was nowhere at all for it to go in there other than out the door, which hadn't opened. So she wasn't at all sure either sighting had been real. She was starting to doubt she'd ever seen it at all, in fact.

Even so, she'd bought a bone-in lamb shoulder the other night. It was marked down at the end of the day, but it was still enough to blow out her grocery budget for the week, and she'd left it by the bins in some gesture of thanks for what the dog had done. *If* it had done it. She didn't know why a dog would help her, or that a dog *could* help her, but she'd left the lamb for it anyway. The neighbourhood cats would be happy, if nothing else.

"The world's just as it was," she said aloud. "Things got weird for a bit, but it's done now. *I'm* done."

The DCI chewed chocolate for a while before answering, and Adams took a sip of coffee. She felt too hot, and she hoped she wasn't getting an infection of some sort. So far the antibiotics the hospital had pumped into her seemed to have staved everything off, but she still wasn't entirely convinced she hadn't caught Weil's disease anyway. It would explain things rather nicely. Or most things, anyway.

"The world was never as it was," the DCI said finally. "You know that, Adams. And you don't strike me as the wilfully ignorant sort."

"I'm wilfully lots of things," Adams said. "Including a police officer. There's more than enough human stuff to deal with. I don't need Yorkie bars."

The DCI watched her for a moment longer, rolling the wrapper from her chocolate Santa between her fingers slowly, then nodded. "I see. Well, take some time off. You're not ready to come back—"

"I *am*," Adams protested, although she thought that

mostly she didn't want to be at home thinking about bridges and dogs and Yorkie bars.

"That's for me to decide, and I can see you're not. Think about things a bit while you're off. I'm going to see you get DI over this, so you'll have more freedom, too. Run your own investigations." She cocked her head at Adams.

Adams clutched her mug a little tighter. "I get DI if I deal with Yorkie bars?"

The DCI seemed to consider it, then shook her head. "No. I can't have anyone in half-hearted. Bloody Harry's a liability because he knows about Yorkie bars, but he flat out refuses to admit it. I'm not having another Harry around the place. So you get DI either way, and you either deal with Yorkie bars, or you stay the hell away from any case that has even a whiff of them. I'm not bribing you to do this. I'm just saying that I need good people for it. And you're good sorts, DS Adams."

"Thanks," Adams said, wondering if she should mention the fact that Harry not only knew about Yorkie bars, he appeared to be rather invested in making sure they stayed in circulation. Then she decided that if she was out, she was out. She fished in her pocket instead. "Do you want the duck?"

The DCI gave her a blank look as Adams held the little metal duck up for consideration. "Why the hell would I want a duck?"

"Well, it's a …" Adams thought of the police diver, her hands cold as the Thames as she'd folded her fingers over Adams', and the strange river scent of her as she wrapped the blanket tight in the launch. There were more than Yorkies in the world, just as there were more than bridges, and it wasn't her place to tell tales. Although she might just tell a Harry-themed tale to the diver, if she could find her.

"Never mind." Adams pocketed it again, comforted by the

smooth contours of its body.

The DCI picked the chocolate Santa up and held it out to her. "Take that. You might choose not to see them, but that doesn't mean they won't choose to see you."

"I won't need it."

"You might," the DCI said, and after a moment Adams took the Santa. "Now get that foot healed up before I see you again." She turned back to her computer, and Adams watched her for a moment, then hobbled back out the door and into the office, the cheap foil of the wrapper too hot under her fingers.

"WELL?" Zahid asked.

"On leave until my foot's healed," she said, dropping into her seat and switching the computer on.

"Looks like it."

"I just want to check something." She waited for it to finish booting up, looking at the framed photos on the walls. Tower Bridge. Blackfriars. She shivered and looked back at the screen, logging herself in. DI. DI was nice. She glanced at the bridge photos again, then opened the police jobs board, scrolling down the listings. Lots of local stuff, moving between departments. Oxford wanted a new DS, but she was going to be a DI. She couldn't quite be excited about it. It didn't feel like something she'd earned. Southampton needed a DI, but they had a bloody great harbour. There'd be bridges for miles, or at least docks and cranes, and she didn't fancy them, either. She kept scrolling, almost passing one before scrolling back up.

Leeds.

Leeds was inland, wasn't it? There could be a canal, of course – she vaguely remembered hearing something about a

Leeds-Liverpool canal. Couldn't have very big bridges over a canal, though. She leaned back in her chair.

"Zahid, you been to Leeds?"

"What?"

"Have you been to Leeds?"

"What, just 'cause I'm Muslim and we all come from Bradford?" Adams raised her eyebrows at him, and he grinned. "Nah. I'm Sheffield, me."

"So you don't know if there's any bridges? In Leeds, I mean."

"Bridges?"

"Yeah. You know – is there a river?"

Zahid frowned. "Dunno, really. Don't think so. There's the canal, though."

"How big's a canal bridge?"

"Big enough for the canal? I don't bloody know. Why? You got a bridge fetish suddenly?"

"Opposite, really," she said, and clicked the listing. Leeds. Yorkshire. Smaller than London, but still a decent city. And no river, so no big bridges. And canals couldn't be too bad. Shallow little things, really. She wondered if the DCI would put in a good word for her. She deserved that, at least.

Leeds. A sudden shiver of anticipation shot down her spine. There couldn't be much trouble in *Leeds.* Not of the sort she was worried about, anyway.

Just a nice, ordinary job. Dealing with nice, *ordinary* cases, robberies and assaults and maybe the odd murder, arresting people and not worrying about bloody things that go bump in the night. No *Yorkie bars.* She hit *Apply.*

Leeds. *Perfect.*

THANK YOU

Lovely people, thank you so much for dipping into the murky waters of DI Adams' backstory with me. I've known since the first Beaufort book that *something* definitely happened in London, but it's taken a little while for me to discover just what. And when I finally did (Adams really is quite fiercely private), it was unfortunately during the strange upheaval of 2021, when I left the UK and came back to NZ for six weeks, only to find myself still here almost two years later.

Ahem. Life-planning is similar to book-planning for me. Largely unknown and prone to change without notice.

Anyhow, what that meant was that the rough draft of *What Happened in London* languished in a notebook in the UK for much longer than was intended (because I still like writing by hand at times, even if it means I can rarely read what I've written when I come back to it). So there has been a little delay getting Adams' story down.

But now here we are, and I hope so much that you've enjoyed it! I think Adams might have quite a lot to say now that we've got that whole bridge awkwardness out of the way, so keep your ducks and Yorkie bars handy. There's more to come.

And I have a small request …

If you did enjoy this book, I'd very much appreciate you taking the time to pop a review up at your favourite retailer or book review site. Especially as this is the first instalment in a potential new series, I'd love to know if it's something you want to see more of.

Reviews are basically magic for authors. Magic of the helpful duck kind, rather than the *snap-snap-snap* kind, too. More reviews mean more people see our books in online stores, meaning more people buy them, so giving us the ability to write more stories and send them back out to you, lovely readers. Less vicious circle, more happy story circle.

Plus it allows us to keep our chocolate supplies well stocked, and we all know that's *vital.*

Thank you again so much for reading. If you'd like to send me a copy of your review, toastie-related recipes or theories, or anything else, drop me a message at kim@kmwatt.com. I'd love to hear from you!

Until next time,

Read on!

Kim

THERE'S ONLY BLOODY BRIDGES

There weren't meant to be bridges

And that's not all there is ...

DI Adams thought things would be better up north. Smaller bridges. Fewer toastie-pushers. A new and hopefully less dog- and Yorkie-fixated DCI.

But the North has its own ideas …

Discover just what awaits Up North for DI Adams in your free short story download!

Scan above to claim your copy, or head to the link below:
https://readerlinks.com/l/3095857/d1rm

THIS NECKLACE ISN'T JUST A NECKLACE ...

Walk softly, and carry a very big stick ...

DI Adams might've left the bridges (some of them, anyway) in London. She might have even left a few monsters behind (but not all). And she would very much like to believe that

Leeds is just a city, with normal city problems that she can arrest people for.

She'd *like* for all this to be true, but she's police. She follows the evidence. And the evidence says that *nothing* about this case is normal.

No, this case could bring down the north unless she stops it.

Her, the invisible caffeine-addicted dog, the duck, and a very big stick ...

ABOUT THE AUTHOR

Hello lovely person. I'm Kim, and in addition to the Gobbelino London tales I also write other funny, magical books that offer a little escape from the serious stuff in the world and hopefully leave you a wee bit happier than you were when you started. Because happiness, like friendship, matters.

I write about baking-obsessed reapers setting up baby ghoul petting cafes, and ladies of a certain age joining the Apocalypse on their Vespas. I write about friendship, and loyalty, and lifting each other up, and the importance of tea and cake.

But mostly I write about how wonderful people (of all species) can really be.

If you'd like to find out the latest on new books, learn about giveaways, discover extra reading, and more, jump on over to www.kmwatt.com and check everything out there.

Read on!

amazon.com/Kim-M-Watt/e/B07JMHRBMC
bookbub.com/authors/kim-m-watt
facebook.com/KimMWatt
instagram.com/kimmwatt
x.com/kimmwatt

ACKNOWLEDGMENTS

Lovely people, it would be basically impossible to thank everyone who has helped me get this book to you. Or, not impossible, but you'd be bored before you got halfway through, and the print costs would just go *way* up.

So I'll keep it as short and sweet as I can (which isn't very. I'm a writer, after all).

Firstly, thank *you,* lovely reader. Thank you for dipping into a tale about the power of ducks and chocolate, and for considering the mysteries of toasties and the hidden things we try not to see. Thank you for joining me.

As always, thank you so much to my beta readers, who received the manuscript for this when I was full of my first cold in *years,* and kindly ignored the above-average typo quotient and corrected the muddled headcounts of missing children (I would be a *terrible* teacher. I was losing kids all over the place).

To my wonderful editor and friend Lynda Dietz, of Easy Reader Editing, who I would recommend to *everyone,* only I don't want to because I want to keep her for my books. Kidding. Sort of. As always, all good grammar praise goes to Lynda, while all mistakes are mine. Find her at www.easyreaderediting.com for fantastic blogs on editing, grammar, and other writer-y stuff.

Thank you to Monika from Ampersand Cover Design, who works magic. Find her at www.ampersandbookcovers.com

And last simply because that's the way the writing of this worked, thank you to my lovely friends (some of whom are family as well), both online and off. I'm a very lucky human to have so many wonderful people in my corner, and none of this would ever have been possible without your continuing support, occasional nagging/scolding (usually related to sleep patterns and work habits), and endless humour. I love you all.

Thank you all for coming on this strange adventure with me.

See you next time! (And watch those bridges …)

Kim x

ALSO BY KIM M. WATT

The Gobbelino London, PI series

"This series is a wonderful combination of humor and suspense that won't let you stop until you've finished the book. Fair warning, don't plan on doing anything else until you're done ..."

- Goodreads reviewer

The Beaufort Scales Series (cozy mysteries with dragons)

"The addition of covert dragons to a cozy mystery is perfect...and the dragons are as quirky and entertaining as the rest of the slightly eccentric residents of Toot Hansell."

– Goodreads reviewer

Short Story Collections

Oddly Enough: Tales of the Unordinary, Volume One

"The stories are quirky, charming, hilarious, and some are all of the above without a dud amongst the bunch ..."

- Goodreads reviewer

The Cat Did It

Of course the cat did it. Sneaky, snarky, and up to no good – that's the cats in this feline collection, which you can grab free by signing up to the newsletter. Just remember – if the cat winks, always wink back …

The Tales of Beaufort Scales

Modern dragons are a little different these days. There's the barbecue fixation, for starters … You'll get these tales free once you've signed up for the newsletter!

Printed in Great Britain
by Amazon

57156517R00169